LEVEL 1

NTC's Basic JAPANESE

LYNN WILLIAMS

National Textbook Company
a division of *NTC Publishing Group* • Lincolnwood, Illinois USA

All cover photos courtesy of Japan National Tourist Organization.

1994 Printing

This edition first published in 1992 by National Textbook Company,
a division of NTC Publishing Group, 4255 West Touhy Avenue,
Lincolnwood (Chicago), Illinois 60646-1975

Manufactured in the United States of America.

3 4 5 6 7 8 9 VP 9 8 7 6 5 4 3

CONTENTS

Note:
In the writing of *hiragana* and *katakana,* space has deliberately been left between words and particles to facilitate understanding of the structures for beginners. At the next level, particles are linked to the previous word, according to Japanese convention.

INTRODUCTION

NTC's Basic Japanese is the product of years of experience presenting the Japanese language in classrooms around the world and aims at responding to the widely felt need for a truly communicative Japanese textbook series. The resulting textbooks thus provide a variety of lively, stimulating, communicative activities that will help students acquire a firm foundation in Japanese and motivate them to continue their study of the language.

The first textbook covers nine Topics: Greetings; In the Classroom; School Life; Time, Days, and Numbers; The Weather; Myself and Others; Families and Friends; Homes and Daily Activities; and Health. Each of the Topics is further divided into specific Units, which provide considerable lesson-plan flexibility for teachers, depending on the amount of class time at their disposal.

The textbook has been designed to be completed within one year, though the sample practice material and extension activities provided will enable teachers to extend the course beyond a year, depending on the number of hours a week Japanese is being taught.

From the beginning, all four language skills (speaking, listening, reading, and writing) are developed and reinforced. At the same time, students are introduced to cultural material that is essential to making real progress in the Japanese language. Students are encouraged to communicate from the very first day, using the Japanese they know to talk about themselves and the world around them. All aspects of the series, including grammar, vocabulary, cultural information, reading and writing activities, are designed for a communicative teaching environment.

Teachers and students alike will find this textbook both accessible and convenient to use. All Topics are presented in such a way that students may easily review and practice material on their own. The textbook also aims at accommodating a variety of learning styles and approaches, thus enabling students to work through material at their own pace, with ample opportunity for review and mastery. The exercises in the course also contribute to the goal of relative autonomy and can be completed by students with little assistance from an instructor. They are also designed to uncover any problems students may be having, so they can then ask for help on these points.

Detailed explanatory notes on grammar and usage enable this text to be used as a self-study book, when that approach is necessary.

Teachers will notice that certain grammatical items are introduced only partially. This technique helps students develop an intuitive knowledge of usage, before they go more deeply into the complexities of a particular structure or pattern. The author has done her best to avoid jargon or linguistic labels, since students grasp grammatical structures more easily and quickly without the use of such language. At the same time, those seeking to attain a more academic level can easily substitute more advanced grammatical labels, where necessary.

Units move at a pace designed to insure that students make real progress in communication. In addition, numerous extension activities vary routines, as well as provide material for review and reinforcement.

Activities and exercises encourage *individual* work and augment the role plays and group work. Regardless of their length, activities provide students with the opportunity to communicate normally without long preparation.

While great care has been taken to insure that all the basics normally covered are dealt with in this course, each unit also provides a rich variety of materials and activities to amplify the basics and to allow teachers and their students the flexibility to suit their own time, pace, and classroom situation. At first glance, some activities may appear too simple. Nonetheless, in practice, they have proven to reinforce with considerable effectiveness the areas they were designed to review. Teachers will also be delighted to learn that the textbook allows for a variety of individual teaching styles. The wide range of activities provided in each Topic encourages teachers to personalize material by means of their own methods and approaches.

Hiragana and Katakana are gradually introduced throughout the course, with the option of teaching these systems from a chart or in groups of syllables, in order to avoid confusion over those that are similar in shape. Students are encouraged to *master* Hiragana and become familiar with Katakana. To attain this goal, numerous review items, along with checkpoints, will help them master the syllabaries gradually, completely, and enthusiastically.

The language taught throughout the course is generally colloquial and in daily use. However, you may find that better and more popular ways exist to express certain ideas. Nevertheless, given the controlled grammar and vocabulary in the course, the author has chosen to stress the more practical and manageable structures. At the end of the course, students will have a solid base for practical communication and will have been equipped to take on more complex colloquial forms and more extended grammar. Also, after completing the book, students should be able to write and read Hiragana with ease. Some Kanji is presented for interest, while a good start is made on Katakana. Students are also expected to read and understand Kana passages. Review exercises, however, are still mostly offered in Roomaji, for the sake of efficiency.

A vocabulary checklist appears at the end of this book, in addition to other useful reference items, including a Kanji checklist (for recognition only), a calendar for learning how to say the days of the month in Japanese, lists of endings for counting people and ages, as well as complete Hiragana and Katakana charts.

FURTHER READING

Benedek, Dezso and Junko Majima, *EasyKana.* Knoxville: The HyperGlot Software Company. (A software program for Hiragana and Katakana practice.)

Benedek, Dezso and Junko Majima. *KanjiMaster.* Knoxville: The HyperGlot Software Company. (A software program for Kanji practice.)

De Mente, Boye. *Discovering Cultural Japan.* Lincolnwood, IL: Passport Books. (A travel companion that explains key Japanese cultural traits – and how to best enjoy Japan.)

De Mente, Boye. *Everything Japanese.* Lincolnwood, IL: Passport Books. (A comprehensive A to Z Encyclopedic overview of all things Japanese.)

Kaneda, Fujihiko. *Easy Hiragana.* Lincolnwood, IL: Passport Books. (A comprehensive worktext for practicing Hiragana.)

Kataoka, Hiroko C. and Tetsuya Kusumoto. *Japanese Cultural Encounters.* Lincolnwood, IL: Passport Books. (More than 50 cultural situations are presented in a problem solving format.)

Lampkin, Rita and Osamu Hoshino. *Easy Kana Workbook.* Lincolnwood, IL: Passport Books. (Provides Hiragana and Katakana practice along with Japanese sentence building.)

Schwarz, Edward A. and Reiko Ezawa. *Everyday Japanese.* Lincolnwood, IL: Passport Books. (Book and audiocassette language program with many cultural notes and illustrated vocabulary.)

Walsh, Len. *Read Japanese Today.* Tokyo: Tuttle Books. (Explains Kanji origins, meanings, readings, and examples of usage.)

Welch, Theodore F. and Hiroki Kato. *Japan Today!* Lincolnwood, IL: Passport Books. A concise A to Z compendium covering all aspects of Japanese culture, society, and customs. Also includes an audiocassette.)

Wells, Tina and Aoi Yokouchi. *Easy Katakana.* Lincolnwood, IL: Passport Books. (A comprehensive worktext for practicing Katakana.)

TOPIC ONE greetings

Introduction

ACHIEVEMENTS

By the end of this topic you will be able to:
- Greet and bid farewell to others at appropriate times.
- Inquire about health and respond to simple inquiries about your own health.
- Introduce yourself and others.
- Ask who someone is.
- Ask what nationality someone is, and tell people your nationality.

おはよう ございます
Ohayoo gozaimasu
Good morning

STUDY

- One of the first things you will notice about Japanese people is that they usually bow to each other when they meet. The bow is called ***Ojigi***. The lower the bow, the more important is the situation, or the more formal is the relationship between the people. When friends meet, the bow often becomes just a nod of the head.

  As people meet and bow, they greet each other. Before 10:30 am they say:

お は よ う　ご ざ い ま す
O ha yo o　*go za i ma su*　Good morning

The phrase means "Good morning" but, as in many other Japanese phrases, it has an important underlying meaning: "I'm so pleased that you are up and about so that I may have the pleasure of meeting you this morning" is a free interpretation.

- During the day, from 10:30 a.m. to 5:00 p.m., the greeting is:

こ ん に ち　は
Ko n ni chi　*wa*　Good day/Good afternoon/Hello

- After 5:00 p.m., the greeting is:

こ ん ば ん は
Ko n ba n wa Good evening

Note: In the examples above, the top line is written in ***hiragana***. The "letters" in each word have been spaced so that you can easily see how they correspond to the letters directly beneath them, which are written in ***roomaji***.

ACTIVITIES

- Practice the three phases above, until you know them well. Look at the *Simple pronunciation guide for hiragana* below to familiarize yourself with the sounds. Find the *hiragana* syllables in the *Hiragana chart* on p. 6. Use these phrases as often as you can when meeting other students and your teachers – a language is for communicating!

- Tonight when you get home, try out the phrase below.

た だ い ま
ta da i ma I'm home!

And before you go to bed, try the following phrase:

お や す み な さ い
O ya su mi na sa i Sleep well!

Welcome to *Nihongo*. You have just begun an exciting, fascinating adventure into the study of a language, a people, and a culture very different from your own.

SIMPLE PRONUNCIATION GUIDE FOR *JAPANESE*

- All the sounds are short.
- The vowel sounds are as follows:
  a as in *f**a**ther*
  i as in *macaron**i***
  u as in *fl**u**te*
  e as in ***e**dge*
  o as in *s**o**l**o***
- If a vowel is doubled, e.g. *oo,* a long sound results. This is like two beats in music. For example, *T**oo**ky**oo***.
- *If two consonants are doubled (or occur together) e.g. the* ***nn*** in *ko**nn**ichi wa,* both must be pronounced. In the case of ***tt*** or ***pp***, linger over saying them to give, as it were, two beats. For example, *KASE**TT**O*.

Learning a language

日　本　語
Ni hon go
Japanese language

日本語

In learning any language it is important to communicate with others and it is great to be able to do so. Using this course you will be able to talk about many things very quickly and feel a real satisfaction in making yourself understood.

The easiest way to learn is in realistic situations, so don't be afraid to try out what you know on Japanese visitors and other people studying Japanese. You will make mistakes, but everyone does from time to time. People will be delighted that you have tried to communicate and they will be patient, and eager to help you. In return you may be able to help them.

SOME STUDY TIPS

- Learn new vocabulary thoroughly the day you first encounter it. Learn its sound, its meaning, and its spelling.

- Make yourself small cards (or buy a packet of blank cards) and write English on one side and Japanese on the other. If you make a hole through one corner of each card you will be able to hang your cards on a string or keyring. This makes it very easy to read through all the words you know every day so that you don't forget them. It's exciting too, to see how quickly the number of words you know grows.

- If you do get behind in remembering vocabulary, you suddenly have a large pile to learn. Instead of being fun it becomes a chore. So, keep at it every day.

- Keep your work neat and tidy, with clear headings so that you can find what you want easily.

- Spelling is very important. At some stage you will want to write words in Japanese script and it will be necessary to have the spelling correct. You may be expressing something very different if you have the spelling wrong!

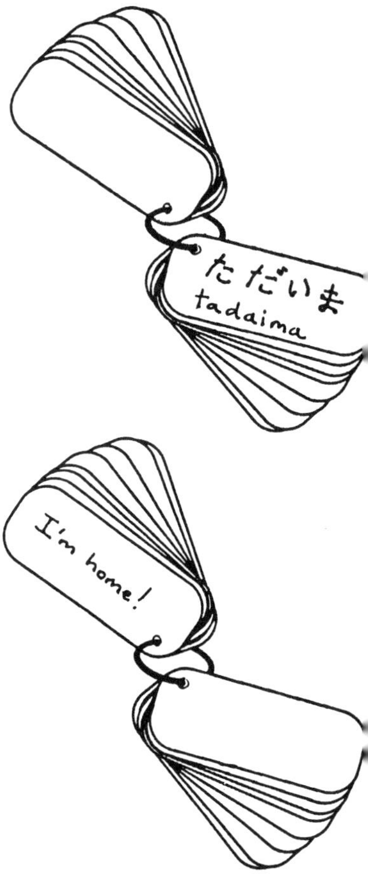

Greetings song

Sensei Ohayoo
Minasan Ohayoo
Kyoo mo tanoshiku
Benkyoo shimashoo

Sensei konnichi wa
Minasan konnichi wa
Kyoo mo tanoshiku
Benkyoo shimashoo

Sensei konban wa
Minasan konban wa
Kyoo mo tanoshiku
Asobimashoo

Writing Japanese

ひらがな	**カタカナ**	**漢字**
hiragana	***katakana***	***kanji***

Hiragana, katakana, and *kanji* are the three Japanese scripts.

Hiragana

This is a beautiful flowing style of writing. The Japanese developed it over a period of several hundred years. It has been used ever since they started to write their language down, instead of passing on stories, history and information only by word of mouth.

This is what the words you have learned look like in *hiragana*:

おはよう ございます　こんにちは
O ha yo o　go za i ma su　ko n ni chi　wa

こんばんは　おやすみなさい
ko n ba n　wa　O ya su mi　na sa i

If you practice writing these phrases, as well as saying them, you will quickly learn to write *hiragana.*

The *Hiragana chart* on p. 6 shows you how to write the symbols. If you would like to do so, learn the chart by heart, but for the present you may just like to copy the words that you have learned.

Hiragana was originally written with a brush called a *fude* and ink was made from soot. The art of writing like this is called *shodoo* (calligraphy). Many people worldwide practice calligraphy in various styles of script as an art form.

Originally Japanese was written downwards, starting from the right of the page, and read downwards. Nowadays, it is also often written across the page from left to right.

日本人の　こどもは　六さいに　なると　小学校に　入ります。　小学校で　六年かん
べんきょうします。　小学校の　つぎに　中学校に　入ります。　中学校で　三年かん
べんきょうします。　中学三年を　おわってから　学校を　やめたい人は　やめても　いい
です。　しかし　日本の　こどもは　たいてい　中学校で　やめないで　こうとう学校に　入ります。

橋本、初日は5位

総合 500メートル2位、3000メートルは8位

世界女子スケート

【ハーグ（オランダ）八日＝ロイター】スピードスケートの一九八六年女子世界選手権は八日、当地で開幕。第一日は五百㍍、三千㍍の二種目を行った。日本期待の橋本聖子（富士急）は五百㍍で42秒06をマークして二位、三千㍍は4分45秒97で八位になり、二種目得点89・721で昨年と同じ五位につけた。

最初の五百㍍はやや風はあったが、まずまずのコンディション。カリン・カニア（旧姓エンケ＝東ドイツ）が41秒13で首位。昨年四種目すべてに勝ち完全優勝したアンドレア・エーリッヒ（旧姓シェーネ＝東ドイツ）は五位と出遅れた。

二種目得点のトップは五百㍍、三千㍍とも一位を占めたカニアで85・758点。他の日本勢は関ナツエ（三協精機）が94・601点で二十六位、浅尾恵子（三協精機）は三千㍍で走路妨害のため失格した。

◇

日本の女子選手が世界選手権五百㍍で二位に入ったのは一九八〇年の長屋真紀子（当時、三協精機）以来四人目。橋本は昨年の世界選手権（サラエボ）一日目は五百㍍三位、三千㍍七位で初日五位につけた。二日目の千五百㍍、五千㍍とも七位で総合成績で七位になり、一九六三年の長久保初枝以来の一けた成績を残した。

今季の橋本は二十二、三日、軽井沢で開かれる世界スプリント一本に絞って調整してきただけに、長距離の練習不足は否めない。日本選手の総合成績過去最高は四位（一九三六年、第一回大会の滝三七子）である。

▽五百㍍ ①カリン・カニア（東ドイツ）41秒13②橋本聖子（富士急）42秒06③ブレア（米）42秒11④トカルチック（ポーランド）42秒22⑤エーリッヒ（東ドイツ）42秒47⑥王秀麗（中国）42秒48㉑関ナツエ（三協精機）44秒35㉗浅尾恵子（三協精機）45秒11

（共同）

▽三千㍍ ①カリン・カニア（東独）4分27秒77②エーリッヒ（東独）4分29秒41③ブレーム（東独）4分34秒86④ファンヘニップ（オランダ）4分36秒55⑤シェーンブルン（東独）4分39秒00⑥フィセル（オランダ）4分43秒60⑧橋本聖子（富士急）4分45秒97㉕関ナツエ（三協精機）5分1秒51（浅尾恵子＝三協精機＝は走路妨害で失格）

（UPI共同）

▽二種目得点 ①カリン・カニア（東独）85・758②エーリッヒ（東独）87・371③ブ

五百㍍で二位になった橋本聖子（富士急）のラストスパート ＝ロイター・サン

Katakana

Katakana is a much sharper, straighter style of writing, used mainly for words that were not known in Japan before Europeans visited the country. For example, the Portuguese introduced bread to Japan in the 1600s and since then the Japanese have called it *PAN* – from the Portuguese word for bread.

Other words infiltrated the language, particularly after 1868 when the Emperor Meiji started to encourage contact with other countries. In the past several decades a multitude of foreign words have been absorbed into Japanese, e.g. *DOA* for door. The Japanese previously had no swinging doors like the ones we use. They had sliding paper screens called *shooji* to close entrance ways and divide rooms, and wooden storm shutters called *amado* to keep out rain.

The main uses for *katakana* are thus for words of foreign origin; foreign personal names and place names; and names of some plants and animals.

HIRAGANA CHART

		a	i	u	e	o
		あ *a*	い *i*	う *u*	え *e*	お *o*
G゛	K	か *ka*	き *ki*	く *ku*	け *ke*	こ *ko*
Z゛	S	さ *sa*	し *shi*	す *su*	せ *se*	そ *so*
D゛	T	た *ta*	ち *chi*	つ *tsu*	て *te*	と *to*
	N	な *na*	に *ni*	ぬ *nu*	ね *ne*	の *no*
B゛/P°	H	は *ha*	ひ *hi*	ふ *fu*	へ *he*	ほ *ho*
	M	ま *ma*	み *mi*	む *mu*	め *me*	も *mo*
	Y	や *ya*		ゆ *yu*		よ *yo*
	R	ら *ra*	り *ri*	る *ru*	れ *re*	ろ *ro*
	W	わ *wa*				を *o*
						ん *n*

KATAKANA CHART

		a	i	u	e	o
		ア *a*	イ *i*	ウ *u*	エ *e*	オ *o*
G゛	K	カ *ka*	キ *ki*	ク *ku*	ケ *ke*	コ *ko*
Z゛	S	サ *sa*	シ *shi*	ス *su*	セ *se*	ソ *so*
D゛	T	タ *ta*	チ *chi*	ツ *tsu*	テ *te*	ト *to*
	N	ナ *na*	ニ *ni*	ヌ *nu*	ネ *ne*	ノ *no*
B゛/P°	H	ハ *ha*	ヒ *hi*	フ *fu*	ヘ *he*	ホ *ho*
	M	マ *ma*	ミ *mi*	ム *mu*	メ *me*	モ *mo*
	Y	ヤ *ya*		ユ *yu*		ヨ *yo*
	R	ラ *ra*	リ *ri*	ル *ru*	レ *re*	ロ *ro*
	W	ワ *wa*				ヲ *o*
						ン *n*

Katakana syllables have the same sounds phonetically as *hiragana* syllables, but the style of writing is different, to satisfy those Japanese who did not want foreign words written in their own traditional script. Below are three examples of words in *katakana*.

ド ア	レ ス ト ラ ン	コ カ	コ ー ラ
DO A	*RE SU TO RA N*	*KO KA*	*KO O RA*
door	restaurant	Coca	Cola

The *katakana* syllabary is shown in the chart on p. 7.

Katakana words occur interspersed among *hiragana*. See if you can identify the *katakana* words in the sentence below which has both *hiragana* and *katakana*.

ブラウン　せんせい　は　にほん　に　いきます。

Kanji

Kanji were introduced into Japan from China around the 6th century, and represent ideas pictorially. They are fascinating to learn.

If you are interested, look in the list of books for further reading, on p. xii, for a book that tells you the stories behind kanji.

日　*ni*　This is the *kanji* for the sun or day.

本　*hon*　This is the *kanji* for the origin of things.

The Japanese called their country *Nihon*, "The Land of the Rising Sun", because it was further east than any other country they knew of in those days. Their national flag shows a red circle on a white background.

And you are now learning *nihongo*, the Japanese language:

日 本 語
ni hon go

There are thousands of *kanji*. Japanese people learn 1,800 in their basic schooling (as well as *hiragana* and *katakana*), and through their lives gradually learn more and more in order to study and to read novels and work-related papers. Eventually, you will be able to read sentences like the one below in which all three forms of script are used:

ブラウン　せんせい　は　日本　に　いきます。

Both *hiragana* and *katakana* were developed from *kanji*. By simplifying certain *kanji*, the *hiragana* syllabary was formed. And by finding *kanji* with the same pronunciation, and then taking out a small part of the *kanji*, the katakana syllabary was developed.

あ安　い以　う宇　え衣　お於

Hiragana* come from simplified *kanji

ア阿　イ伊　ウ宇　エ江　オ於

Katakana* come from part of the *kanji

Roomaji

Roomaji (spelling Japanese words with the English [Roman] alphabet) was developed to help foreign people learn Japanese more quickly, and is particularly helpful for those who don't need to learn to read and write Japanese.

Roomaji is useful for us, but the Japanese use it mostly in places like train stations, to help foreigners find their way around. In fact, most Japanese find it very hard to read.

Japan: the country

Looking at the following maps will help give you a better understanding of Japan and the Japanese way of life.

Japan: main islands, major cities, and closest neighbors

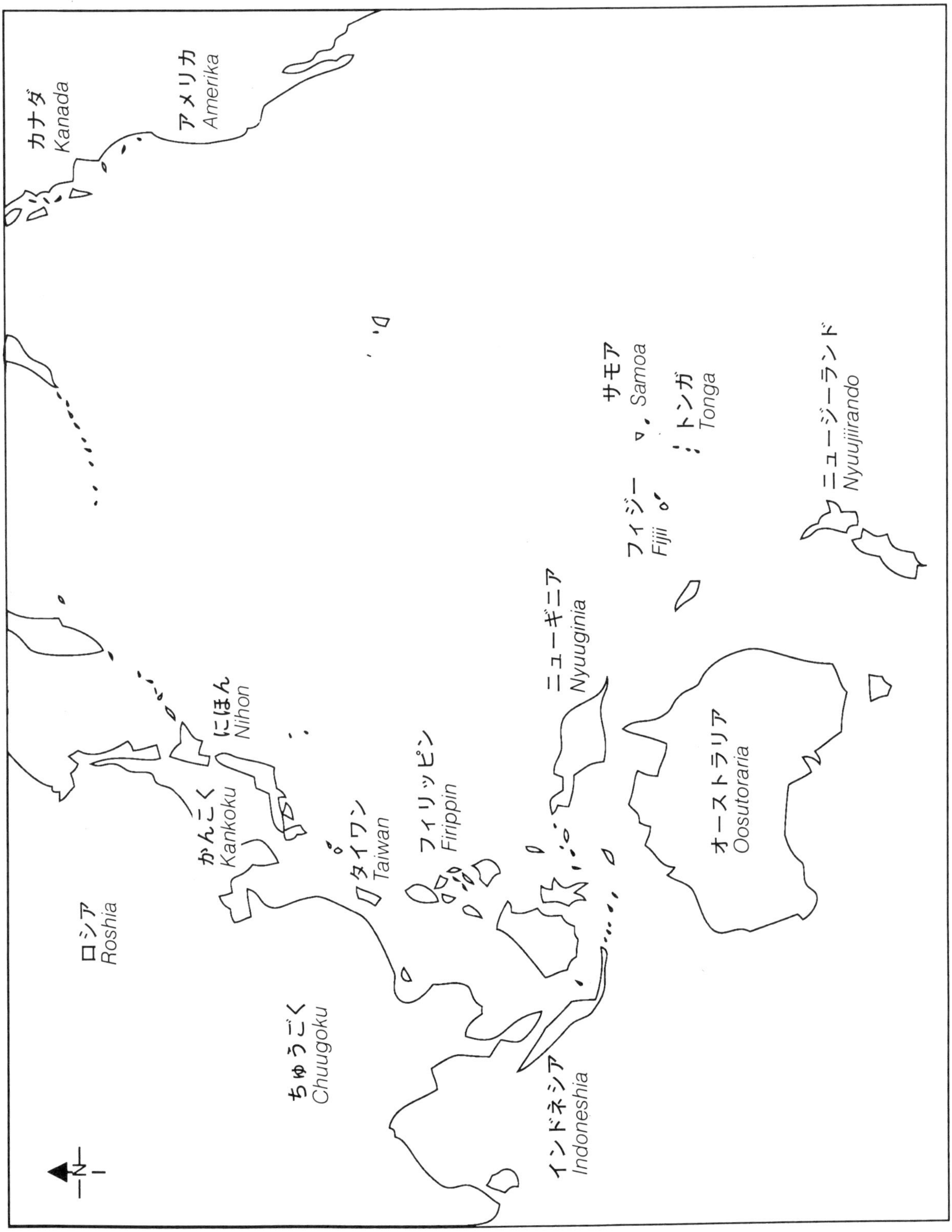

Japan's position in the Pacific

ACTIVITIES

Map of Japan

- Learn the names of the four main islands. Remember that there are also about three thousand small islands in what the world calls Japan.
- Notice the location of the largest cities. Why do you think that they were established there?
- Who are Japan's closest neighbors? How far away are they?
- Draw a map of Japan, and label the four main islands and the major cities.

Map of the Pacific region

Notice that most of the country names on this map of the Pacific region are written in *katakana*, which is generally used for foreign place names. Now look at the photographs below. They will tell you something about Japan's climate.

Summer

Winter

In summer, most places are very hot and humid while northern and mountainous areas are just comfortably warm. In winter most of Japan is very cold, while Kyushu is quite mild.

There are great contrasts too between the city and country. Although it is a very crowded country, there are large areas of mountains and forests and peaceful, quiet places. Even in the bustling cities, it is possible, mostly around temples and shrines, to find natural areas where the noise of the city can hardly be heard.

There are many contrasts between city and country.

Writing practice

- Learn how to write "Japan" in *hiragana*:

にほん *nihon* Japan

Note the way that each *hiragana* syllable corresponds to the *roomaji* version:

に	ほ	ん
ni	*ho*	*n*

1 This syllable is *ni* に

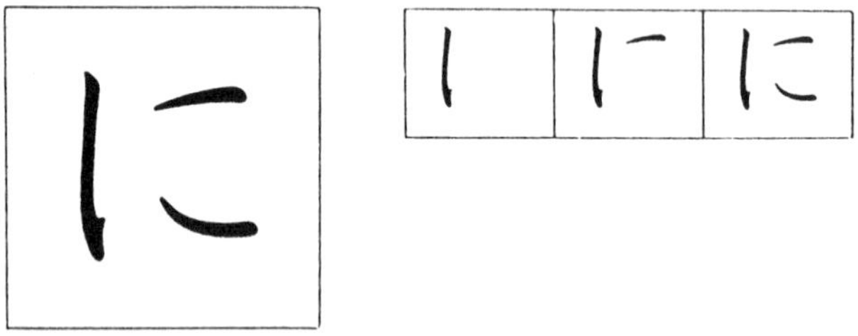

Pick out the syllable that is not written correctly in the line of syllables below.

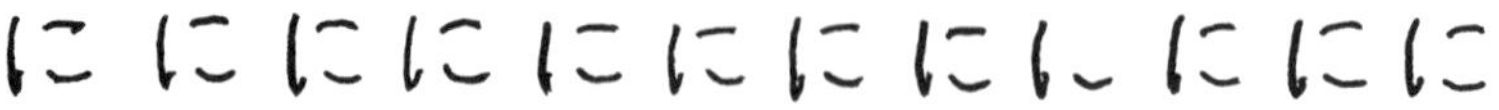

Practice writing the syllable *ni* until you are sure that you can do it without looking at the sample. Be careful to get the balance of the shape right. The chart at the back of the book also shows you how to write the syllables.

2 *ho* is written like this ほ

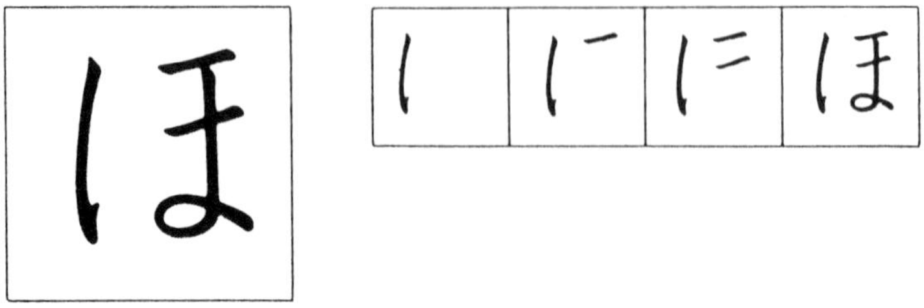

Practice as you did with *ni*.
Try reading aloud the line of *hiragana* below:

ほ に ほ ほ ほ に に に に ほ に ほ に

3 *n* is written like this ん

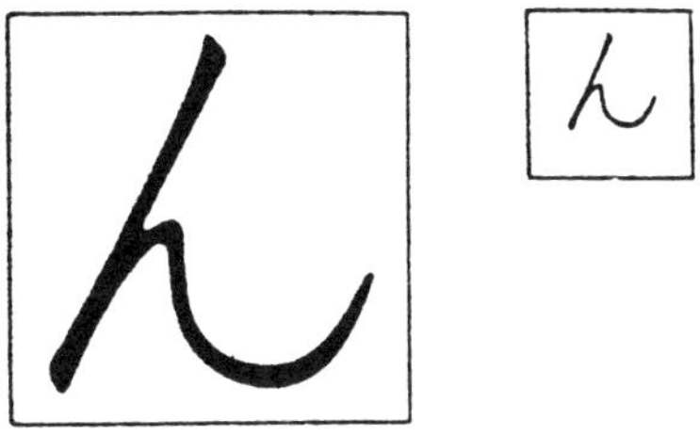

It is the last syllable on the *hiragana* chart and sounds like the "n" in "ham'n eggs".

Practice reading and writing it.

From the line of *hiragana* syllables below pick out the three that you need for *nihon*.

ま さ に か し ん は ら ほ み せ

- The word for "book" is *hon*. See if you can write it correctly without looking back. Write it many times until you are sure that you know it well.
- One of the words for "person" is *nin*. Write it, using the syllables you know. You now know 3 of the 46 basic *hiragana*. Well done!
- On the cover of your notebook you may like to write *nihongo* in *kanji*. Check with your teacher how to write it.

日本語

Reading practice

- See if you can read the following out loud without making a mistake. How fast can you go?

にほんんほにほんにんんにほにん

Vocabulary checklist (Topic One: Introduction)

Here is a checklist of all the vocabulary introduced in Topic One, Introduction.

List One contains words that you **must** learn. List Two contains interest words that will be useful in later Topics but are not essential at the moment.

List One

ひらがな	*hiragana*	hiragana
か	*ka*	(question marker)
かんじ	*kanji*	kanji
カタカナ	*KATAKANA*	katakana
こんばん　は	*konban wa*	Good evening
こんにち　は	*konnichi wa*	Good day/Good afternoon/Hello
にほん	*nihon*	Japan
にほんご	*nihongo*	Japanese language
おはよう　ございます	*Ohayoo gozaimasu*	Good morning
おじぎ	*Ojigi*	bow
おやすみ　なさい	*Oyasumi nasai*	Sleep well!
ただいま	*tadaima*	I'm home!

Learn the list above thoroughly before you cotinue. You may also like to practice writing the words in *hiragana.*

List Two

(Katakana words, when written in *roomaji*, have been written in capital letters to help you remember always to write that word in *katakana.)*

あまど	*amado*	sliding shutters
ドア	*DOA*	door
ふで	*fude*	brush
コカ　コーラ	*KOKA KOORA*	Coca Cola
めいじ	*Meiji*	Meiji (name of Emperor, 1867 – 1912)
パン	*PAN*	bread
レストラン	*RESUTORAN*	restaurant
しょどう	*shodoo*	Japanese calligraphy
しょうじ	*shooji*	paper screens

Japanese place names

ほっかいどう	*Hokkaidoo*	(northern island)
ほんしゅう	*Honshuu*	(largest island)
きゅうしゅう	*Kyuushuu*	(southern island)
しこく	*Shikoku*	(smallest of the four main islands)

ひろしま	*Hiroshima*	Hiroshima
きょうと	*Kyooto*	Kyoto
ながさき	*Nagasaki*	Nagasaki
なら	*Nara*	Nara
おおさか	*Oosaka*	Osaka
さっぽろ	*Sapporo*	Sapporo
とうきょう	*Tookyoo*	Tokyo

Other place names

アメリカ	*AMERIKA*	America
ちゅうごく	*Chuugoku*	China
フィリッピン	*FIRIPPIN*	Philippines
ハワイ	*HAWAI*	Hawaii
インドネシア	*INDONESHIA*	Indonesia
カナダ	*KANADA*	Canada
かんこく	*Kankoku*	Korea
ニュージーランド	*NYUUJIIRANDO*	New Zealand
オーストラリア	*OOSUTORARIA*	Australia
ロシア	*ROSHIA*	Russia
サモア	*SAMOA*	Samoa
タイワン	*TAIWAN*	Taiwan

Unit 1

こんにち　は、ジェレミ　です
konnichi wa, JEREMI desu
Hello, I'm Jeremy

NEW WORDS

です	*desu*	is/are
あなた	*anata*	you
げんき	*genki*	fine, well
おひさしぶり　です　ね	*Ohisashiburi desu ne*	Haven't seen you for ages
おかげ　さま　で	*Okage sama de*	Thank you for asking . . .
さん	*san*	Mr./Mrs./Miss, etc.
せんせい	*sensei*	teacher, master
ああ	*aa*	Oh

STUDY

By the end of this unit you will be able to give your name, exchange greetings, and make some conversation.

- **Introducing yourself simply**
  You know how to greet people at various times of the day, now learn how to tell them your name.
  It is very simple: Just tell them your name and add *desu,* for example: *Mary desu. John desu.*
  Don't pronounce the *u* on the end of *desu.*
  You can now understand the following introductions:

Konnichi wa, JEREMI desu.	こんにち　は、ジェレミ　です。
Konnichi wa, PIITAA desu.	こんにち　は、ピーター　です。

- Here is the beginning of a conversation between two people who haven't met for a long while.

Haruko:

じろう　さん。	*Jiroo san!*	Jiroo!
おはよう　ございます、	*Ohayoo gozaimasu,*	Hello,
おひさしぶり　です　ね。	*Ohisashiburi desu ne.*	I haven't seen you for ages.
おげんき　です　か。	*Ogenki desu ka.*	How are you?

Jiroo:

ああ　はるこ　さん。	*Aa Haruko san!*	Oh Haruko!
おかげ　さま　で	*Okage sama de*	Thank you for asking,
げんき　です。	*genki desu.*	I'm fine.
あなた　は。	*Anata wa.*	How about you?

Haruko:

げんき　です。	*Genki desu.*	I'm fine.

- Jiroo and Haruko are common Japanese first names. Jiroo means "Number Two Son", and Haruko means "Spring Child". The *ko* on the end of Haruko is a very frequent ending on girls' names, meaning "child" or "little one". *Haru* is the word for "spring".

- Notice the word *san* that follows the name when they speak to each other. It is like "Mr./Mrs./Miss/Master" in English, and it is used after everyone's name, except your own when you are talking about yourself.

- When you speak of, or to, a teacher, you must use their name followed by ***sensei*** (teacher) to show respect for their status. (Status in Japan is very, very important.)

- You will notice that Haruko says *Ogenki desu ka* when inquiring about Jiroo, but only *Genki desu* when talking of her own health. If you want to ask after someone else's health you put in the *O* to show respect. It is called an "**honorific O**". Never put in the *O* when speaking of yourself. More of the honorific *O* later. For the moment learn the phrases as they are and practice using them with your friends.

- You will learn about *wa* later. Just learn *anata wa* as a phrase, for the moment. (Be careful, though. It cannot be used for addressing superiors.)

ACTIVITIES

- Practice calling your friends by their names, followed by *san*.

- Introduce yourself to the people on either side of you.

- Practice the conversation example above, substituting different greetings for different times of day. Act it out if you can. Pay special attention to the sounds. Check if you are not sure.

- Check with your teacher how to pronounce your name correctly in Japanese.

- Practice the following two dialogues.

1

Brett:	ジョン　さん　こんばん　は。	*JON san konban wa.*
	おげんき　ですか。	*Ogenki desu ka.*

John:	ブレシト　さん、　おひさしぶり です　ね。おかげ　さま　で げんき　です。	*BURETTO san, Ohisashiburi desu ne. Okage sama de genki desu.*

2

Smith:	すずき　せんせい　です　か。	*Suzuki sensei desu ka.*
Suzuki:	はい　すずき　です。 スミス　さん　です　か。	*Hai Suzuki desu.* *SUMISU san desu ka.*
Smith:	スミス　です。 おげんき　です　か。	*SUMISU desu.* *Ogenki desu ka.*
Suzuki:	おかげ　さま　で　げんき　です。 あなた　は。	*Okage sama de genki desu. Anata wa.*

(Suzuki is a common Japanese surname.)
(*SUMISU* is the Japanese for Smith.)

1
Brett: Good evening, John. How are you?
John: Brett, I haven't seen you for ages. I'm fine thanks.

2
Smith: Are you Mr. Suzuki the teacher?
Suzuki: Yes, I'm Suzuki. Are you Mr. Smith?
Smith: I'm Smith. How are you?
Suzuki: I'm fine, thanks. How about you?

Ka is the equivalent of our question mark, so *Suzuki san desu* "I am Mr. Suzuki" becomes "Are you Mr. Suzuki?" if you say *Suzuki san desu ka.*

Only ask people how they are if you know they have been sick or you haven't seen them for a while.

- How would you say the following in Japanese?

1 How are you, Mrs. Brown?
2 John, I haven't seen you for ages.
3 Thank you for asking, I'm fine.
4 Are you Mr. Suzuki? (the teacher)
5 How about you?
6 Good morning, I'm Smith.
7 Good afternoon, how are you?
8 Good evening, teacher.
9 Good night.
10 I'm home!

です
desu
is/are

NEW WORDS

では　ありません	*dewa arimasen*	is not/are not
なん　です　か	*nan desu ka*	What is it?
ねこ	*neko*	cat
いぬ	*inu*	dog
うち	*uchi*	house
はな	*hana*	flower
えんぴつ	*enpitsu*	pencil
くるま	*kuruma*	car
でんわ	*denwa*	telephone
かさ	*kasa*	umbrella
かばん	*kaban*	bag/briefcase
き	*ki*	tree
りんご	*ringo*	apple
やま	*yama*	mountain
ほん	*hon*	book

STUDY

- Japanese verbs are very simple in structure.

  です
  desu (Remember: don't pronounce the *u*) means:
  I am　　You are
  He is　　She is　　It is
  You are (plural)
  We are　　They are
  Pronouns are much less often used than in English. They do exist, but for the present we will not use them.

- You learned the word *sensei*.

  せんせい　です
  Sensei desu can mean:
  I am a teacher.
  You are a teacher.
  He/she is a teacher.
  You (plural) are teachers.
  We are teachers.
  They are teachers.
  Notice there is no difference in the Japanese for plurals. It sounds confusing, but in practice the context tells you who is being spoken about.

- The negative of *desu* is ***dewa arimasen***: では　ありません
So, to say "I am not a teacher", you say *sensei dewa arimasen.*
This is the formal way of saying the negative, and is very polite. There are, however, more colloquial ways to say "is not" that you will learn later.

- なん　です　か　***nan desu ka***　What is it?
Notice that *ka* marks a question.

ACTIVITIES

- Using the objects pictured on p. 21 and 22, ask and answer questions, for example:

Ask: *Nan desu ka.*	Answer: (name of object) + *desu*
Ask: *Neko desu ka.* (Is it a cat?)	Answer: (positive) *Neko desu.* (It's a cat.)
	Answer: (negative) *Neko dewa arimasen.* (It's not a cat.)

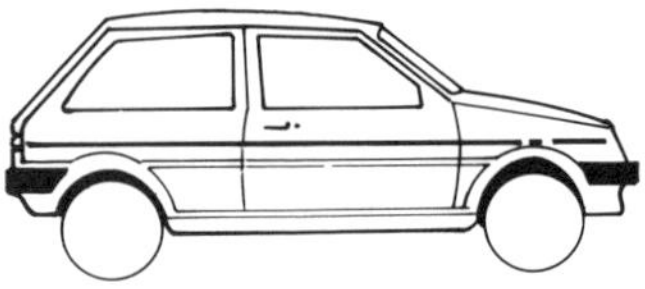

- Make up a conversation: You meet someone you haven't seen for a long time who is carrying a box in which something seems to be moving. You say hello, say that you haven't seen him/her for ages, ask after health and then ask, pointing at the box "What is it?". The person replies.

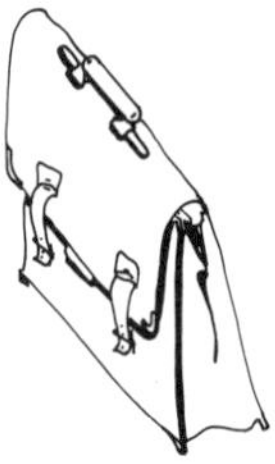

- What would you say in response to the illustrations, using *desu* and *dewa arimasen*? Make a sentence for each picture.

だれ　です　か
dare desu ka
Who are you?

NEW WORDS

だれ	*dare*	who
みなさん	*minasan*	everyone/everybody
いいえ	*iie*	no
はい	*hai*	yes
せいと	*seito*	pupil (student)

STUDY

Study the short dialogues below.

• ピーター　さん　です　か。	*PIITAA san desu ka.*	Are you Peter?
はい　ピーター　です。	*Hai, PIITAA desu.*	Yes, I'm Peter.
• だれ　です　か。	*Dare desu ka.*	Who are you?
ピーター　です。	*PIITAA desu.*	I'm Peter.
• ピーター　さん　です　か。	*PIITAA san desu ka.*	Are you Peter?
いいえ　ピーター　さん　では　ありません。	*Iie, PIITAA san dewa arimasen.*	No, I'm not Peter.
• だれ　です　か。	*Dare desu ka.*	Who is it?
ピーター　です。	*PIITAA desu.*	It's Peter.

In the last conversation it is obvious that Peter himself is answering because he has not used *san* after his name. Remember the rule: never use *san* when referring to yourself.

ACTIVITIES

- Work with a friend who can answer positively or negatively to questions like: *Taroo san desu ka, Michiko san desu ka.*

- You need a number of cards corresponding to the number of people in your group. All except one are blank – this has the name Jiroo on it.

  Give out the cards. Do not tell anyone if you have the Jiroo card or not. Everyone goes around the group greeting each person in turn with 1) a greeting appropriate to the time of day and 2) *Jiroo san desu ka* ("Are you Jiroo?") until he is found.

  The person who finds him calls out loudly *Minasan, Jiroo san desu!* ("Everybody, it is Jiroo!"). If you are not Jiroo you answer, *Jiroo san dewa arimasen, (ROBIN) desu.*

  Take back the cards, reshuffle, and redistribute for another game.

- **Extension:**
  When Jiroo has been found, people can ask how he is, and say they haven't seen him for ages or ask if he is a student.

すみません が、あの ひと は だれ です か
Sumimasen ga, ano hito wa dare desu ka
Excuse me, who is that person over there?

NEW WORDS

すみません が	*sumimasen ga*	Excuse me, but . . .
あの	*ano*	that (over there)
ひと	*hito*	person
どうも	*doomo*	very much
ありがとう ございます	*arigatoo gozaimasu*	Thank you

STUDY

- Read the following dialogue.

Ishikawa: すみません が、あの ひと は だれ です か。
Sumimasen ga, ano hito wa dare desu ka.

Yamada: あの ひと は ブラウン せんせい です。
Ano hito wa BURAUN sensei desu.

Ishikawa: ありがとう ございます。
Arigatoo gozaimasu.

- ***Sumimasen*** is a word used very frequently in many different situations. You use it when you want to make your way through a crowd or to attract someone's attention, or to say "Excuse me" as in the conversation above. The ***ga*** means "but" in this situation and really means "Excuse me, **but** could you please help me?" We do the same sort of thing in English when we don't finish sentences assuming that the person we are speaking to will know what we mean.

- ***Arigatoo gozaimasu*** is often shortened to *arigatoo* for "Thanks" or lengthened to *doomo arigatoo gozaimasu* for "Thank you very very much indeed". In some parts of Japan the *u* on the end of words like *desu* and *gozaimasu* is pronounced, but Tokyo standard pronunciation does not pronounce the *u*.

- ***Hito*** is just one word for person. There are several others which you will learn later.

- *Ano hito wa* "(talking about) that person over there". The particle ***wa*** signals what you are talking about.

  The Japanese always say what they are talking about before continuing. Teachers often employ the same tactic. If a teacher calls out "Open the door, Keri", Keri may only take notice of her name, having been dozing before! If the teacher calls out "Keri, open the door", there is more chance that she will get the whole message.

Reading practice

Here are dialogues for reading practice. Read them on your own or with a friend. Take care to pronounce them carefully. Don't forget to double the time for double syllables. Imagine they are beats of music and give each syllable its due.

1 Mariko is a friend of Keri's mother, and Mariko has not seen Keri for some time.

Keri:	まりこ さん、こんにち は。	*Mariko san, konnichi wa.*
Mariko:	ああ、ケリ さん です か。	*Aa, KERI san desu ka.*
Keri:	はい、ケリ です。	*Hai, KERI desu.*
Mariko:	おひさしぶり です ね。 おげんき です か。	*Ohisashiburi desu ne.* *Ogenki desu ka.*
Keri:	おかげ さま で げんき です。あなた は。	*Okage sama de genki desu.* *Anata wa.*
Mariko:	げんき です。	*Genki desu.*

2 Kenji is looking for a student named Ichiroo, but chooses the wrong person.

Kenji:	いちろう さん です か。	*Ichiroo san desu ka.*
MAAKU:	いいえ、いちろう さん では ありません。 マーク です。 あの ひと は いちろう さん です。	*Iie, Ichiroo san dewa* *arimasen. MAAKU desu.* *Ano hito wa Ichiroo san* *desu.*
Kenji:	ありがとう ございます。	*Arigatoo gozaimasu.*

1

Keri : Hello, Mariko.
Mariko : Oh, is it Keri?
Keri : Yes, I'm Keri.
Mariko : I haven't seen you for ages. How are you?
Keri : (Thanks for asking) I'm fine. How about you?
Mariko : I'm fine.

2
Kenji : Are you Ichiroo?
Mark : No, I'm not Ichiroo. I'm Mark. That person over there is Ichiroo.
Kenji : Thank you.

Check your understanding

Check your understanding of the following:

1		
BOBU:	すみません　が　あの　ひと　は　だれ　です　か。ブラウン　せんせい　です　か。	*Sumimasen ga ano hito wa dare desu ka. BURAUN sensei desu ka.*
Rie:	いいえ、ブラウン　せんせい　では　ありません。　スミス　せんせい　です。	*Iie, BURAUN sensei dewa arimasen. SUMISU sensei desu.*
2		
PIITAA:	じろう　さん　です　か。	*Jiroo san desu ka.*
Jiroo:	はい、じろう　です。	*Hai, Jiroo desu.*
PIITAA:	こんにち　は、　ピーター　です。	*Konnichi wa, PIITAA desu.*

1
Bob : Excuse me, who is that person over there? Is it Brown (the teacher)?
Rie : No, it's not Brown (the teacher). It's Smith (the teacher).

2
Peter : Are you Jiroo?
Jiroo : Yes, I'm Jiroo.
Peter : Hello, I'm Peter.

ACTIVITIES

- Practice the conversations above with a friend.

- Practice your Japanese:
  1 How would you ask someone if she is Sachiko?
  2 How would you say "Good evening" to your teacher?
  3 What would you say if you met your friend at 8:30 a.m.?

4 How would you ask your friend if he or she is well?
5 How would you answer if someone asked you if you are well?
6 What greeting would you use if you met Mr. Smith at midday?
7 First thing in the morning you greet your mother. What do you say?
8 Say "Goodnight, sleep well" to someone.
9 How would you ask "Who is it?" if someone comes to your door?

- Work with a friend. Make up a conversation that uses as much as possible of the Japanese you have learned so far. Practice it until you can speak it naturally without looking at your book.

- Try out your conversation on other people. Ask them questions in English afterwards to see if they have really understood.

Writing practice

Hiragana

- Learn to write あなた　の (*anata no*):

  あ　な　た　の
  a　na　ta　no

  Practice the four syllables until you are sure that you can recognize and write them.

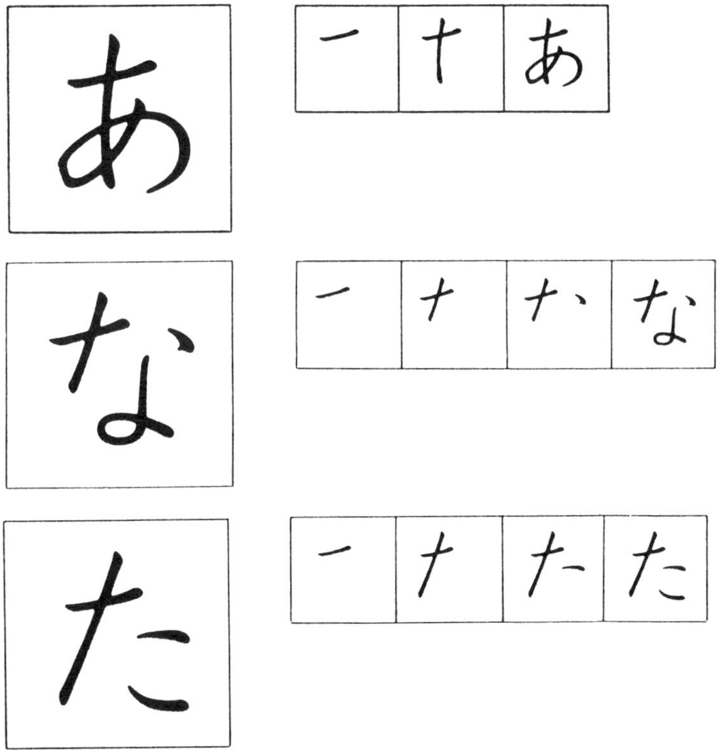

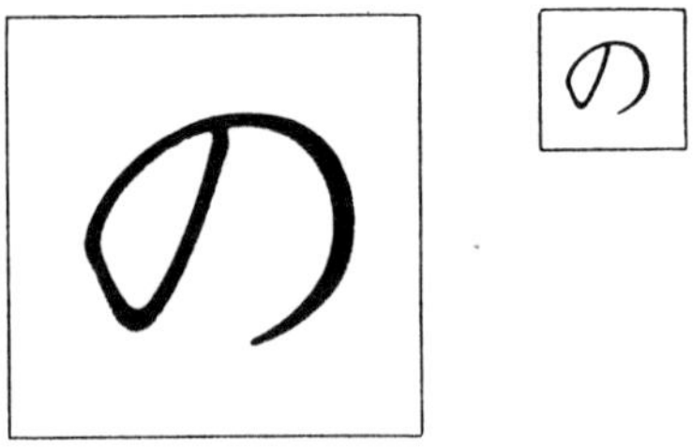

- Identify *ho, n, ni,* and *a* from the line below:

  ま は た ん ほ あ お も し に な の

- Here are some *roomaji* words to change into *hiragana*:
  anata (you) *ano* (that over there) *nan* (what)

EXERCISE

You now know the *hiragana* for *n, ho, ni, a, na, ta, no*. Now see if you can identify them in the following words:

a	1	2	3	4			
	せ	ん	せ	い			
b	1	2	3	4	5	6	7
	お	や	す	み	な	さ	い
c	1	2	3	4			
	に	ほ	ん	ご			
d	1	2	3	4	5		
	こ	ん	に	ち	は		
e	1	2	3	4	5		
	こ	ん	ば	ん	は		
f	1	2	3	4			
	た	だ	い	ま			
g	1	2	3	4			
	ひ	ら	が	な			
h	1	2	3	4			
	か	た	か	な			
i	1	2	3				
	か	ん	じ				
j	1	2	3				
	に	ほ	ん				

Vocabulary checklist (Topic One: Unit 1)

List One (Essential)

あなた	*anata*	you
あの	*ano*	that over there
ブラウン	*BURAUN*	Brown (name)
ありがとう　ございます	*arigatoo gozaimasu*	Thank you very much
だれ	*dare*	who
です	*desu*	is/are
では　ありません	*dewa arimasen*	is not/are not
どうも	*doomo*	very much
げんき　です	*genki desu*	am/is/are well
はい	*hai*	yes
ひと	*hito*	person
か	*ka*	(question marker)
みなさん	*minasan*	everybody/everyone
なん	*nan*	what
なん　です　か	*nan desu ka*	What is it?
おひさしぶり　です　ね	*Ohisashiburi desu ne*	Haven't seen you for ages
おげんき　です　か	*Ogenki desu ka*	How are you?
おかげ　さま　で	*Okage sama de*	Thank you for asking
げんき　です	*genki desu*	I'm fine
さん	*san*	Mr./Mrs./Master/Miss
せいと	*seito*	pupil (student)
せんせい	*sensei*	teacher
すみません　が	*sumimasen ga*	Excuse me, but. . .
スミス	*SUMISU*	Smith (name)
すずき	*Suzuki*	Suzuki (name)
は	*wa*	(topic particle meaning "talking about . . ." Note: the *wa* particle uses the *ha* syllable when you write it in *hiragana*)

List Two (Useful but not essential at this stage)

でんわ	*denwa*	telephone
えんぴつ	*enpitsu*	pencil
はな	*hana*	flower
ほん	*hon*	book
いぬ	*inu*	dog
かばん	*kaban*	bag, briefcase
かさ	*kasa*	umbrella
き	*ki*	tree
くるま	*kuruma*	car
ねこ	*neko*	cat

りんご	*ringo*	apple
うち	*uchi*	house (your own house)
やま	*yama*	mountain

TIPS FOR LEARNING VOCABULARY

There are many different ways of learning vocabulary:

- Some people like to write words out over and over until they know them.
- Others like to do it by word association — imagining crazy associations to help them to remember.
- Another way is to write words onto cards, string cards together on a keyring and read them over in spare moments.
- If you can develop a photographic memory, it is helpful for other subjects too. You may like to practice looking hard at the written word for 20 seconds, then shut your eyes and see if you can "see" the word written behind your eyelids. If it is a word that can easily be pictured, like "cat" imagine a cat by the side of the written word. A few seconds later try to recall the image. It takes practice but this is a very useful skill to develop.
- Recording words onto a tape cassette is also a good way of learning for some people, but remember that it is important to learn the correct spelling too.

You will develop your own "best" way.

Unit 2

お なまえ は なん です か
O namae wa nan desu ka
What is your name?

NEW WORDS

なまえ	*namae*	name
わたし	*watashi*	I/me
の	*no*	(belonging to)

STUDY

- By the end of this unit you will be able to: tell people your name more formally; ask other people's names; ask who things belong to; and tell people what is yours.

- You learned a very simple way of introducing yourself in Unit 1. Here is another way to ask someone else's name and a more formal way of giving your own:

  お なまえ は なん です か。 *O namae wa nan desu ka.*
  はるこ です。 *Haruko desu.*
  What is your name?
  It's Haruko.

- The *O* is an "honorific *O*" which shows respect for the person to whom you are speaking.

- To tell someone your name more formally, you would say
  わたし の なまえ は はるこ です。
  Watashi no namae wa Haruko desu.
  My name is Haruko.

- The ***no*** works like an English apostrophe. It means "belonging to" and is called a particle, so *watashi no namae* means "the name belonging to me" or "my name".

- The ***wa*** is like a sign to tell you that the words in front of it are the topic of the sentence. You can think of it as saying "talking about . . .". It is also called a particle.

  It is always written with the syllable **は** *(ha)* although this seems strange.
  O namae wa . . . (talking about) your name . . .
  Watashi no namae wa . . . (talking about) my name . . .

ACTIVITY

- Practice asking the names of people in your group, and tell them your own.

わたし の です
Watashi no desu
It's mine

NEW WORDS

ペン	*PEN*	pen
だれ	*dare*	who

STUDY

- Look at the following sentence:

  わたし の ねこ です。 *Watashi no neko desu.* It's my cat.

  If you leave out the noun, *neko*, the sentence becomes:
  Watashi no desu (It is mine).

- The question we ask can also leave out the noun, when we understand what is being asked about, for example:

だれ の ねこ です か。	*Dare no neko desu ka.*	Whose cat is it?
だれ の です か。	*Dare no desu ka.*	Whose is it?

ACTIVITIES

- Send one student out of the room after he/she has taken a really good look around at articles on people's desks. Choose an article that he/she should have seen clearly, and bring it to the front of the class.

  He/she re-enters, and the group shows the object, asking *Dare no desu ka.* He/she tries to remember, and may guess right away, answering, for example, *MERII san no desu.* But the student may have to go around the group asking *Anata no desu ka.* ("Is it yours?") or *(SUZAN) san no desu ka* ("Is it Susan's?") until the owner is discovered.

  Keep a count of his/her guesses on the board.

  If you have time to play several games, the overall winner is the one who guesses most quickly.

- Mini quarrel: argue with a friend over who owns something, for example:

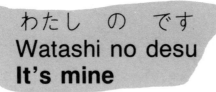

Watashi no PEN desu.	It's my pen.
Iie, watashi no desu.	No, it's mine.

Anata no dewa arimasen.	It's not yours.
Iie, watashi no desu.	No, it's mine.

EXERCISE

Construct sentences using the patterns in the following examples, and write them in your book.

1	*Watashi no desu.*	It is mine.
2	*Anata no desu ka.*	Is it yours?
3	*Watashi no (neko) desu.*	It is my (cat).
4	*(Neko) wa watashi no desu.*	The (cat) is mine.
5	*(Hon) wa anata no desu.*	The (book) is yours.
6	*(Hana) wa watashi no dewa arimasen.*	The (flowers) are not mine.
7	*(Enpitsu) wa anata no dewa arimasen.*	The (pencils) are not yours.
8	*(Suzuki) san no desu.*	It is (Suzuki's).
9	*(BURAUN) san no desu ka.*	Are they (the Browns')?
10	*Watashi no desu ka.*	Is it mine?

なまえ は なん です か
namae wa nan desu ka
What's its name?

NEW WORDS

うま	*uma*	horse
うさぎ	*usagi*	rabbit
ひつじ	*hitsuji*	sheep
うし	*ushi*	cow, bull
くま	*kuma*	bear
ぶた	*buta*	pig

STUDY

- By the end of this unit you will be able to ask the Japanese names of objects and animals.

- Read the following dialogue aloud with two friends:

Haruko:	じろう　さん、　おはよう ございます。　あの　ねこ は　だれ　の　です　か。	*Jiroo san, Ohayoo gozaimasu. Ano neko wa dare no desu ka.*
Jiroo:	わたし　の　では ありません。ピーター さん　の　です。	*Watashi no dewa arimasen. PIITAA san no desu.*
Haruko:	ピーター　さん、あの　ねこ は　あなた　の　です　か。	*PIITAA san, ano neko wa anata no desu ka.*
PIITAA:	はい、わたし　の　ねこ です。	*Hai, watashi no neko desu.*
Haruko:	ねこ　の　なまえ　は　なん です　か。	*Neko no namae wa nan desu ka.*
PIITAA:	ねこ　の　なまえ　は スミス　です。	*Neko no namae wa SUMISU desu.*

Haruko Good morning, Jiroo. Whose is that cat over there?
Jiroo : It's not mine. It's Peter's.
Haruko : Peter, is that cat over there yours?
Peter : Yes, it's my cat.
Haruko : What is the cat's name?
Peter : The cat's name is Smith.

- **Note**: There is no honorific *O* before the question *Namae wa nan desu ka* when we are discussing an animal or thing.

- When you want people to know clearly what you are talking about, you give the topic, follow it with *wa*, and then continue, for example:
  Neko no namae wa . . . nan desu ka.
  Talking about the cat's name . . . what is it?

ACTIVITIES

- Make up your own conversation like the one above. Instead of "cat", use an animal from the list on p. 35.

- Practice until you are sure you know the words well, then act out the conversation for your group, without looking at your book.

- Write out the conversation in your book.

うま
uma

うさぎ
usagi

ひつじ
hitsuji

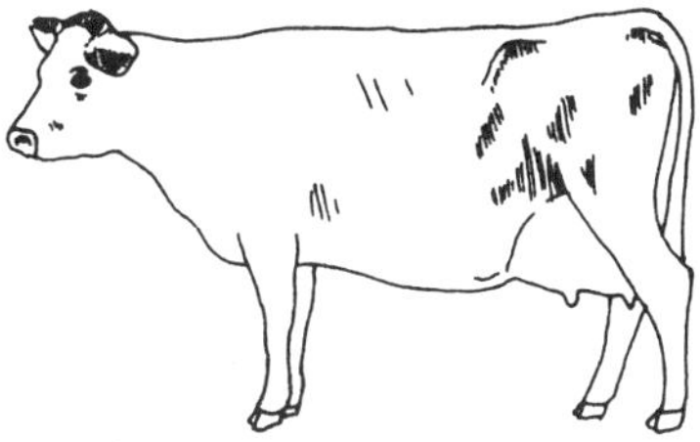

うし
ushi

くま
kuma

ぶた
buta

にほんご　の　なまえ　は　なん
です　か

nihongo no namae wa nan
desu ka

What is its Japanese name?

STUDY

- This is one way to ask for the name of something in Japanese:
  Nihongo no namae wa nan desu ka.
  What is its name in Japanese?
  The reply will be:
  ....desu.
  It's....................
  or
  Nihongo no namae wa ....desu.
  Its Japanese name is ....

ACTIVITY

- Point to one of the animals and ask someone the question above.
  They can answer using either of the patterns above.

EXERCISE

Using words learned previously, you can make sentences like these:

Anata no hon desu ka.
Is it your book?

Iie watashi no hon dewa arimasen.
No, it's not my book.

Watashi no kuruma desu.
It's my car.

Hanako san no hana desu.
They are Hanako's flowers.

Nihongo no namae wa "hon" desu.
The Japanese name is "hon".

Inu no namae wa "ROVER" desu.
The dog's name is Rover.

- Make ten sentences like these, and write them in your book. Use *roomaji.*

STUDY

- **Japanese verbs always go at the end of a sentence.**
  You may have noticed that in Japanese the verb goes right at the end of a sentence except if the question marker *ka* is present and takes the last place. So a Japanese sentence literally translated means:
  Anata no hon desu.
  You belonging to book (it) is.
  Try reading the sentence above from the right-hand side, and it will make better sense in English:
  "It is a book belonging to you."
  It is important when you put a Japanese sentence into English that you make the English sound as natural as possible.

Unit 3

はじめまして　どうぞ　よろしく
hajimemashite doozo yoroshiku
Pleased to meet you

NEW WORDS

はじめまして	*hajimemashite*	(For the first time)
どうぞ　よろしく	*doozo yoroshiku*	Pleased to meet you

STUDY

Read the following dialogue aloud with a friend. You will understand it without an English translation.

BURAUN:	こんにち　は。 スミス　さん　です　か。	*Konnichi wa.* *SUMISU san desu ka.*
SUMISU:	はい、スミス　です。	*Hai, SUMISU desu.*
BURAUN:	わたし　の　なまえ　は ブラウン　です。 はじめまして　どうぞ よろしく。	*Watashi no namae wa* *BURAUN desu.* *Hajimemashite* *doozo yoroshiku.* [bows]
SUMISU:	はじめまして。	*Hajimemashite.* [bows]

- ***Hajimemashite*** means "I am meeting you for the first time." and corresponds to "How do you do?" or "I'm pleased to meet you" and we use it when we first meet someone.

  Doozo yoroshiku literally means "Please be good to me" and can also be used for "How do you do?". Either of the expressions can be used to say "How do you do" but often they are used together, as in the dialogue above: *Hajimemashite doozo yoroshiku.* Underlying the expression is the idea ". . . and I hope you will forgive me in advance for anything that I may do in the future which may distress or offend you".

さよなら
sayonara
saying goodbye and thank you

NEW WORDS

さよなら	*sayonara*	goodbye
さようなら	*sayoonara*	goodbye
じゃ　また	*ja mata*	see you
どうも	*doomo*	very much

STUDY

- **Goodbye**

  さよなら
  Sayonara Goodbye
  This is said when the parting is likely to be for an extended period. Do not use it to a member of your family, unless you don't expect to see him/her again.

  さようなら
  Sayoonara Goodbye
  This is said to your school principal, or on a formal occasion.

- じゃ　また
  Ja mata See you/Goodbye

  Ja means "Well then", "In that case".
  mata means "again".
  Use *Ja mata* to say goodbye to someone your own age or younger.

- **Thank you**
  You have already learned the following expressions:
  Arigatoo gozaimasu. Thank you.
  Doomo by itself is used as an informal way to say "Thanks".

ACTIVITIES

- Use the examples on p. 37 and above to make up your own conversation with someone you haven't met before.
  Imagine you meet at the station. Greet and introduce yourself. Point to luggage, and ask if it belongs to him/her. He/she says yes or no. You walk off to the hotel, possibly carrying heavy luggage!
  Put as much into the conversation as you can without asking for any new words. On the way, ask about the person's health. Mime putting him/her into a taxi, and say goodbye.

- Write the conversation you have just acted out, on paper. Cut out the sentences as strips. Check against the example.

- Mix up the sentences in the conversation you have written and ask a friend to sort it out into logical order again.
- Stick the sentences in their correct order into your book.

Check your understanding

What do the following sentences mean?

1 *Ogenki desu ka.*
2 *Ohisashiburi desu ne.*
3 *Onamae wa nan desu ka.*
4 *Okage sama de genki desu.*
5 *Dare desu ka.*
6 *Anata no desu ka.*
7 *Watashi no neko desu.*
8 *Jiroo san wa dare desu ka.*
9 *Hajimemashite doozo yoroshiku.*
10 *Konnichi wa, minasan.*
11 *BURAUN sensei desu.*

すみません　が、　どこ　の　かた　です　か

sumimasen ga, doko no kata desu ka

Excuse me, what nationality are you?

NEW WORDS

じん	*jin*	person
にん	*nin*	person
かた	*kata*	person (very polite)
なにじん	*nanijin*	(what person)
どこ	*doko*	where

Countries

Below are the names of some countries.

アメリカ	*AMERIKA*	America
オーストラリア	*OOSUTORARIA*	Australia

カナダ	*KANADA*	Canada
イギリス	*IGIRISU*	England
ドイツ	*DOITSU*	Germany
フランス	*FURANSU*	France
オランダ	*ORANDA*	Holland
インド	*INDO*	India
イタリア	*ITARIA*	Italy
ニュージーランド	*NYUUJIIRANDO*	New Zealand
ロシア	*ROSHIA*	Russia
ホンコン	*HONKON*	Hong Kong
メキシコ	*MEKISHIKO*	Mexico
スペイン	*SUPEIN*	Spain

- Notice that the names above are written in *katakana. DOITSU* is the only one that doesn't sound familiar. It comes from the German word "Deutsche".

ACTIVITIES

- Using a map of the world, show your friends where each of the countries in the list above is. Using the language you know, you can say, for example:
  AMERIKA desu.
  ROSHIA dewa arimasen, DOITSU desu.

- Ask questions like: *INDO desu ka.*
  and answer: *Hai, INDO desu.* or *Iie, INDO dewa arimasen.*

STUDY

Person

- The word used when describing nationality is:

じん	***jin***	**person**

To give your nationality, just add *jin* to your country name, e.g.:

アメリカじん です。
AMERIKAjin desu. I am an American.

ACTIVITIES

- Look at a map again and practice the nationality words with a friend. Point at countries on the map and take turns describing the nationality.

- Ask your neighbors about their nationality, asking, for example:
  AMERIKAjin desu ka. Are you American?
  They can answer:
  Hai, AMERIKAjin desu. or *Iie, AMERIKAjin dewa arimasen.*

The *kanji* for "person" is 人
One explanation for this *kanji* is:
"No one in the world can exist alone. Everybody needs others as they go through life".
Here is a simplified person: ノ
And here are the others supporting the person: ㇏
Together they make the *kanji*: 人

Note that the *kanji* can be read as *jin* or as *nin*. Later you will learn about the different readings of *kanji*. For now, just remember that there are various ways to pronounce the same *kanji*.

人

- Go around the room meeting people. Greet them. Ask their names. Tell them your own. Ask how they are. Answer their inquiries about your own health. Ask what nationality they are. Tell them your nationality. Say goodbye.

- Write down a conversation in *roomaji* based on the outline in the previous activity. If you want to do it in *hiragana*, do so copying words carefully from the text. Remember when you write your nationality that only the country itself is in *katakana*.

  e.g. アメリカ じん (*jin* in *hiragana*)
  アメリカ 人 (*jin* in *kanji*)

STUDY

- **Asking about nationality**

  A more formal way of asking a person's nationality is:

  どこ の かた です か。

  Doko no kata desu ka. Where are you from?/What is your nationality?

  doko means "where", *kata* is a polite word for *jin* (person).

- A less formal way of asking the question is:

  なにじん です か。

  Nanijin desu ka. Where are you from? (What person are you?)

ACTIVITIES

- Go around the room again, asking either :
  Doko no kata desu ka., or
  Nanijin desu ka.
  (Remember: to both questions you answer . . . *jin desu.*)

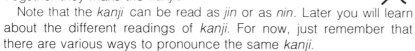

- In groups of four or five:
  One person thinks of a nationality and writes it secretly on paper.
  The rest of the group have to guess which nationality has been chosen by asking *ROSHIAjin desu ka*, etc. until they find out. The person who has chosen the nationality answers either *Hai, ROSHIAjin desu* or *ROSHIAjin dewa arimasen.*
  The group may ask only five questions. If they don't guess in that time, the person has a second turn. If their chosen nationality is guessed, the person who guessed it takes a turn to choose a nationality.

FORMAL AND LESS FORMAL

Doko no kata desu ka is a very polite way of saying "Where do you come from?" or "What nationality are you?" It is safe to use when speaking to anyone.

Nanijin desu ka is an expression you would use only among your own friends, or people your own age, but it has the same meaning.

You will remember two more expressions that have two levels of formality:

さようなら *Sayoonara*	and	じゃ また *ja mata*

Learning Japanese, you will become very aware of different levels of formality. We actually have the same formality in English, but because it is our native language, we do it naturally, and tend not to be so aware of it (unless we have to do something like meet the president, when we need to find out how to address him particularly politely!).

Kata is a very polite word for *jin* (person), and a third word you know for person is *hito.* All of them are polite, but *kata* is the most polite.

ACTIVITIES

- Look at these examples:
  Ano hito wa dare desu ka.
  Ano kata wa dare desu ka.
  Which is more polite?

- Discuss the following:
  "Politeness is of very high importance is Japan. Japanese people, 120 million of them living in a small country, have to learn to respect one another's privacy and to be considerate and polite at all times, if society is to run smoothly."

EXERCISES

- Read the following:

1 *Sensei, Ohayoo gozaimasu. JON san desu. AMERIKAjin desu.*
2 *MAIKU san, konnichi wa. Ohisashiburi desu ne. Ogenki desu ka.*
3 *Tadaima.*
4 *Minasan, BURAUN sensei desu.*
5 *MERISSA san, konban wa.*
6 *Ogenki desu ka. Okage sama de genki desu.*
7 *Hajimemashite doozo yoroshiku.*
8 *Arigatoo gozaimasu. Doomo arigatoo gozaimasu.*
9 *Oyasumi nasai.*
10 *FURANSUjin desu.*
11 *Onamae wa nan desu ka.*
12 *Watashi no namae wa SUZAN desu.*
13 *Sensei dewa arimasen.*
14 *Seito desu ka.*
15 *Ja mata.*

- Match the sentences above with the ones below:

A Are you a student?
B What's your name?
C Goodnight and sleep well.
D Thank you. Thank you very much.
E How are you? I'm fine thank you (for asking).
F I'm home.
G Good afternoon, Mike. I haven't seen you for ages. How are you?
H Good morning, teacher. This is John. He's American.
I He's French.
J My name is Susan.
K I'm not a teacher.
L I'll see you again.
M I'm pleased to meet you (for the first time).
N Everybody, this is Mr. Brown (teacher).
O Good evening, Melissa.

Check your understanding

How many of the following sentences can you understand?

あの　かた　は　アメリカじん　です。	*Ano kata wa AMERIKAjin desu.*
あの　ひと　は　フランスじん　です。	*Ano hito wa FURANSUjin desu.*
オーストラリアじん　です　か。	*OOSUTORARIAjin desu ka.*
わたし　は　ドイツじん　です。	*Watashi wa DOITSUjin desu.*
あなた　は　オーストラリアじん　です　か。	*Anata wa OOSUTORARIAjin desu ka.*
わたし　は　フランスじん　では　ありません。	*Watashi wa FURANSUjin dewa arimasen.*
ロシアじん　では　ありません。	*ROSHIAjin dewa arimasen.*

スペインじん　です　か。	*SUPEINjin desu ka.*
メキシコじん　です。	*MEKISHIKOjin desu.*
イギリスじん　です。	*IGIRISUjin desu.*

Meishi

Below are *meishi* or name cards. *Meishi* are very important in Japan and are exchanged when you meet someone for the first time as part of the introduction.

Japanese people always give their surnames when being introduced. Students in school are called by their surnames. Friends and families use first names.

From the cards on p. 46 you can learn some common Japanese names. People's first names are in brackets and whether they are male or female is indicated with M or F.

Just as English names like "Baker" came from the occupation of a person's forebears, or as "Underhill" was derived from the place where people lived, Japanese names have meanings, for example:
take means "bamboo",
shita means "under".
So originally the Takeshita family must have lived "under the bamboo", perhaps on a slope below a stand of bamboo.
Ishi means "stone",
gawa or *kawa* means "river".
So probably, the Ishigawa family came from a place near a stony river.

ACTIVITIES

- Choose a name card for yourself. (These can be photocopied and cut up.) When you are asked *Onamae wa nan desu ka,* you can answer, for example, *Takeshita desu* or *Takeshita Hanako desu,* remembering to say the first name after the surname. Or you can say *Watashi no namae wa Takeshita Hanako desu.*

  You can also say "I'm a person belonging to Nagasaki" with *Nagasaki no hito desu.*

- The group sits in a circle and one person asks the question *Onamae wa nan desu ka.* His or her neighbor answers, then asks the next person in the circle the question until everyone in the group has had a turn. Ask about nationality using questions like: *(Nihonjin) desu ka,* to which the answer would be *Hai (nihonjin) desu,* or *Iie (nihonjin) dewa arimasen. FURANSUjin desu.* Use the nationality cards on p. 47 as well.

- When all the nationality cards are on the table, one of you can be the questioner, and ask *(AMERIKAjin) wa dare desu ka.* The first one to find the card asked for calls out *AMERIKAjin wa (SUMISU) san desu.* The caller then asks the next question until all the cards have been "won". The winner is the person who has picked up the most cards.

  (You will probably have lots of ideas for using these cards to play simple games that will help you to use your Japanese. Invent your own, but check the Japanese phrases and vocabulary with your teacher before you use the game to avoid repeating incorrect grammar and spelling.)

HITACHI

株式會社 日立製作所

宣伝部 海外宣伝グループ

松村賢吾

郵便番号一〇一

東京都千代田区神田駿河台四丁目六番地

東京（〇三）二五八－一一一一（大代表）

（〇三）二五八－二三九八（直通）

ファクシミリ 二五五－六二〇一

千葉みどり

〒339 岩槻市諏訪3－3－9－502

TEL 0487（94）1835

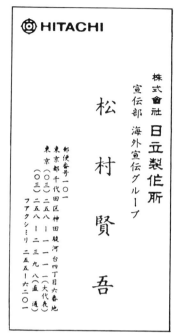

めいし
meishi

わたなべ けいこ **WATANABE (Keiko)** とうきょう **TOOKYOO** **(F)**	たなか さつき **TANAKA (Satsuki)** なごや **NAGOYA** **(F)**	いそだ けいこ **ISODA (Keiko)** ひろしま **HIROSHIMA** **(F)**
いのうえ まさお **INOUE (Masao)** さっぽろ **SAPPORO** **(M)**	いしだ ともこ **ISHIDA (Tomoko)** おおさか **OOSAKA** **(F)**	すずき いちろう **SUZUKI (Ichiroo)** ふくおか **FUKUOKA** **(M)**
わずか たろう **WAZUKA (Taroo)** ながさき **NAGASAKI** **(M)**	やまだ くみこ **YAMADA (Kumiko)** よこはま **YOKOHAMA** **(F)**	たにざき としお **TANIZAKI (Toshio)** にいがた **NIIGATA** **(M)**
ふじた はなこ **FUJITA (Hanako)** きょうと **KYOOTO** **(F)**	そま まさる **SOMA (Masaru)** くらしき **KURASHIKI** **(M)**	おぬき かおる **ONUKI (Kaoru)** おかやま **OKAYAMA** **(M)**
こばやし みゆき **KOBAYASHI (Miyuki)** こうべ **KOOBE** **(F)**	さとう さちこ **SATOO (Sachiko)** ふくやま **FUKUYAMA** **(F)**	ひらおか しんご **HIRAOKA (Shingo)** なら **NARA** **(M)**

Note: *Meishi* are often written in Japanese on one side and English on the other, particularly for people who do business with English-speaking countries. The *meishi* above have both languages together and have been simplified for easy use.

You will find that any Japanese-made business card, whether for a foreigner or for a Japanese national, will be printed with the name in its

Suzuki Masahiro *Nihon* (M)	Green Jock *NYUUJIIRANDO* (M)	Tscherner Hans *DOITSU* (M)
Smith Robin *AMERIKA* (F)	Le Croix Pierre *FURANSU* (M)	Rossini Maria *ITARIA* (F)
Connors Jane *OOSUTORARIA* (F)	Lim Choon *TAIWAN* (M)	Hunter Simon *KANADA* (M)
Lozano Minerva *MEKISHIKO* (F)	Verner Lucy *IGIRISU* (F)	Vives Francesca *SUPEIN* (F)
Costatino Mario *ITARIA* (M)	Wu Agnes *HONKON* (F)	Sison Jun *FIRIPPIN* (M)

usual order, i.e., if the name is normally written first-name-first, it will be printed that way on the *meishi,* but if it is normally written last-name-first, as Japanese names are, that will be the order printed on the *meishi.*

Writing practice

わ　　え　　し　　ま
wa　　*e*　　*shi*　　*ma*

Look carefully at the examples and practice writing the syllables.

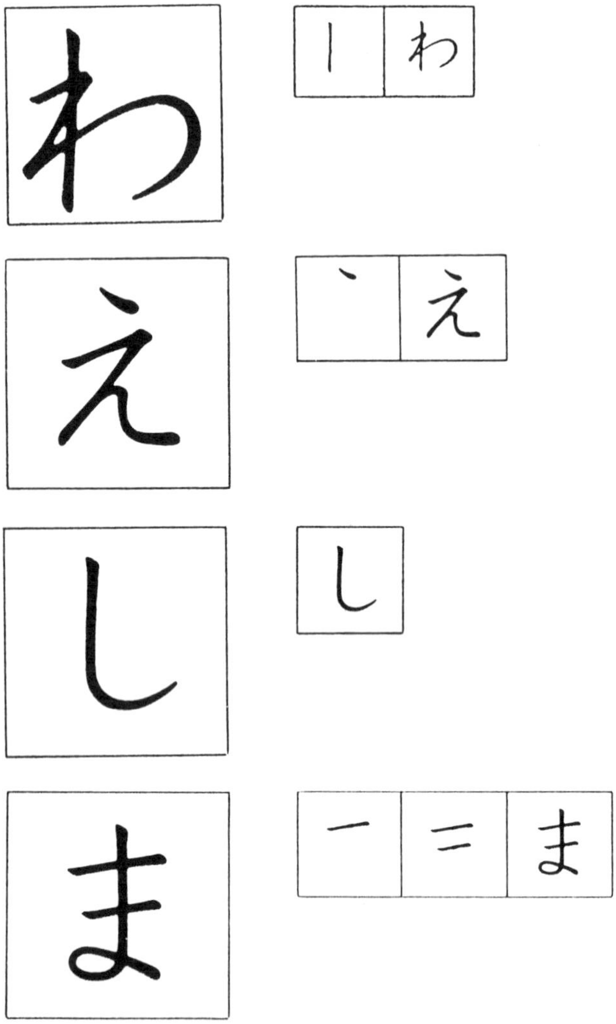

Now there are many words that you can write in *hiragana*. Try the following:

わたし *watashi*	の *no*	なまえ *namae*
あなた *anata*	の *no*	なまえ *namae*
にほん *Nihon*	ほん *hon*	なし *nashi* (Japanese pear)

しま *shima* (island)	なま *nama* (raw)	え *e* (picture)

Find the *hiragana* words that you know in this puzzle:

ら	し	ね	ま	こ	に	ほ	ん	り	せ	そ	え	と	ゆ	よ
み	ほ	ん	な	も	さ	む	お	ろ	れ	は	ひ	じ	ん	ふ
か	き	す	せ	く	う	い	わ	た	し	に	ね	へ	め	や
り	る	わ	あ	な	た	け	を	ん	し	こ	の	ち	て	つ

(You now know 11 *hiragana*)

Round up time!

Here are some suggestions for activities that will help you to realize how much you know.

- With a group of friends, make up a quiz from information to be found in this unit. For example:
  "What was the name of the Emperor of Japan in 1868?"
  "What does *konnichi wa* mean?"
  "How should you spell *Ohayoo gozaimasu*?"
  Challenge another group to a quiz – take turns being quizmaster.
- On the blackboard, brainstorm information that you have learned about Japan. Keep a tally of how much information you have remembered. (Let everyone join in, or play it as a team game.)
- Vocabulary game. "I'm thinking of a word that begins with . . .". The person who guesses first chooses the next word. Only use words learned in this topic.
- Play "hangman" with your friends using Japanese words you have learned in this unit.

Vocabulary checklist (Topic One, Units 2 and 3)

List One (essential)

アメリカ	*AMERIKA*	America
どこ　の　かた　です　か	*Doko no kata desu ka*	What nationality are you?/Where are you from?
ドイツ	*DOITSU*	Germany
どうも　ありがとう　ございます	*doomo arigatoo gozaimasu*	Thank you very much.

フランス	*FURANSU*	France
はい	*hai*	yes
はじめまして　どうぞ よろしく	*hajimemashite doozo yoroshiku*	Pleased to meet you for the first time
ホンコン	*HONKON*	Hong Kong
イギリス	*IGIRISU*	England
いいえ	*iie*	no
インド	*INDO*	India
イタリア	*ITARIA*	Italy
じゃ　また	*ja mata*	See you! Bye!
カナダ	*KANADA*	Canada
メキシコ	*MEKISHIKO*	Mexico
なまえ	*namae*	name
なにじん　です　か	*nanijin desu ka*	What nationality? (informal)
にん、じん、ひと、かた	*nin/jin/hito/kata*	person
の	*no*	(particle meaning "belonging to")
ニュージーランド	*NYUUJIIRANDO*	New Zealand
お	*O*	(honorific to show respect)
オーストラリア	*OOSUTORARIA*	Australia
オランダ	*ORANDA*	Holland
ペン	*PEN*	pen
ロシア	*ROSHIA*	Russia
さよなら	*Sayonara*	Goodbye
さようなら	*Sayoonara*	Goodbye (formal)
スペイン	*SUPEIN*	Spain
は	*wa*	(particle to show topic)
わたし	*watashi*	I/me

List Two (useful but not essential at this stage)

うま	*uma*	horse
うさぎ	*usagi*	rabbit
ひつじ	*hitsuji*	sheep
うし	*ushi*	cow, bull
くま	*kuma*	bear
ぶた	*buta*	pig

TOPIC TWO in the classroom

Introduction

ACHIEVEMENTS

By the end of this topic you will have learned:

- about the Japanese education system;
- the names of common classroom objects;
- how to ask what something is called in Japanese;
- more *hiragana*;
- how to tell people about "this" and "that";
- to give and understand simple instructions;
- how to ask people to give things to you;
- how to ask people to do things for you.

From kindergarten to university

Japanese children begin compulsory schooling at the age of six. Sixty-four per cent of them, however, attend nursery schools and kindergarten before that. Many of those also attend English classes several times a week!

Kindergarten schools are called ***yoochien***. Even kindergarten children wear uniforms and take pride in being part of a group.

At six, children enter ***shoogakkoo***, Primary school. They spend their next six years there. They learn *hiragana, katakana,* and a basic 800 *kanji*

Yoochien **children**

Shoogakkoo **pupils**

小学校

中学校

高等学校

as well as subjects similar to those studied in American schools. They don't usually study English formally until they enter high school; but the desire to be good at English, and the parental feeling that children will not succeed in getting good jobs unless they have good English, prompts most of them to attend private English lessons right through Primary School.

Shoogakkoo is written with the *kanji* for "small": 小（しょう） *shoo* and the *kanji* for school: 学校（がっこう） *gakkoo*

Between *shoogakkoo* and high school, students attend ***chuugakkoo***. *Chuugakkoo* is a Middle or Intermediate School equivalent to an American Junior High School.

Chuu is written like this in *kanji*: 中
That *kanji* means "middle".

Students are legally allowed to leave school after *chuugakkoo*. They are then fifteen years old.

At fifteen they enter ***kootoogakkoo*** (High school) and remain there until they go to work or enter university at eighteen or nineteen.
Kootoo is written with the *kanji* for "high": 高（こう）*koo* and the *kanji* for grade: 等（とう）*too*.

Ninety-four per cent of Japanese students, according to a recent survey, continue to *kootoogakkoo*, because education is seen to be the only way, in such a large and competitive society, to get a good job with reasonable long-term prospects. A good job depends on good school results, and on which schools and university or other educational institutions you have attended.

Because of this, the majority of Japanese parents plan their children's education very carefully and set goals for them to achieve. For many children, the expectation of the parents is so high that the students live their whole school lives under tremendous pressure. They often attend cram schools called ***juku*** at night after attending school all day. When they arrive home again they do enormous amounts of homework. They frequently have to leave home at 7 a.m. to catch trains and buses to school, so there are many who are perpetually tired. **There are 20,000 cram schools in Tokyo alone.**

***Chuugakkoo* students**

***Kootoogakkoo* students**

大学

Thirty-seven per cent of Japan's students eventually enter university or ***daigaku***. Being accepted into the university of your choice is very important. In comparison with school days, once they have entered university the pressure eases and students spend their university years learning how to socialize.

Dai is written with the *kanji* for "big": 大 (だい).

Gaku is the *kanji* for "school": 学 (がく).

In the classroom

As there are so many students in a class, in some schools practical work is often impossible. In a science class, for example, the students may never do a practical experiment themselves, but watch the teacher demonstrate by means of an overhead projector, in an ordinary classroom.

Art classes, too, often take place in ordinary classrooms. The opportunity to experiment or to show individual creative ability is often very limited.

***Juku* class**

***Kootoogakkoo* art class**

Unit 1

きょうしつ
kyooshitsu
Classroom

NEW WORDS

ボールペン	*BOORUPEN*	ballpoint pen
ちず	*chizu*	map
え	*e*	picture
えんぴつ	*enpitsu*	pencil
はこ	*hako*	box
いす	*isu*	chair
かばん	*kaban*	bag/briefcase
かみ	*kami*	paper
こくばん	*kokuban*	blackboard
きょうしつ	*kyooshitsu*	classroom
ノート	*NOOTO*	notebook
つくえ	*tsukue*	desk

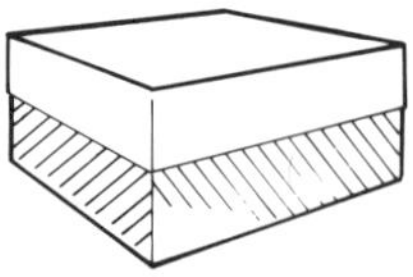

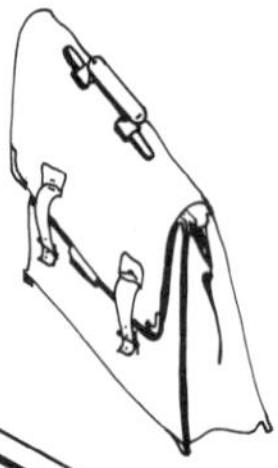

STUDY

- By the end of this unit you will be able to: act upon and give simple instructions; and say what things are in the classroom.

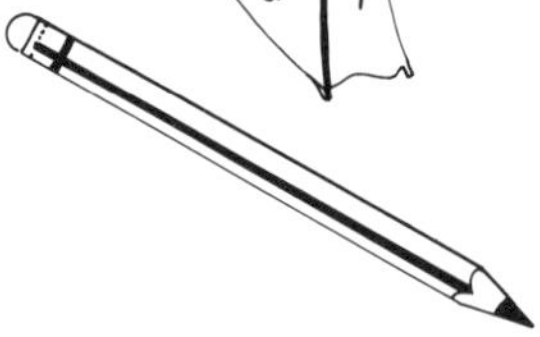

- じゃない　です　　*janai desu*　　is not/are not

  Janai (desu) is an informal alternative to *dewa arimasen*. The negative of *tsukue desu* (It is a desk) is *tsukue dewa arimasen*. Or, in an informal situation, e.g. between schoolfriends, we can say ***tsukue janai (desu)***.

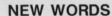

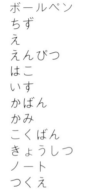

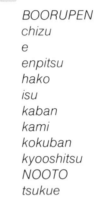

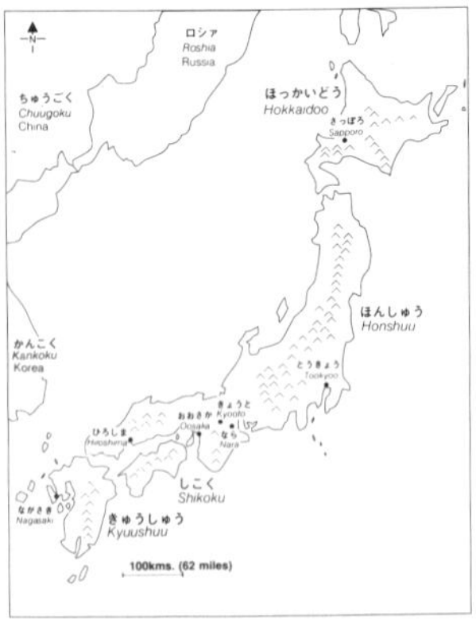

- In Topic One you learned how to ask what things are, and what things are called in Japanese. For example:

  Nan desu ka.　　What is it?
  Tsukue desu.　　It's a desk.

  Nihongo no namae wa nan desu ka. What is its Japanese name?
  Nihongo no namae wa tsukue desu. Its Japanese name is *tsukue*.

  Review these phrases. Now use the same patterns but in the negative, e.g. *tsukue dewa arimasen / tsukue janai desu.*

ACTIVITIES

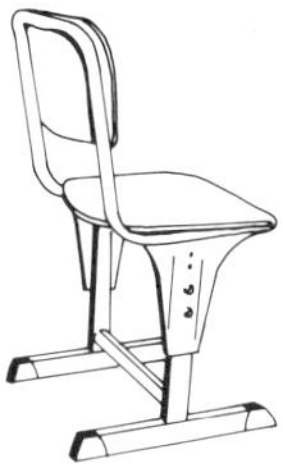

- Practice the phrases above with the words in the *New words* section.
- Match all of the illustrations in the margin with the appropriate Japanese word in the *New words* section.
- With a neighbor take turns making a sentence for each illustration. Make sentences in the negative too.

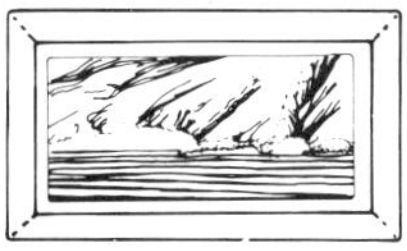

- Can you understand the following dialogues?

MAAKU: *Watashi no namae wa MAAKU desu. AMERIKAjin desu.*
Jiroo: *Watashi no namae wa Jiroo desu. Nihonjin desu.*
MAAKU: [Pointing to object] *Nihongo no namae wa nan desu ka.*
Jiroo: *Nihongo no namae wa tsukue desu.*
MAAKU: *Arigatoo gozaimasu.*

Kiri is looking at the things on Toshiki's desk.
KIRI: *Enpitsu desu ka.*
Toshiki: *Iie, enpitsu dewa arimasen. PEN desu.*

Toshiki could have said, *enpitsu janai desu* if it was an informal situation. But if Kiri was talking to an adult more formally, *dewa arimasen* would be a very formal, polite way to answer her.

How well do you think they know each other from the conversation above? In Japanese you can do a lot of easy detective work on the relationships between people if you know about the different levels of formality.

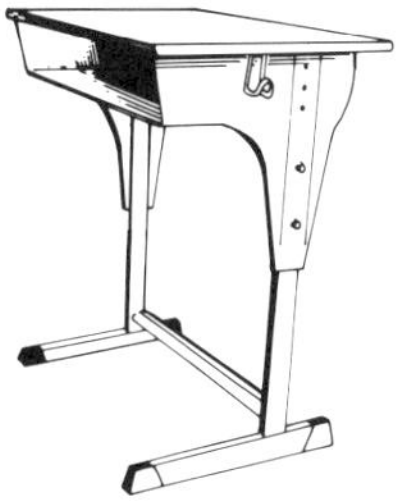

EXERCISES

- Here are some review conversations for you to check your memory:

A: あの ひと は だれ です か。 *Ano hito wa dare desu ka.*
B: ブラウン さん です。 *BURAUN san desu.*
A: ブラウン さん は どこ の かた です か。 *BURAUN san wa doko no kata desu ka.*
B: オーストラリアじん です。 *OOSUTORARIAjin desu.*

A: だれ の いぬ です か。 *Dare no inu desu ka.*
B: ピーター さん の です。 *PIITAA san no desu.*
A: にほん の いぬ です か。 *Nihon no inu desu ka.*
B: はい、 にほん の いぬ です。 *Hai, Nihon no inu desu.*

A: ほん は だれ の です か。 *Hon wa, dare no desu ka.*
B: わたし の じゃない です。 *Watashi no janai desu.*
A: あなた の です か。 *Anata no desu ka.*
C: いいえ、 わたし の では ありません。 *Iie, watashi no dewa* arimasen.

A:	ああ、ジョン　さん　おはよう ございます。おひさしぶり　です ね。おげんき　です　か。	*Aa, Jon san Ohayoo gozaimasu. Ohisashiburi desu ne. Ogenki desu ka.*
B:	おかげ　さま　で　げんき　です。 なん　です　か。	*Okage sama de genki desu. Nan desu ka.* (pointing to ground.)
A:	わたし　の　ノート　です。 ありがとう　ございます。	*Watashi no NOOTO desu. Arigatoo gozaimasu.*

- Listen as your teacher reads the conversations and try to really hear the sounds correctly so that your own pronunciation improves.
- Practice reading the conversations aloud with others. Be careful with pronunciation.
- Listen to one of the conversations read by your teacher and see if you fully understand.
- Write the English translation of the conversations in your book.
- Make up similar conversations of your own and act them out.

Writing practice

ka か　*to* と　*mi* み　*se* せ　*i* い

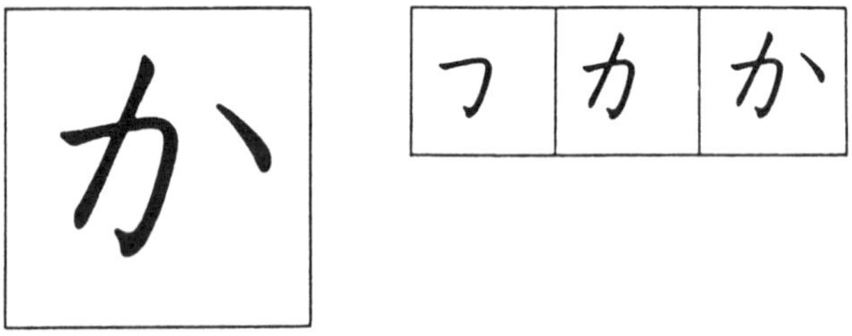

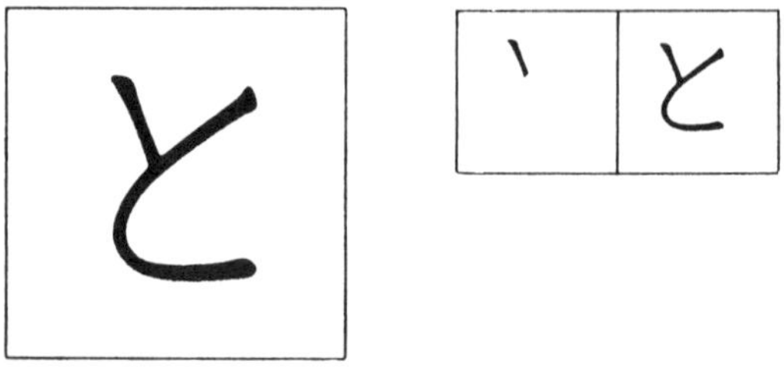

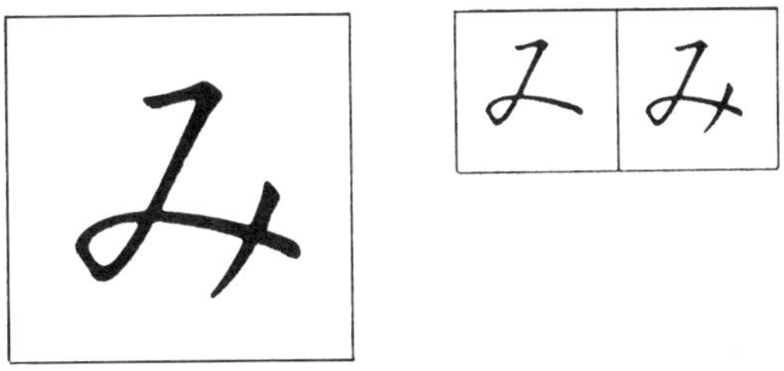

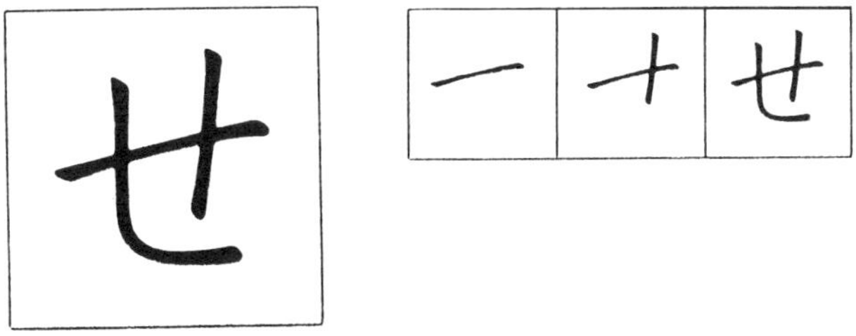

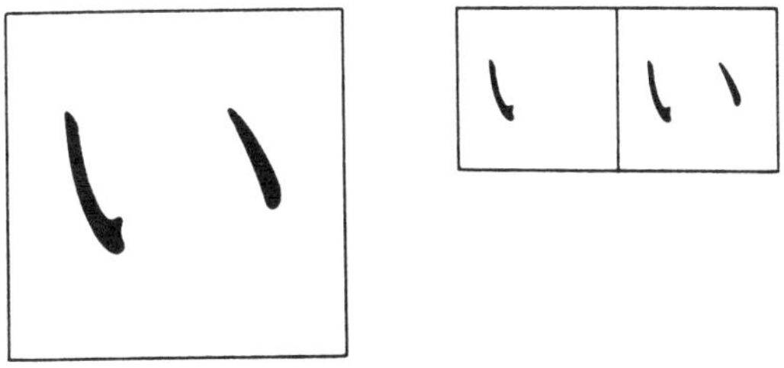

- Practice writing the syllables above until you are sure that you can read them and identify them.

- Write the following words:
  kami *seito* *sensei*

- Find the new *hiragana* in the line below. How many times does each one occur?
  き み も そ か と せ と い ま ら ち さ ふ ひ せ か い

  Don't forget to keep practicing the syllables that you learned previously.

- Read the following words aloud:
  かみ せいと せんせい みせ せかい

- Pick out the words you know from the following selection:
  にまん かみ せいと もらさ あなた わたし ひふ

It may help you to remember the *hiragana* shapes if you link them in your mind with an object. The more ridiculous the association the more likely you are to remember it.

In groups try to work out ways for people to remember the *hiragana*. The artist of the group could draw the associations. Share them with the rest of the class.

Below are two examples of associations – for *wa* and *ka*. (The girl is crying "wa!")

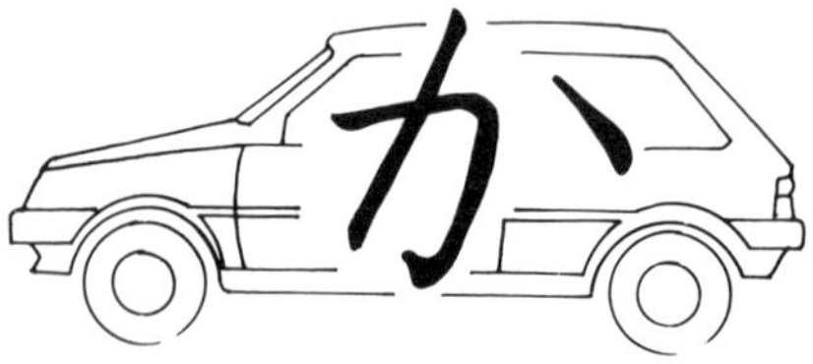

Unit 2

これ は なん です か
kore wa nan desu ka
What is this?

NEW WORDS

これ	*kore*	this
それ	*sore*	that
まんが	*manga*	comic (book, or magazine)
しんぶん	*shinbun*	newspaper
ざっし	*zasshi*	magazine

STUDY

- In Topic One you learned that the particle *wa* signals what you are talking about. So when you say: ***Kore wa nan desu ka*** it means "What is this?", or literally: "Talking about this thing here, what is it?"
  Some people find it helps to remember ***kore*** if they think of it as "this thing here".

- ***Sore*** means "that" and refers to something closer to the person you are talking with than to yourself, just as the English word "that" does.
  We can ask:

  これ　は　なん　です　か。
  Kore wa nan desu ka.　　What is this?

  The answer will be, for example:

  それ　は　ちず　です。
  Sore wa chizu desu.　　That is a map.

讀賣新聞
THE YOMIURI SHIMBUN
第38868号
(日刊) ©読売新聞社1984年
9月15日 土曜日
昭和59年(1984年)
発行所 読売新聞社
東京都千代田区大手町1-7-1
郵便番号100
電話(03)242-1111
郵便振替口座東京4-612

長野地震 山崩れ被害拡大

1人死に28人不明

旅館や工場 車の

王滝村 道路寸断、救助難航

十四日朝発生した長野県西部を震源とする強い地震の被害は、時を追って広がり、がけ崩れなどが各所で起きた震源地の同県木曽郡王滝村を中心に、同日夜までに死者一人、行方不明二十八人、負傷八人にのぼっている。政府は、同村に災害救助法を適用、また、吉村長野県知事の要請を受けて、自衛隊松本駐屯部隊の隊員百人が同日午後、同村に救助出動し、余震の続く村内で、土砂にのまれた行方不明者の捜索・救出活動に当たっている。今回の地震は、同村近くを走る隠れた枝状活断層が引き起こしたとみられ、気象庁は、この地震を「昭和五十九年長野県西部地震」と命名した。

（関連記事22・23面、解説9面、写真3面にも）

えぐられた村 地震によるがけ崩れでえぐられた王滝村松越地区（本社ヘリから）

「長野県西部地震」と命名

【長野】震源地に近い王滝村の被害は同日午後から夜にかけてさらに広がり、十五日午前一時現在、長野県警本部がまとめたところによると、死者一人、行方不明者二十八人となった。長野県は十四日午後、「木曽地震県災害対策本部」（本部長・吉村知事）を設置した。

被害は同村内三か所で起きた大規模な土砂崩れによるものが中心。このうち大又川が御岳湖に流入する河口付近では、両岸背後の山が幅百五十㍍、高さ二百㍍にわたって崩れたため、同川右岸の同村森林組合作業所と左岸のおんたけ生コン会社の工場や事務所、そのわきの城田建材会社が土砂に直撃され、同組合職員、樋孝義さん(五三)ら四人と、おんたけ生コン会社作業員藤本たきよさん(四九)ら五人、建材会社の作業員三人の計十二人が行方不明となった。

この現場から西へ約十㌔の滝越地区では、民家二戸が地震の揺れでつぶれ、うち一軒の中にいた望月みさをさん(六五)が死亡した。

同地区東側の濁川温泉でも旅館一軒が、土砂崩れで姿を消し、経営者の半場久江さん(五〇)と長男夫婦、孫の計四人が行方不明になっている。

このほか、滝越地区では、同郡上松町、森下誠一さん(…三)ら王滝林業の作業員…が、同日朝から車二台に分…して同地区に仕事に出たま…同夜になっても避難場所に…を見せていない。

また、同林業の王滝村東…本志郎さん(五〇)ら五人も同…早朝、同村の三浦貯水池の…白谷の作業現場に向かった…まま同夜になっても連絡がと…ず、行方不明となってい…

他の場所でも住民一人と…行人一人が行方不明にな…ど、行方不明者は合わせ…二十八人。雨でゆるんだ地…のため、小さな土砂崩れ…地で起きており、被害が…っている。

同村の道路は、いたる…

▶14日午後9時「ひまわ…

災害救助

長野県西部地震で土砂…被害が出た同県木曽郡王…に対し、厚生省は、十四…後、災害救助法を適用し…

◇

長野県警が同日午後九…

く…

いずきんにだ…が奉納される。古式の歌…踊りの面影をとどめると…究者も注目している。

Japanese people read a great deal. Comics, magazines, and newspapers tend to be more popular than novels, and everyone enjoys reading them while traveling or waiting for trains and buses. Even adults often read comics in Japan.

Japanese popular books are mostly smaller than ours to make them easier to carry around.

ACTIVITIES

- Using the illustrations on pages 54 and 55 and the photos in this unit, point to each object. Using the phrases on p. 60, ask and answer questions.

- Now use the same illustrations to tell your partner:
  Kore wa watashi no PEN desu.
  Your partner can also question you, asking:
  Kore wa anata no kaban desu ka.
  or *Sore wa anata no desu ka.*
  Your answer will of course be either:
  Hai, watashi no desu or *Iie, watashi no janai desu.*

- See how many things you can now answer to the question *Nan desu ka.*
  One person starts off the chain by asking the question. Try to go around the group answering ". . . . *desu*" without anyone repeating an object. (The faster you go the better!)

- One person holds up an object and asks *Kore wa nan desu ka*. The group in turn answer *It's not a (book)* with *(Hon) janai desu* etc.
  The last person gives the object its name with *desu* e.g. *PEN desu.*

- *Anata no desu ka.*
  Pass an object from one to another around the group asking in turn: *Kore wa anata no desu ka.* or *Anata no (PEN) desu ka.*
  Everyone, except the last person, says it is not theirs.

- You see someone in the street who has just dropped something. You go up to him or her and say:
  "Excuse me, please, but . . . is this yours?" The person answers either Yes or No (in which case you either continue to try to find the owner or give up!).
  You may like to act this out. Maybe it will lead to you introducing yourself to the stranger.

- You could extend the conversation with the stranger by asking his or her nationality, and by telling your own nationality before saying goodbye.

- Write a conversation based on the two activities above.

- One person is chosen to go around the room pointing to objects and asking *Koré wa nan desu ka.* The group replies with *Sore wa. . . desu.*

Unit 3

たって　ください
tatte kudasai
Please stand

NEW WORDS

たって　ください	*tatte kudasai*	Please stand
すわって　ください	*suwatte kudasai*	Please sit
みて　ください	*mite kudasai*	Please look
きいて　ください	*kiite kudasai*	Please listen
よんで　ください	*yonde kudasai*	Please read

STUDY

- At the end of this unit you will be able to understand, respond to and give simple instructions.
- Learn the new phrases above just as they are. We'll look at the grammar involved in a later unit.
- ***Kudasai*** cannot be used to say "Please" on its own, as we do in English. The underlying meaning of *kudasai* is "please do me the honor of doing this for me" and it implies that you will be giving the person something they want by following their instruction. It's a polite way to ask someone to do something for you.

ACTIVITY

This is a version of "Simon Says" (five minutes).

Everyone stands and one person calls instructions as above, e.g.
mite (look) *kudasai*: stare straight ahead
kiite (listen) *kudasai*: cup one hand behind the ear
tatte (stand) *kudasai*: stand up
suwatte (sit) *kudasai*: sit down
The last one to obey the instruction is "out" and goes to the front of the room to help spot others. When someone is out, call out his/her name followed by *san*. Play fast to see if you can stump someone!

Tatte kudasai

- Extension: use the following instructions in the game.
  Tatte mite kudasai Stand and look
  Tatte kiite kudasai Stand and listen
  Suwatte kiite kudasai Sit and listen
  Suwatte mite kudasai Sit and look

Unit 4

これ　を　ください
kore o kudasai
Please may I have this?

NEW WORDS

どうぞ	*doozo*	here you are
ふでばこ	*fudebako*	pencil case (originally a brush case in Japan)
ごみばこ	*gomibako*	garbage can
けしごむ	*keshigomu*	eraser
ものさし	*monosashi*	ruler
これ　を　ください	*kore o kudasai*	Please give me this (thing). Please, may I have this ?

STUDY

- The ***o*** in the phrase *Kore o kudasai* is another particle. You have already learned the topic particle *wa* and the particle *no* ("belonging to"). *O* is the object particle, and follows the object or thing that you are talking about.

  The *hiragana* syllable **を** is only used for the particle *o*.

- We can substitute any object for *kore*, for example:

ほん　を　ください。	*Hon o kudasai.*	Please give me the book.
ペン　を　ください。	*PEN o kudasai.*	Please give me the pen.

  It is an object that you need, therefore you put the ***o*** particle in after the name of the object.

A: これ　を　ください。	*Kore o kudasai.*	Please, may I have this?
B: どうぞ。	*Doozo.*	Here you are.

  Underlying the word *doozo* is the understanding that you are pleased to be able to do this small thing for another person – that, in fact, you feel honored to be able to do it!

- **It is very important to sort out in your own mind why you are using the particles**. They are very relevant clues to the exact meaning of Japanese sentences.

  Think about the way you have used them up to this point:
  Hon o kudasai. "Please, give me the book". or "Please, may I have the book?" Ask yourself **who** is being spoken to? The answer is **you**,

therefore you are the **topic**. What is the object wanted? The answer is the book. Therefore, in a very explicit sentence we would say:
Anata wa hon o kudasai.

Here is another example:
Nihongo o benkyoo shimasu.
We assume that I am talking about myself, but it could be any other person who studies Japanese if we are not there to realize that all the build-up conversation (the context) has been about my activities. So, to make it absolutely clear I could say:
Watashi wa *nihongo o benkyoo shimasu.*
I am the topic and the object of the inquiry is the subject I study. If I want to say that it is Mark who studies Japanese, he becomes the **topic** and I say:
MAAKU *san wa nihongo o benkyoo shimasu.*

ACTIVITIES

- With a neighbor see how many things you can ask for in Japanese, using the pattern above.

- Ask your neighbor for objects from the word list. When they are handed to you, your neighbor will say "Here you are". Don't forget to say "Thank you"!

  Here are some examples to help you to see if you have got it right:

ほん　を　ください。	*Hon o kudasai.*	Please, may I have the book ?
どうぞ。	*Doozo.*	Here you are.
ありがとう。	*Arigatoo.*	Thanks.
ノート　を　ください。	*NOOTO o kudasai.*	Please, may I have the notebook?
どうぞ。	*Doozo.*	Here you are.
ありがとう。	*Arigatoo.*	Thanks.
わたし　の　ペン　を　ください。	*Watashi no PEN o kudasai.*	Please, may I have my pen?
どうぞ。	*Doozo.*	Here you are.
ありがとう。	*Arigatoo.*	Thanks.

Writing practice

そ	れ	こ	て	は
so	*re*	*ko*	*te*	*ha*

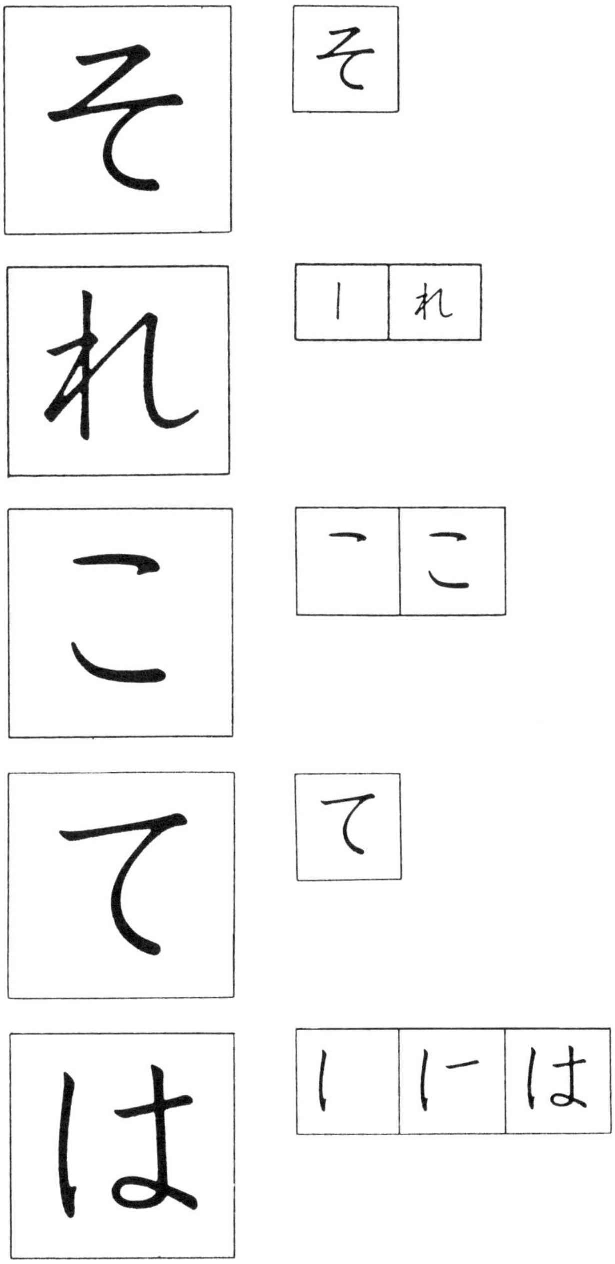

- Find associations for the syllables above if it helps you, or just practice writing them over and over if that is easier.
  Write them on small cards and keep looking at them in spare moments and you will be surprised how quickly you will learn them.

- Try the following activities with the syllables.
  Read them aloud and clap the rhythm.
  Draw them in the air.
  Picture them in your mind and further develop your photographic memory.

- Think about all the *hiragana* you now know:

に	ほ	ん	あ	な	た	の	わ	ま	せ		
ni	*ho*	*n*	*a*	*na*	*ta*	*no*	*wa*	*ma*	*se*		
え	と	い	れ	こ	を	か	み	し	そ	て	は
e	*to*	*i*	*re*	*ko*	*o*	*ka*	*mi*	*shi*	*so*	*te*	*ha*

Write the ones that rhyme with:

ほ	た	み	せ
ho	*ta*	*mi*	*se*

- Look at your vocabulary lists and pick out words that you can write in *hiragana*. How many can you write without looking at the *hiragana* example? Test yourself and then check against the *hiragana* column in the vocabulary lists.

A *manga* page

Unit 5

あれ／どれ
are/dore
that over there/which

NEW WORDS

あれ	*are*	that over there
どれ	*dore*	which (out of several things)

STUDY

- You already know *kore* "this", and *sore* "that". **あれ *are*** is used for things that are away from both speaker and listener.

- **どれ *dore*** is used to ask "which?" or "which one?" when talking about more than two things.
  To ask "which one?" you can use *dore* by itself (the voice rises in a questioning way). Or you can ask **Dore desu ka** "which (one) is it?"
  To answer the question *Dore desu ka* you could say *kore* or *sore* or *are*, depending on the position of the object. Usually you would also point to the object, to make it clearer.

- We can ask "Please, may I have that thing over there?" using
  あれ　を　ください　　*Are o kudasai.*
  This is the same pattern as ones you now know, for example:
  これ　を　ください　　*Kore o kudasai*
  "Please, may I have this?" / "Please give me this"
  and,
  それ　を　ください　　*Sore o kudasai*
  "Please, may I have that thing over there?"

ACTIVITIES

- The teacher has an object. Practice as follows:
  Student 1　*Sore o kudasai.*
  Teacher:　*Kore desu ka. Doozo.*
  Student 1:　*Arigatoo.*
  Student 2:　*Sore o kudasai.*
  and so on until you have returned the object to the teacher.

- Work in pairs. Ask each other for things, or ask what things are, using *kore, sore, are*, and *dore*.

Unit 6

かいて　ください
kaite kudasai
please write

NEW WORDS

かいて　ください	*kaite kudasai*	please write

STUDY

- Note the spelling of *kaite* in *kaite kudasai*. Don't confuse it with *kiite* (きいて) meaning "listen". Also be careful with pronunciation. Remember that *kaite* will be written かいて and cannot possibly be pronounced the same way as *kiite* (きいて). Learning to write words in *hiragana* will help you to keep them more clearly separated in your mind.

- **Using the instructions you know**
  You have learned several instruction phrases, for example: よんで　ください *yonde kudasai* please read. Now you can be more specific and include a noun, for example:
  ***hon** o yonde kudasai, **manga** o yonde kudasai*
  Remember that the particle *o* is put after the object you are talking about.

NOOTO o yonde kudasai.	Please read the notebook.
Zasshi o yonde kudasai.	Please read the magazine .
Hon o mite kudasai.	Please look at the book.
Manga o yonde kudasai.	Please read the comic.

- You could be asked to look at **your** books:
  あなた の ほん を みて ください。 ***Anata** no hon o mite kudasai.*

ACTIVITIES

- Make up some instructions for other people to follow using the above patterns.

- Now you can ask people to write words in *roomaji* and have a spelling test! Make a list of ten words to test your friends. Take turns testing each other. Here is the sentence pattern:

  「にほん」を」 かいて ください。 *"Nihon" o kaite kudasai.*
  「ボールペン」 を かいて ください。 *"BOORUPEN" o kaite kudasai.*

  Write *katakana* words (those written in capital letters) that you have learned in *roomaji.*

Check your understanding

- How would you say the following in Japanese?
  Remember: in English we say "Please, may I have . . .?" as an alternative to "Please give me". In English that means that a question mark is needed. In Japanese it is not necessary because the "Please give me" version is being used.
  (The particle you need is given at the end of the line.)

  1 Please, may I have the newspaper? (Please give me the newspaper) (*o*)
  2 What is this? (*wa*)
  3 May I have that, please? (*o*)
  4 Please look. (don't use a particle)
  5 Stand up, please. (don't use a particle)
  6 This is a comic. (*wa*)
  7 Please give me that (over there). (*o*)
  8 Is this a garbage can? (*wa*)
  9 That is not a garbage can. (*wa*)
  10 This is not Debbie's book. (*wa*)
  Write your answers to the sentences above. After you have checked your answers so that you are sure you are correct, test your friends.

Answers

1 *Shinbun o kudasai.*
2 *Kore wa nan desu ka.*
3 *Sore o kudasai.*
4 *Mite kudasai.*
5 *Tatte kudasai.*
6 *Kore wa manga desu.*
7 *Are o kudasai.*
8 *Kore wa gomibako desu ka.*
9 *Sore wa gomibako dewa arimasen. (janai desu)*
10 *Kore wa DEBBI san no hon dewa arimasen. (janai desu)*

Now see how many of the following you can figure out. Check your work on the next page.

1	たって ください。	*Tatte kudasai.*
2	みなさん、おはよう ございます。	*Minasan, Ohayoo gozaimasu.*
3	せんせい、 ほん を ください。	*Sensei, hon o kudasai.*
4	ジェーン さん、 ノート を ください。	*JEEN san, NOOTO o kudasai.*
5	みなさん、 すわって ください。	*Minasan, suwatte kudasai.*
6	リチャード さん、 なん です か。	*RICHAADO san, nan desu ka.*
7	ペン です か。	*PEN desu ka.*
8	いいえ、ペン では ありません。	*Iie, PEN dewa arimasen.*
9	ねこ は わたし の です。	*Neko wa watashi no desu.*
10	あなた の ものさし です か。	*Anata no monosashi desu ka.*
11	わたし の えんぴつ です。	*Watashi no enpitsu desu.*
12	みて ください。	*Mite kudasai.*
13	いす です。	*Isu desu.*
14	つくえ では ありません。	*Tsukue dewa arimasen.*
15	わたし の きょうしつ です。	*Watashi no kyooshitsu desu.*
16	だれ の しんぶん です か。	*Dare no shinbun desu ka.*
17	ちず は にほん の ちず です か。	*Chizu wa nihon no chizu desu ka.*
18	アメリカ の ちず です。	*AMERIKA no chizu desu.*
19	あの かた は フランスじん です か。	*Ano kata wa FURANSUjin desu ka.*
20	あなた は にほんじん です が。	*Anata wa Nihonjin desu ka.*
21	わたし の なまえ は リサ です。	*Watashi no namae wa RISA desu.*
22	あなた の なまえ は サイモン です か。	*Anata no namae wa SAIMON desu ka.*
23	フィリップ さん の ざっし です。	*FIRIPPU san no zasshi desu.*
24	まんが じゃない です。	*Manga janai desu.*
25	だれ の えんぴつ です か。	*Dare no enpitsu desu ka.*

If you cover the *roomaji* you may like to see how many of the *hiragana* words you are able to recognize.

1 Please stand.
Good morning, everyone.
3 Teacher, may I have the book, please?
4 Jane, please give me the notebook.
Please sit down, everybody.
6 Richard, what is it?
7 Is it a pen?
8 No it's not a pen.
9 The cat is mine.
10 Is it your ruler?
11 It's my pencil.
12 Look, please.
13 It's a chair.
14 It's not a desk.
15 It's my classroom.
16 Whose newspaper is it?
17 Is the map a map of Japan?
18 It's a map of America.
19 Is that person over there French?
20 Are you Japanese?
21 My name is Lisa.
22 Is your name Simon?
23 It's Philip's magazine.
24 It's not a comic.
25 Whose pencil is it?

Unit 7

まど　を　あけて　ください
mado o akete kudasai
Please open the window

NEW WORDS

まど	*mado*	window
あけて　ください	*akete kudasai*	Please open
しめて　ください	*shimete kudasai*	Please close
ドア	*DOA*	door

STUDY

Sensei: おはよう　ございます。 *Ohayoo gozaimasu.*
スー　さん　まど　を　あけて　ください。 *SUU san mado o akete kudasai.*
ベン　さん　ドア　を　しめて　ください。 *BEN san DOA o shimete kudasai.*
みなさん、すわって　ください。 *Minasan, suwatte kudasai.*

Teacher: Good morning.
Sue, please open the window.
Ben, please close the door.
Please sit down, everyone.

- Doors and windows are things that you cannot pick up and give someone, but are objects just the same. The thing (object) we want to open is the window, *mado*, so it is followed by the ***o*** particle just the same as any other object.

- ***Mado o akete kudasai*** means in literal translation "the window open please". In natural English, "Please open the window".

  Now you can enjoy asking your friends to do many things at your bidding! The following sentences may help:

  きょうしつ　の　まど　を　しめて　ください。 *Kyooshitsu no mado o shimete kudasai.*
  ドア　を　あけて　ください。 *DOA o akete kudasai.*
  ケリ　さん　かばん　を　しめて　ください。 *KERI san kaban o shimete kudasai.*

Please close the classroom window.
Please open the door.
Keri, please close the bag.

ACTIVITIES

- work with a partner:
  See how many instructions you can give your partner without running out of ideas, and then switch roles.

- Write a list of as many instructions as you can.

- Add on more instructions to your game of "Simon Says" and play it fast.

- Make up a scene with a group of friends in which a teacher enters the classroom, gives a greeting appropriate to the time of day, and asks various pupils to do something. They respond appropriately. It is a Japanese lesson. They ask the names of classroom objects. They are then given some work to do. At the end of the lesson they say "Thank you" and "Goodbye". Try to use all the grammar structures that you have learned.

Song

Musunde hiraite

Musunde hiraite
Te o utte musunde
Mata hiraite
Te o utte
Sono te o ue ni
Musunde hiraite
Te o utte musunde

Musunde hiraite
Te o utte musunde
Mata hiraite
Te o utte
Sono te o shita ni
Musunde hiraite
Te o utte musunde

Extension

- Make two sets of picture cards of all the words that you know in Japanese. Spread the cards face upwards on a desk. One person calls out the Japanese names and the players race to be the first to pick up the correct card.
  Or you can use the cards face down. Players take turns turning over a card and making up a sentence containing that word.

- Make a set of word cards with all the words you know. Don't put the English on the card. Use them to test yourself. Or turn them face down and, with a partner, take turns turning them over and saying the word. If you know it, the card becomes yours. If you don't, put it back face down again. See who can win the most.

- The class divides into groups. Each group needs two envelopes and a pair of scissors. Each group receives a photocopy of the *Vocabulary checklist (Topic Two)*.
  Cut up the words and put English in one envelope, *hiragana, katakana* and *roomaji* (still joined in a strip) in the second envelope. Label the envelopes clearly to keep for further use.
  1 Each person in turn takes out one strip from the Japanese word envelope, gives the English equivalent if he / she can and makes up one sentence with the word. Try to extend yourself.
  2 Match the words in the two envelopes. You may like to compete with other groups to see who matches all the words first.

Vocabulary checklist (Topic Two)

List One (Essential)
Introduction

ようちえん	*yoochien*	kindergarten
しょうがっこう	*shoogakkoo*	primary school
ちゅうがっこう	*chuugakkoo*	junior high school
こうとうがっこう	*kootoogakkoo*	senior high school
じゅく	*juku*	cram school

Unit 1

ボールペン	*BOORUPEN*	ballpoint pen
ちず	*chizu*	map
え	*e*	picture
えんぴつ	*enpitsu*	pencil
はこ	*hako*	box
いす	*isu*	chair

かばん	*kaban*	bag
かみ	*kami*	paper
こくばん	*kokuban*	blackboard
きょうしつ	*kyooshitsu*	classroom
ノート	*NOOTO*	notebook
ペン	*PEN*	pen
つくえ	*tsukue*	desk
じゃない です	*janai desu*	(informal negative of *desu* "is not")
わたし	*watashi*	I/me
の	*no*	(particle meaning "belonging to")
なまえ	*namae*	name
アメリカ	*AMERIKA*	America
じん	*jin*	person
ありがとう ございます	*arigatoo gozaimasu*	Thank you
あの	*ano*	that (over there)
だれ	*dare*	who
どこ の かた です か	*doko no kata desu ka*	What nationality are you?

Unit 2

これ	*kore*	this
まんが	*manga*	comic
しんぶん	*shinbun*	newspaper
それ	*sore*	that
ざっし	*zasshi*	magazine

たって ください	*tatte kudasai*	Please stand
すわって ください	*suwatte kudasai*	Please sit
みて ください	*mite kudasai*	Please look
きいて ください	*kiite kudasai*	Please listen
よんで ください	*yonde kudasai*	Please read

Unit 4

どうぞ	*doozo*	here you are
これ を ください	*kore o kudasai*	Please give me this

Unit 5

あれ	*are*	that (over there)
どれ	*dore*	which (of more than two things)

Unit 6

かいて ください	*kaite kudasai*	Please write

Unit 7

まど	*mado*	window
あけて　ください	*akete kudasai*	Please open
しめて　ください	*shimete kudasai*	Please close
ドア	*DOA*	door

List Two
(useful but not essential)

ふでばこ	*fudebako*	pencil case
ごみばこ	*gomibako*	garbage can
けしごむ	*keshigomu*	eraser
ものさし	*monosashi*	ruler

TOPIC THREE
school life

Introduction

ACHIEVEMENTS

By the end of this topic you will be able to tell people:
- what you study at school;
- what you like and dislike;
- what you do in your free time.

The school year

The Japanese school year begins in April with an entrance ceremony and finishes in March with end of year exams.

Students attend school five and a half days a week, from eight-thirty to three-thirty, or four o'clock. After school there are often compulsory club activities, such as ***ikebana*** (flower arranging), ***shodoo*** (calligraphy), martial arts like ***juudoo***, ***kendoo*** and ***karate***, and sports activities.

Lessons in Japanese schools tend to be very formal and follow a government specified framework, using textbooks supplied by the government. Formal tests are given twice a term.

Ikebana

***Shodoo* class**

***Juudoo* class**

***Kendoo* class**

The average class size is forty-five students so there is little opportunity for individual attention in class. Teachers spend a lot of time out of school hours counselling, coaching and answering queries from students. Students are also helped by the ***senpai-koohai*** system. Older students (***senpai***) look after and help a younger student (the ***koohai***). The relationship formed often lasts right through life. They will help each other at work and in social life.

Classmates – ***dookyuusei*** – remain close, too. Strong bonds are made within class groups and students may attend class reunions all their lives.

An interesting feature about Japanese schooling is that students are responsible for cleaning their own schools on a roster system. It is a matter of great pride to do the job well to maintain the school's cleanliness and tidiness.

Group pride and responsibility are stressed and group activities to strengthen the bonds are encouraged. When students leave school and enter the work force they will expect to have the same sort of involvement with colleagues during and after work time, and the same sort of responsibility to their employers.

***Dookyuusei* look after each other**

Older students look after younger ones

Unit 1

べんきょう　します
benkyoo shimasu
I study/I will study

NEW WORDS

べんきょう　します	*benkyoo shimasu*	study
ちがいます	*chigaimasu*	polite way of saying "you're wrong"
ドイツご	*DOITSUgo*	German language
えいご	*eigo*	English language
フランスご	*FURANSUgo*	French language
じゃ　また	*ja mata*	See you!
にほんご	*nihongo*	Japanese language
はなします	*hanashimasu*	speak
れんしゅう　します	*renshuu shimasu*	practice
します	*shimasu*	do
そう　です　か	*soo desu ka*	Is that so?/Really?
そう　です	*soo desu*	Yes, I am/That is so/ I agree
なにご	*nanigo*	What language(s)?

STUDY

- Read through the following conversation. (Maki sees Taroo going into the school library one morning.)

Maki:	おはよう　ございます。	*Ohayoo gozaimasu.*	Good morning.
Taroo:	おはよう　ございます。	*Ohayoo gozaimasu.*	Good morning.
Maki:	なに　を　します　か。	*Nani o shimasu ka.*	What are you going to do?
Taroo:	べんきょう　します。	*Benkyoo shimasu.*	Study.
Maki:	ああ　そう　です　か。 じゃ　また。	*Aa soo desu ka.* *Ja mata.*	Really? See you.
Taroo:	じゃ　また。	*Ja mata.*	Bye.

- Verbs are action or "doing" words.
  します *shimasu* do.
  Shimasu means "do" but, as you saw with *desu*, there are many ways to translate one Japanese verb:
  I/He/She/You will do;
  We/You/They will do;
  I am going to do;
  He/She is going to do;
  You are going to do;
  We/You/They are going to do.
  How you translate the verb depends on the context. If you are speaking to someone it is assumed that you are talking about yourself, unless you specifically state another person.

- The ***shi*** part of the word *shimasu* is called the **stem**, and means "do". The **second part of the word** tells you the **tense** (when the action happens or has happened). In this case ***masu*** is the second part and always indicates **future** action or **habitual** action.
  Masu is referred to as the ***masu* ending.**

- *Shimasu* therefore means "do" or "will do." (We say "I study history" meaning that this is what we usually do — an habitual action. If we say "I will study history", future action is assumed.)
  Many words are put with *shimasu* to say things like "do study". In the dialogue above Maki uses ***benkyoo shimasu***. This is translated as "study".
  Renshuu shimasu means "do practice" but is translated as "practice".

- In Topic One you learned nationalities and the name of countries. Now you can add the language.
  By putting ***go*** on the end of a country's name you can say what the language is, e.g.

ドイツご	*DOITSUgo*	German
イタリアご	*ITARIAgo*	Italian
にほんご	*Nihongo*	Japanese
フランスご	*FURANSUgo*	French

  Do the same with all the country names that you know except English, which is ***eigo*** and learn this one very carefully. ***IGIRISUjin* speak *eigo***!
  Remember that all the names of countries except Japan, Korea and China that are in your vocabulary are written in *katakana*.

- In Topic Two you learned the particle *o* – the object particle. It is used after the names of languages, too.
  Nihongo ***o*** *benkyoo shimasu.* I study Japanese.
  Eigo ***o*** *hanashimasu.* I speak English.

- ***Nanigo*** means "What language?". So we can ask:
  Nanigo o benkyoo shimasu ka.
  What languages do you study?

- Imagine there is a group of people talking. One person asks the others about the languages they study. I want to make sure that everyone knows that I am the one who studies Japanese. I could say:
  Watashi wa (Speaking of myself) *nihongo o benkyoo shimasu.* I am the topic and Japanese is the thing I study. By putting in ***watashi wa*** I make sure that people don't assume that all of us study Japanese.

- ***Hanashimasu*** (speak/talk) is used to express "I speak (English)" or whatever your native language is. It is not used for languages that you are learning. For those, use the verb *benkyoo shimasu.*
  For example:
  FURANSUjin wa FURANSUgo o hanashimasu.
  Nihonjin wa nihongo o hanashimasu, eigo o benkyoo shimasu.

ACTIVITIES

- Practice using all the names of languages followed by the particle *o* and *benkyoo shimasu.*

- Write down five sentences in the same pattern.

- Play a guessing game. Divide into small groups. One person chooses a language and writes it secretly on paper. The others have five turns to find out which language is on the paper by asking:
  Anata wa (nihongo) o benkyoo shimasu ka. "Do you study Japanese?" (The meaning is "talking about you – do you study Japanese?") **You** are the topic so I make sure that you understand that by using ***anata wa***. And in the answer I use ***watashi wa*** to show that I am talking about myself and no one else: *Hai watashi wa (nihongo) o benkyoo shimasu* or *Iie chigaimasu* (Sorry, you're wrong!)

- ***Renshuu shimasu*** is used in the same way as *benkyoo shimasu.* Someone may ask you: *Nani o shimasu ka* "What are you going to do?"
  Nani is the same word as *nan* that you have learned already, but if you say *Nan o shimasu ka* it sounds a bit jerky. The Japanese, who like things to be flowing, have put on an "*i*" to make it sound more pleasant.
  Work with a partner. Practice asking each other *Nani o shimasu ka,* and answer either that you are going to study one of the languages or practice one of the languages.

  Practice telling a partner what native language is spoken by different nationalities.

Unit 2

ピアノ を れんしゅう します
PIANO o renshuu shimasu
I'm going to practice piano

NEW WORDS

ピアノ	*PIANO*	piano
ギター	*GITAA*	guitar
バイオリン	*BAIORIN*	violin
フルート	*FURUUTO*	flute
かがく	*kagaku*	science
ちり	*chiri*	geography
おんがく	*ongaku*	music
れきし	*rekishi*	history
しゃかい	*shakai*	social studies
すうがく	*suugaku*	math
たいいく	*taiiku*	physical education

STUDY

Kenji meets Sumiko outside the music room:

Kenji:	こんにち は。なに を します か。	*Konnichi wa. Nani o shimasu ka.*
Sumiko:	ピアノ を れんしゅう します。	*PIANO o renshuu shimasu.*
Kenji:	そう です か。	*Soo desu ka.*
Sumiko:	はい そう です。さよなら。	*Hai, soo desu. Sayonara.*

ACTIVITIES

- Practice the conversation above with a partner. Keep practicing until you know all the vocabulary really well and can substitute the names of instruments easily.

- Practice the same sort of conversation using school subjects.

- Make up a conversation in which you meet a new student:
  Greet.
  Introduce yourself.
  Ask the student's name and nationality.
  Give your own nationality.
  Make noises like "Is that so" appropriately through the conversation! Japanese people do that a lot.
  Ask what the student studies.
  Say goodbye and "See you again".

- Write a conversation like the one you have practiced, in your book. You will probably want to say, "I study Japanese and Math and English", and so on. Do it this way, using や ***ya***:
  Nihongo ***ya*** *suugaku* ***ya*** *eigo o benkyoo shimasu.* The *ya* means "and" when you are giving a list. It assumes "and other things" because obviously you do a lot of other things as well. Put *o* after the last thing in your list.

Unit 3

テニス　を　します　か
TENISU o shimasu ka
Do you play tennis?

NEW WORDS

バレーボール	*BAREEBOORU*	volleyball
スポーツ	*SUPOOTSU*	sports
テニス	*TENISU*	tennis
フットボール	*FUTTOBOORU*	football
サッカー	*SAKKAA*	soccer

STUDY

Kumiko:

テニス　を　します　か。	*TENISU o shimasu ka.*	Do you play tennis?

Reiko:

はい、　テニス　を　します。	*Hai, TENISU o shimasu.*	Yes, I do.
あなた　は。	*Anata wa.*	How about you?

Kumiko:

はい、　テニス　を　します。	*Hai, TENISU o shimasu.*	Yes, I play tennis.

- All the new words are written in *katakana* because they are games that were not known in Japan until this century. The instrument names that you have learned are written in *katakana* for the same reason.

- Looking at the conversation above you will see that *shimasu* can also be used to say "play" when talking of sports.

- Later you will learn different verbs for "play" connected with different instruments. At the moment you can only say you **practice** an instrument.

- There is a word for "play" (*asobimasu*) as in "The children are playing" but the Japanese don't use it when talking about sports or playing instruments. Sports and music are taken seriously. You do them to the best of your ability. Hence the word "play" suggests a less serious attitude.

ACTIVITIES

- Practice asking a partner "What do you play?" with *Nani o shimasu ka*, or ask *PIANO o renshuu shimasu ka* "Do you practice the piano?" etc.

- Make posters of various activities, putting the Japanese names on them large and boldly, for your classroom wall.

- Make booklets for others to read using any of the vocabulary and grammar structures that you now know. Before you write the final version check that your spelling and grammer are correct. You don't want to confuse others or consolidate wrong patterns for them (or for yourself).

- Update your vocabulary cards.

Unit 4

なに が すき です か
nani ga suki desu ka
What do you like?

NEW WORDS

…が すき です	. . . *ga suki desu*	I like . . .
…が きらい です	. . . *ga kirai desu*	I dislike . . .
…が すき じゃない です	. . . *ga suki janai desu*	I don't like . . . (not as strong as *kirai*)

STUDY

- Learn the phrases above just as they are for now. が *ga* is another particle that, among other things, is used for emotions – you'll learn about it later.

- Read through the following dialogue:

Mariko:	スポーツ が すき です か。	*SUPOOTSU ga suki desu ka.*	Do you like sports?
Kenichi:	はい、 スポーツ が すき です。	*Hai, SUPOOTSU ga suki desu.*	Yes, I like sports.
Mariko:	テニス が すき です か。	*TENISU ga suki desu ka.*	Do you like tennis?
Kenichi:	いいえ、 バレーボール が すき です。	*Iie, BAREEBOORU ga suki desu.*	No, I like volleyball.
Mariko:	そう です か。 バレーボール が きらい です。	*Soo desu ka. BAREEBOORU ga kirai desu.*	Is that so. I hate volleyball!

ACTIVITIES

- Work in a group. Everyone in the group takes turns saying what they like or dislike doing.

- Work in a small group. Using the cards you have made before (objects, names, activities, etc.), take turns picking up a card and saying something about it, e.g. you pick up a card with *hana* (flower) on it, and construct a sentence with that word in it.

  Examples of constructions you can try are below:

  Hana desu.
  Neko dewa arimasen, inu desu.
  Kore wa kaban desu.
  SUPOOTSU o shimasu.
  Suugaku o shimasu.
  IGIRISUjin desu.
  Nihongo o benkyoo shimasu.
  PIANO o renshuu shimasu.
  Taiiku ga suki desu.
  Ano hito ga kirai desu.
  Suugaku wa suki janai desu.

  Try not to use a pattern that anyone else has used. If you do you are "out".

- On your own, shuffle or mix up your vocabulary cards and pick out ten at random. Construct a sentence to write in your book for each one.

Check your understanding

- Identify the following *hiragana* syllables (without looking them up!).

  に　え　と　な　ま　の　ほ　れ　し
  そ　か　ん　た　み　こ　は　せ　あ

- Read the following words and give their *roomaji* equivalents:

  はな　　　みなさん
  あなた　　なまえ

- Write five words in *hiragana* with *roomaji* underneath to show what you intend the word to be.

- Here are some words in *roomaji*. Put them into *hiragana*.

  kasa　　*ano*
  kami　　*kata*
  mikan　　*shimasu*

- Now look at the *hiragana* chart on p. 6 and see if you were correct. Make a note to work hard on the ones you got wrong.

  It's a good idea every day to pick out something you haven't quite mastered and practice it – not only *hiragana* but grammar or vocabulary as well.

Unit 5

バスケットボール　を　しません
BASUKETTOBOORU o shimasen
I don't play basketball

NEW WORDS

バスケットボール	*BASUKETTOBOORU*	basketball
くん	*kun*	pal/friend (used by males only)
よみます	*yomimasu*	read
ききます	*kikimasu*	listen
レコード	*REKOODO*	records
ラジオ	*RAJIO*	radio
カセット　テープ	*KASETTO TEEPU*	cassette tape
しません	*shimasen*	don't do/won't do
よみません	*yomimasen*	don't/won't read
ききません	*kikimasen*	don't/won't listen
はなします	*hanashimasu*	speak/talk

STUDY

- Masahiro meets Ichiroo. They have not seen each other for a long time since Ichiroo moved to another town.

Masahiro:

おはよう　ございます。
おひさしぶり　です　ね。
おげんき　です　か。

Ohayoo gozaimasu.
Ohisashiburi desu ne.
Ogenki desu ka.

Ichiroo:

ああ　まさ　くん、おはよう。
げんき　です。　あなた　は。

Aa Masa kun, Ohayoo.
Genki desu. Anata wa.

Masahiro:

げんき　です。　なに　を　べんきょう
します　か。

Genki desu. Nani o benkyoo
shimasu ka.

Ichiroo:

にほんご　や　えいご　や　ロシアご
や　すうがく　や　れきし　を
します。　あなた　は。

Nihongo ya eigo ya ROSHIAgo
ya suugaku ya rekishi o
shimasu. Anata wa.

Masahiro:

わたし　は　にほんご　や　れきし
や　ドイツご　を　します。
すうがく　を　しません。
スポーツ　を　します　か。

Watashi wa nihongo ya rekishi
ya DOITSUgo o shimasu.
Suugaku o shimasen.
SUPOOTSU o shimasu ka.

Ichiroo:

はい、スポーツ　が　すき　です。
テニス　や　フットボール　を
します。

Hai, SUPOOTSU ga suki desu.
TENISU ya FUTTOBOORU o
shimasu.

Masahiro:

バスケットボール　を　します
か。

BASUKETTOBOORU o shimasu
ka.

Ichiroo:

いいえ、しません。
バスケットボール　が　きらい
です。

Iie, shimasen.
BASUKETTOBOORU ga kirai
desu.

Masahiro:

ああ　そう　です　か。
バスケットボール　を　します。

Aa soo desu ka.
BASUKETTOBOORU o shimasu.

Check your understanding of the dialogue with the following translation.

M : Hello. I haven't seen you for ages. How are you?

I : Ah, Masa, hello. I'm fine. How about you?

M : I'm fine. What do you study?

I : Japanese, English, Russian, Math and History. And you?

M : I study Japanese, History and German. I'm not studying Math. Do you play sports?

I : Yes, I like sports. I play tennis and football.

M : Do you play basketball?

I : No, I don't. I hate basketball.

M Really? I play basketball.

You may like to see if you can say these things in Japanese without looking at the dialogue.

- ***Yomimasu*** and ***Kikimasu***

These two verbs function the same way as *shimasu. Yomimasu* means "will read" or "read". Therefore *hon o yomimasu* means "I'll read a book/I read books".

Remember all the options you have with *shimasu?* It is the same for every other verb — you/he/she/we/they (read).
Remember that a full sentence could say:

Watashi wa hon o yomimasu.
or
Anata wa REKOODO o kikimasu.

This is correct but usually Japanese leave out *watashi wa* or *anata wa* when it is obvious who the topic is.

REKOODO o kikimasu means "I listen to records" or "I will listen to records".
Here are some examples of things you can now say:

Hon o yomimasu.	I'll read the book.
Watashi no hon o yomimasu.	I'll read my book.
BEN san no manga o yomimasu.	I'm going to read Ben's comic.
Eigo o hanashimasu.	I speak English (as my native language).
FURANSUgo o hanashimasu ka.	Do you speak French (as your native language)?
Ryuuichi san wa shinbun o yomimasu.	Ryuuichi will read the newspaper.
Watashi wa zasshi o yomimasu.	I'll read the magazine.

Hon o yomimasu.	We'll read books.
RAJIO o kikimasu.	I'll listen to the radio.
REKOODO o kikimasu.	I listen to records.
Watashi wa KASETTO TEEPU o kikimasu.	I listen to casette tapes.
Anata wa REKOODO o kikimasu ka.	Do you listen to records?

- Negatives

Shimasen is the negative of ***shimasu***
Yomimasen is the negative of ***yomimasu***
Kikimasen is the negative of ***kikimasu***
Hanashimasen is the negative of ***hanashimasu***
The negative of verbs in Japanese always ends in ***masen***.

You know how to use the ***masu*** form of *shimasu*. That pattern will stay the same for every verb you learn. To make the negative (to say you don't or won't do something) you take off the *masu* from *shimasu* leaving its stem, *shi*, and add on *masen*.

Shimasen means "won't do" or "don't do". So, *benkyoo shimasen* therefore means "don't study" or "won't study".

You now know the following:
FURANSUgo o benkyoo shimasen.
PIANO o renshuu shimasen.
PIITAA san wa FUTTOBOORU o shimasen.
SUU san wa BAIORIN o renshuu shimasen.
Yomimasu, kikimasu and ***hanashimasu*** work in exactly the same way.

Hon o yomimasen.	I won't read the book/I don't read books.
BOBU san wa REKOODO o kikimasen.	Bob doesn't listen to records.
ITARIAgo o hanashimasen.	I don't speak Italian (as my native language).

ACTIVITIES

- With a partner write down twenty different things that you do or don't do. (It doesn't have to be the truth!)
- Update your vocabulary cards.
- Listen as your teacher reads the conversation. Take careful note of pronunciation.
- Practice the conversation with a partner, substituting your own names.
- Practice again substituting different activities.
- With a partner (a different one would be a good idea so that you get used to other ways of thinking, and working with different people) make

up a play that you could act out for the class. Try to use as many constructions and vocabulary items as possible. You will feel surprised perhaps by how much you can now say in Japanese.

- Listen to and watch other people's plays. See how much you can understand and see how many different ways people find for using the same basic vocabulary. Use only the words you know so that the rest of the group can understand your play.

- Work in two teams and see which team remembers the most vocabulary. Each team produces a list of ten words and ten phrases or sentences to test the other team.

Writing Practice

く	さ	へ	ぬ
ku	***sa***	***he***	***nu***

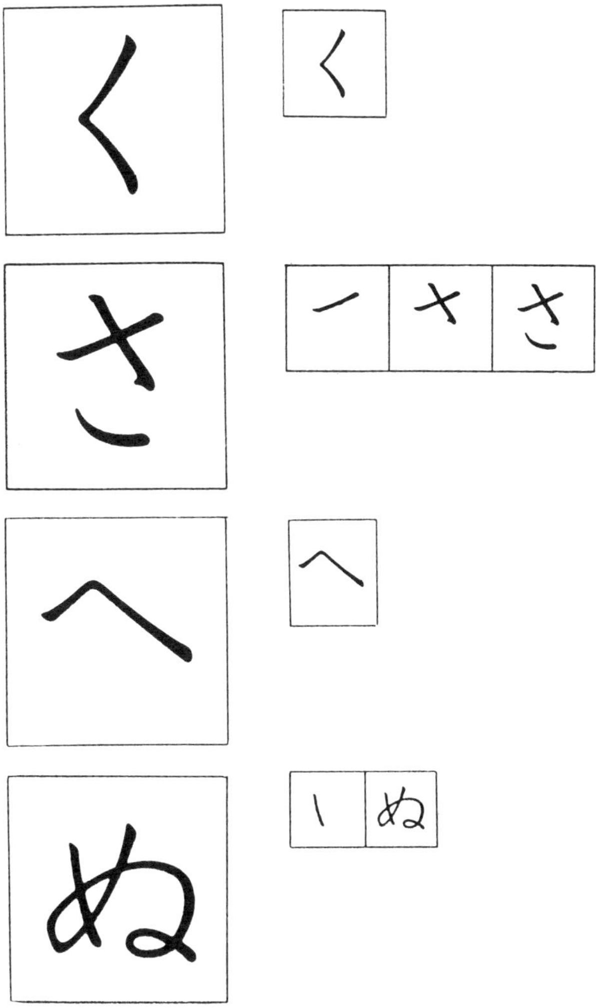

- Practice the syllables above in any way that you have developed for easy learning.

- Look for all the ones you know in the group below:

お	か	さ	た	な	は	ま	ら	や	わ
い	き	く	け	そ	み	の	た	ち	つ
め	ゆ	を	し	す	せ	に	ぬ	ね	む
ひ	ふ	ほ	も	り	る	ろ	お	う	て

- Look at the syllables below:

て	せ	て	く	ぬ	る	て	く
く	て	さ	し	ね	ほ	み	て
む	く	て	く	て	ぬ	て	も
て	し	は	か	り	て	く	そ
あ	て	ぬ	く	す	ひ	ふ	て
く	み	く	ら	さ	き	ま	と

In a collection game Kumi needs 14 *ku* syllables to win, Megumi needs 11 *te* syllables, and Kenji needs 9 *nu* syllables. Who will win?

Vocabulary checklist (Topic Three)

List One (Essential)
Introduction

いけばな	*ikebana*	flower arranging
からて	*karate*	(martial art)
じゅうどう	*juudoo*	(martial art)
せんぱい	*senpai*	special senior friend
こうはい	*koohai*	junior friend of a *senpai*
がっこう	*gakkoo*	school

Unit 1

べんきょう　します	*benkyoo shimasu*	study
ちがいます	*chigaimasu*	You're wrong/I beg to differ
ドイツご	*DOITSUgo*	German language
えいご	*eigo*	English
フランスご	*FURANSUgo*	French
はなします	*hanashimasu*	speak/talk
イタリアご	*ITARIAgo*	Italian
にほんご	*nihongo*	Japanese
れんしゅう　します	*renshuu shimasu*	practice
します	*shimasu*	do/will do
しません	*shimasen*	won't do/don't do
そう　です　か	*soo desu ka*	Is that so?
そう　です	*soo desu*	That's right/That is so
なにご	*nanigo*	What language(s)?

Unit 2

バイオリン	*BAIORIN*	violin
ちり	*chiri*	geography
フルート	*FURUUTO*	flute
ギター	*GITAA*	guitar
かがく	*kagaku*	science
おんがく	*ongaku*	music
ピアノ	*PIANO*	piano
れきし	*rekishi*	history
しゃかい	*shakai*	social studies
すうがく	*suugaku*	math
たいいく	*taiiku*	P.E.
や	*ya*	and (in a list)

Unit 3

バレーボール	*BAREEBOORU*	volleyball
スポーツ	*SUPOOTSU*	sports
テニス	*TENISU*	tennis
フットボール	*FUTTOBOORU*	football
サッカー	*SAKKAA*	soccer

Unit 4

きらい　です	*kirai desu*	I strongly dislike
すき　です	*suki desu*	I like
すき　じゃない　です	*suki janai desu*	I don't like

Unit 5

バスケットボール	*BASUKETTOBOORU*	basketball
はなします	*hanashimasu*	speak/talk
はなしません	*hanashimasen*	don't/won't speak
ききます	*kikimasu*	listen
ききません	*kikimasen*	don't/won't listen
くん	*kun*	good friend (used by males only)
ラジオ	*RAJIO*	radio
レコード	*REKOODO*	record (music)
カセット　テープ	*KASETTO TEEPU*	cassette tape
よみます	*yomimasu*	read
よみません	*yomimasen*	don't/won't read

List Two
Introduction

しょどう	*shodoo*	calligraphy
けんどう	*kendoo*	(martial art)

TOPIC FOUR time, days, and numbers

Introduction

ACHIEVEMENTS

At the end of this topic, you will be able to:

- count to one hundred;
- ask for someone's telephone number and give your own;
- ask and say what day it is;
- ask and say when someone does something;
- ask and say what time it is in hours and half hours.

Time

Time is very important in Japan. When a tour guide says that the bus will pick you up at two minutes past eight o'clock, the driver means exactly that! Often the driver will have permission to stop at a place for only a certain number of minutes, so Japanese people know that they must be there on time because the driver can't wait for them, and tourists soon learn!

Subways, buses and ordinary trains, too, are run very precisely and only have a specific time allowed for passengers to get on and off. Again it is necessary to be there on time and to get on and off trains and buses quickly and safely. If you think about it, it makes sense for safety and for the smooth running of the whole transportation system.

Days

In other ways time is very important to Japanese people.

A great many of them spend more than four hours a day just traveling back and forth to work or school. They spend a large part of each year looking forward to, experiencing and reminiscing over the many festivals that are held frequently through the year in every town and village. You will learn about some of the more famous ones as you go through this course. They provide spiritual times, relaxation, and enjoyment, in a very crowded, busy existence.

A festival day

Leisurely shopping on Sundays

Numbers

Numbers are important, too. Japanese people have a very great awareness of "good" numbers, and auspicious days for doing things. Many of them regularly visit priests at shrines to find out if a particular day would be a good one for whatever they want to do. Around exam times students and their anxious families keep the priests very busy.

House numbers are not very easy to find in Japan because houses are numbered as they are built, not in sequence along a road. Number one may be next to number 79 or even number 263! Thank goodness the policeman knows all the people in his area and can help you find the right house!

Japan now counts years in business and everyday situations by a Western calendar, but there is another way of counting calendar years and days as well. There are special periods of time measurement counted from the beginning of the Emperor's reign. You may pick up a yogurt carton, for example, and notice that its shelf life is shown as a particular month and day, 1-2 *Heisei* because the present Emperor's reign is called the ***Heisei*** period. (*Heisei* means "accomplishment of peace".) The former emperor reigned for 63 years and his reign was called **Shoowa**. The labeling in those days showed the *Shoowa* ("Bright peace") date.

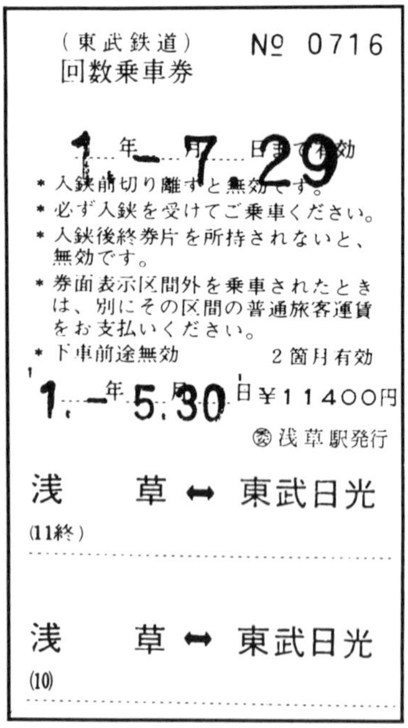

This train ticket is stamped with the *Heisei* date: 1-7-29 (29 July, in year 1 of *Heisei*)

Unit 1

なんばん　です　か
nanban desu ka
What number is it?

NEW WORDS

ばん	*ban*	number
なんばん　です　か	*nanban desu ka*	What number is it?
たす	*tasu*	added to
れい（ゼロ）	*rei/zero* (ZERO)	0
いち	*ichi*	1
に	*ni*	2
さん	*san*	3
し/よん	*shi/yon*	4
ご	*go*	5
ろく	*roku*	6
しち/なな	*shichi/nana*	7
はち	*hachi*	8
きゅう/く	*kyuu/ku*	9
じゅう	*juu*	10
じゅういち	*juuichi*	11
じゅうに	*juuni*	12
じゅうさん	*juusan*	13
じゅうよん	*juuyon*	14
じゅうご	*juugo*	15
じゅうろく	*juuroku*	16
じゅうなな	*juunana*	17
じゅうはち	*juuhachi*	18
じゅうきゅう/く	*juukyuu/ku*	19
にじゅう	*nijuu*	20
にじゅういち	*nijuuichi*	21
さんじゅう	*sanjuu*	30
ひゃく	*hyaku*	100

The Japanese have two sets of numbers used in everyday life. They are used for counting different things.

The first set (shown above) is actually Chinese and was introduced into Japan many centuries ago. The second set is uniquely Japanese and is only used in specific situations for the numbers one to ten. You will learn those later.

STUDY

- You will notice that the number four has two written and uttered forms:
  し ***shi*** and よん ***yon***.
  Shi is associated with death in Japan so there are many situations where a Japanese person prefers to use *yon* for number four. No one wants to be in a hospital room with number four on the door! Japanese are just as superstitious about *shi* as many other people are about number thirteen.

- ***Nana*** and ***shichi*** are alternatives for the number seven and are used, according to tradition, in particular situations. For example, when telling the time and for the month of July, use *shichi*, and when giving the age of seven, *nana* is used with a counter. (Counters will be explained later.)

- ***Kyuu*** and ***ku*** for nine are used in different situations. You will learn to recognize which to use from the context.

ACTIVITIES

- Looking at the numbers above you will see how easy it is to count to 100. Practice counting up to 100 in your head.

- Taking turns with a partner, see if you can count to twenty.

- Try counting up to 100 around the class going as fast as you can.

- Make a pack of cards numbered one to ten. Put your pack with a friend's pack and shuffle them well.
  With a partner take turns turning up one card each. For example, Student *1* turns up number three and calls out *san* and puts the card face up on the desk. Student *2* turns up number five and puts it down either in front or behind the other card (thereby creating two piles) and calls out either thirty-five (*sanjuugo*) or fifty-three (*gojuusan*) depending on which card is first.
  Keep going until you exhaust the pack. Before you play again, shuffle the cards well.

STUDY

- Now let's try some **math** in Japanese!
  Many people in Japan, even though calculators and computers are in everyday use, still prefer to use an abacus, called a ***soroban***, for calculations, and they are incredibly fast.

- **Addition.** When adding two numbers, for example 3 + 5, the pattern is:

  San ***tasu*** *go* ***wa*** *hachi desu.*

阪1・I

（なまえ　　　　　　　　　　　）

20 9. たしざん (1)

34～36ぺえじ

てん

（1つ 10てん）

❖ たしざんを　しましょう。

① 6＋2

② 7＋1

③ 3＋4

④ 4＋2

⑤ 6＋3

⑥ 7＋2

⑦ 4＋5

⑧ 6＋4

⑨ 7＋3

⑩ 9＋1

Tashizan o shimashoo
(Let's do some addition).
A page from a *juku* exercise book.

ACTIVITIES

- Try reading the following examples and giving the answer in Japanese.

1 *ichi tasu san*	11 *hachi tasu go*
2 *ni tasu go*	12 *go tasu kyuu*
3 *san tasu yon*	13 *kyuu tasu roku*
4 *go tasu roku*	14 *ni tasu kyuu*
5 *yon tasu go*	15 *hachi tasu hachi*
6 *juu tasu go*	16 *san tasu kyuu*
7 *juu tasu yon*	17 *juu tasu juu*
8 *san tasu juu*	18 *zero tasu san*
9 *roku tasu san*	19 *zero tasu zero*
10 *kyuu tasu juu*	20 *yon tasu hachi*

- Read the following in Japanese to your partner who will give you the answer in Japanese.

11 + 2	9 + 6	21 + 17
14 + 6	7 + 8	18 + 19
17 + 5	8 + 4	12 + 17
18 + 3	6 + 5	46 + 29
19 + 4	9 + 11	37 + 15
6 + 11	12 + 7	83 + 28

- Have a mini Japanese math quiz. Divide the group into teams. Each team will prepare the addition "sums" using only numbers up to 100 and must, of course, have the answers themselves!

- Number Bingo in Japanese. Use a commercially produced set or make your own. If you make your own, it's a good idea to cover them with plastic and then you can mark off the numbers as they are called with a felt pen. They can be wiped off afterwards, as long as you use waterbased pens, and it saves the hassle of finding enough counters.

- If you have room, put your chairs in a circle. You need one chair less than the total number in your group. Each person receives a number. The teacher calls out two or more numbers. Students with those numbers must leave their chairs and move to another before all the chairs are re-occupied. One person will be left in the middle again.

  If you want everyone to change places, call out *minasan*.

- Keep practicing all the *hiragana* that has been presented so far so, that you don't forget it. See how many number names you can write with the *hiragana* that you know.

Unit 2

あなた の でんわ ばんごう は なん です か
anata no denwa bangoo wa nan desu ka
What is your telephone number?

NEW WORDS

でんわ ばんごう	*denwa bangoo*	telephone number
どう いたしまして	*doo itashimashite*	Don't mention it

STUDY

- Read through the following dialogue.

Keri:
せんせい の でんわ ばんごう は なん です か。 — *Sensei no denwa bangoo wa nan desu ka.*

Sensei:
わたし の でんわ ばんごう です か。 — *Watashi no denwa bangoo desu ka.*

Keri:
はい。 — *Hai.*

Sensei:
ろく さん ぜろ の いち きゅう に いち です。 — *Roku san zero no ichi kyuu ni ichi desu.*

Keri:
ありがとう ございます。 — *Arigatoo gozaimasu.*

Sensei:
どう いたしまして。 — *Doo itashimashite.*

- あなた の でんわ ばんごう は
anata no denwa bangoo wa
This means "talking about your telephone number". Remember the particle *no*, "belonging to"? Note that using the particle *wa* makes sure the listener tunes in to exactly what you are talking about.

- When giving your telephone number you can say:
Watashi no denwa bangoo wa . . . desu.

When giving another person's number we can say:
(SAIMON) san no denwa bangoo wa . . . desu.

- We can give telephone numbers just as in English, but we put ***の no*** after the exchange to show that the number **belongs to** that area. For example: 578-6258.
  This number reads: *go nana hachi* **no** *roku ni go hachi.*

- We can ask about a telephone number in either of the following ways:
  Anata no denwa bangoo wa nan desu ka.
  Denwa bangoo wa nan desu ka.
  In the question *Denwa bangoo wa nan desu ka*, we assume it is our own telephone number that is required. But to make it more explicit, ***Anata no*** *denwa bangoo wa nan desu ka* could have been used (What is **your** telephone number?). This is because a direct translation of *Denwa bangoo wa nan desu ka* could have meant "What is **the** telephone number?" referring to a previous part of the conversation.

ACTIVITIES

- Ask your neighbors to give you their telephone numbers.

- Go around the room. Introduce yourself to two different people.
  Ask about their health.
  Ask if they like a particular activity.
  If they say no, ask if they like something else.
  Ask for their telephone numbers and say goodbye.

- Write a conversation based on the outline above.

- Keep practicing all the *hiragana* that you should know.

- Work around your group, asking for and giving your telephone numbers. (If you prefer to give a false one, that's fine.)

- Read the following telephone numbers out loud together. Remember to insert ***no*** after the area number.
  25-4567
  96-9634
  174-6491
  295-8453
  354-7628

Unit 3

なんようび　です　か
nanyoobi desu ka
What day is it?

NEW WORDS

なんようび	*nanyoobi*	what day?
げつようび	*getsuyoobi*	Monday
かようび	*kayoobi*	Tuesday
すいようび	*suiyoobi*	Wednesday
もくようび	*mokuyoobi*	Thursday
きんようび	*kinyoobi*	Friday
どようび	*doyoobi*	Saturday
にちようび	*nichiyoobi*	Sunday

STUDY

- Read through the following dialogue.

Saburoo:

なんようび　です　か。	*Nanyoobi desu ka.*	What day is it?

Michiko:

すいようび　です。	*Suiyoobi desu.*	It's Wednesday.

Saburoo:

ああ　そう　です　か。	*Aa soo desu ka.*	Really?
ありがとう　ございます。	*Arigatoo gozaimasu.*	Thank you.
すいようび　たいいく　です。	*Suiyoobi taiiku desu.*	Wednesday there's P.E.

- The *kanji* for the days of the week are interesting.

Monday is **moon** day	月	***getsu/****tsuki*	moon
Tuesday is **fire** day	火	***ka/****hi*	fire
Wednesday is **water** day	水	***sui/****mizu*	water
Thursday is **wood** day	木	***moku/****ki*	tree
Friday is **metal** day	金	***kin/****(o)kane*	metal, gold, money

月
火
水
木
金

土
日

Saturday is **earth** day	土	***do/****tsuchi*	earth
Sunday is **sun** day	日	***nichi/****hi*	sun, day

As you can see, the days of the week all take their names from basic things in nature.

You will notice that two different words have been given for each *kanji*. These are called **readings**. As your study continues, you will learn about these. For the present, learn the first reading of each pair.

ACTIVITIES

- Work in a small group. Fill in a program for Kenji. Give him an activity to keep him busy every day of the week.

  Begin: *Kenji san wa, getsuyoobi BASUKETTOBOORU o renshuu shimasu.* Just put Kenji's name with *san* and the day of the week in front of the sentence patterns you know already.

- Make a set of cards of the days of the week. Place them face down on a desk.

  With a partner take turns flipping them over. The first one to turn up *getsuyoobi* leaves it face up and gives a sentence out loud about an activity for that day of the week. No one else can have a turn until *kayoobi* occurs. Make up a sentence as before.

  Keep going until all the cards have been turned up and are lying in order on the desk. The winner is the one who turned up the most.

- Practice putting your own set of cards out in order on your desk.
- When you think you know them well, start with different days and see if you can still get them in the correct sequence.
- Class activity: students in turn call out any day. The class continues the sequence.

Unit 4

きょう　なに　を　します　か
Kyoo nani o shimasu ka
What will you do today?

NEW WORDS

あした	*ashita*	tomorrow
いつも	*itsumo*	always
きょう	*kyoo*	today
こんしゅう	*konshuu*	this week
まいにち	*mainichi*	every day
らいしゅう	*raishuu*	next week
いつ	*itsu*	when?

STUDY

- All of the new words above are put at the beginning of a sentence, in front of what you want to say.

- Read through the dialogue below and see how the words are used.

Saki:	きょう　なに　を　します　か。	*Kyoo nani o shimasu ka.*
Tomoko:	きょう　ギター　を　れんしゅう　します。	*Kyoo GITAA o renshuu shimasu.*
Saki:	あした　なに　を　します　か。	*Ashita nani o shimasu ka.*
Tomoko:	あした　ギター　を　れんしゅう　します。	*Ashita GITAA o renshuu shimasu.*
Saki:	いつも　ギター　を　れんしゅう　します。	*Itsumo GITAA o renshuu shimasu!*
Tomoko:	すいようび　ギター　の　れんしゅう　を　しません。フルート　の　れんしゅう　を　します。	*Suiyoobi GITAA no renshuu o shimasen. FURUUTO no renshuu o shimasu.*

- Did you understand the dialogue perfectly? Check the English translation below.
  "What will you do today?"
  "I'll practice the guitar."

"What will you do tomorrow?"
"I'll practice the guitar."
"You always practice the guitar!"
"I don't play guitar on Wednesdays, I play the flute."

ACTIVITIES

- Make cards of all the new words in this topic. Put a set in a pile face down on the desk. Put the cards you made before in a second pile face down. With a partner, take turns flipping over a card from each pile and make a sentence that includes both words.

EXERCISES

- What do the following sentences mean?
  1 *Itsumo benkyoo shimasu.*
  2 *Konshuu hon o yomimasu.*
  3 *Mainichi eigo o benkyoo shimasu.*
  4 *Raishuu SAKKAA o shimasen.*
  5 *Ashita FUTTOBOORU o shimasu ka.*
  6 *Getsuyoobi BAIORIN o renshuu shimasu.*
  7 *Ashita nanyoobi desu ka.*
  8 *Mokuyoobi desu ka.*
  9 *Doyoobi benkyoo shimasen.*
  10 *Itsu nihongo o benkyoo shimasu ka.*
  11 *Mainichi benkyoo shimasu.*

- With a partner, make up eleven sentences using the patterns above and write them in your notebook. Check that the sentences are correct. Remember the pattern:
  Time word/Object or activity/Particle *o*/ Verb

Unit 5

いま　なんじ　です　か
ima nanji desu ka
What time is it now?

NEW WORDS

ええ	*ee*	(alternative for *hai*. More informal way to say "Yes")
いま	*ima*	now
ばんごはん　の　じかん	*bangohan no jikan*	dinner time
じ	*—ji*	(hour o'clock)
くじ	*kuji*	nine o'clock
よじ	*yoji*	four o'clock
はん	*han*	half

STUDY

- Mr. Brown asks the time from a stranger in the street.

BURAUN:	すみません　が。 こんばん　は。	*Sumimasen ga.* *Konban wa.*
Itoo:	こんばん　は。	*Konban wa.*
BURAUN:	いま　なんじ　です　か。	*Ima nanji desu ka.*
Itoo:	いま　ろくじ　です。	*Ima rokuji desu.*
BURAUN:	ありがとう　ございます。	*Arigatoo gozaimasu.*
Itoo:	どう　いたしまして。	*Doo itashimashite.*

- All of the time words that you have learned so far are general time words, for example:
  "**Mondays** I do . . ."
  "Kumiko studies **every day** . . ."
  This unit teaches you how to tell the time. The next unit tells you how to say that you will do something at a particular time.
  It is very simple to tell the time in hours and half hours in Japanese. Giving exact minutes is more complicated, so that will be introduced in a later unit. Be content for the moment to round time up to the nearest half hour.

To say "It's one o'clock", all you have to do is to put ***ji*** on to the numbers you already know. For example:

いちじ です	***ichiji desu***	It's one o'clock.
にじ です	***niji desu***	It's two o'clock.

There are two exceptions to what you expect.

くじ ***kuji***	(not *kyuuji*)	nine o'clock
よじ ***yoji***	(not *yonji*)	four o'clock

Japanese people are very sensitive to sound combinations and prefer the sounds *kuji* and *yoji*.

- **Half hours**

さんじ はん です か。 *Sanji han desu ka.*
Is it half past three?

ええ、さんじ はん です。 *Ee, sanji han desu.*
Yes, it's half past three.

Just put ***han*** after the hour that you are talking about.

ACTIVITIES

- What's the time? All students stand (*tatte kudasai*). One student comes to the front of the group and secretly decides what time will be "dinner time". The group calls out together *Ima nanji desu ka.*
  Student *1*: (*hachiji desu*)
  The group calls out again and again until Student *1* calls out ***Bangohan no jikan desu*** *Dinner time*. Upon hearing this the group sits down as quickly as possible. The first person to sit takes over at the front. Alternatively, the last person is "out" when all but one have been eliminated.

- With a small group (five people), make up a role play in which two people go to the station to meet someone. They are not sure what he/she looks like so they ask the wrong person at first. They check the time with a person standing nearby. They approach another person who appears to be waiting and greet him/her and ask if it's Mr./Ms. Smith.
  It's the correct person so they introduce themselves (for the first time). They inquire after Mr./Ms. Smith's health, and ask some more questions as they walk off to their car together.

- In Japan you will often come across twenty-four hour time. Airlines, of course, use it and you'll come across it in many other situations. So practice being able to recognize the time that way.
  If someone gives the time as 20:30, would you immediately think 8:30 p.m.? It is necessary to tune in quickly because times at railway stations,

357	473	251	951	1135	253	255	955	257	475	1137	359	259	959	361	477	261	1039	263	479	265	267	269		れっしゃばんごう
普通	普通	準急	普通	特急	準急	準急	普通	準急	普通	特急	普通	準急	普通	普通	普通	準急	特急	準急	普通	準急	準急	準急		れっしゃしゅべつ
				きぬ 135号						きぬ 137号							けごん 39 号							れっしゃめい
会津高原	東武宇都宮	東武宇都宮	東武日光	鬼怒川温泉	東武宇都宮	東武宇都宮	東武日光	新栃木	東武宇都宮	鬼怒川公園	新藤原	新栃木	東武日光	鬼怒川温泉	東武宇都宮	新栃木	東武日光	新鹿沼	東武宇都宮	新栃木	新栃木	新栃木		ゆきさき
—	—	17.45	—	18.00	18.03	18.29	—	18.53	—	19.00	—	19.18	—	—	—	19.45	20.10	20.12	—	20.37	21.20	22.12	発	あさくさ
—	—	18.01	—	↓	18.21	18.46	—	19.11	—	↓	—	19.36	—	—	—	20.01	↓	20.28	—	20.57	21.36	22.29	発	きたせんじゅ
—	—	18.38	—	↓	18.56	19.21	—	19.46	—	↓	—	20.10	—	—	—	20.34	↓	20.58	—	21.29	22.07	22.57	発	かすかべ
—	—	18.43	—	✓	19.02	19.28	—	19.54	—	✓	—	20.18	—	—	—	20.42	✓	21.03	—	21.38	22.12	23.02	発	とうぶどうぶつこうえん
—	—	19.25	—	↓	19.43	20.14	—	20.34	—	↓	—	20.58	—	—	—	21.25	↓	21.44	—	22.21	22.54	23.43	着	しんおおひらした
—	19.21	19.29	—	↓	19.48	20.18	—	20.38	20.54	↓	—	21.02	—	—	21.22	21.30	↓	21.48	—	22.26	22.58	23.47	着	とちぎ
—	19.25	19.39		19.19	19.52	20.25		20.42	20.57	20.14	—	21.09		—	21.25	21.33	21.18	21.52		22.30	23.05	23.51	着	しんとちぎ
—			19.45	19.20			20.26	—		20.15	—	—	21.10	—		—	21.19	21.59		—	—	—	発	しんとちぎ
—			20.05	19.34			20.47	—		20.29	—	—	21.31	—		—	21.33	22.20		—	—	—	着	しんかぬま
			20.29	19.52			21.10	—		20.47	—	—	21.59			—	21.51	═		—	—	—	着	しもいまいち
			20.29	19.55			21.11	—		20.51	—	—	21.59			—	21.52	—		—	—	—	発	しもいまいち
			20.38	20.03			21.19	—		20.59	—	—	22.08			—	22.00	—		—	—	—	着	とうぶにっこう
	19.26	19.44	—		19.57	20.31	—	—	20.58		—	—	—		21.26	—	新栃木で21・26発の東武宇都宮行に接続	—	22.04	—	—	—	発	しんとちぎ
	19.38	19.53	—		20.07	20.40	—	—	21.09		—	—	—		21.36	—		—	22.15	—	—	—	着	みぶ
	19.45	20.00	—		20.14	20.47	—	—	21.16		—	—	—		21.44	—		—	22.22	—	—	—	着	おもちゃのまち
	19.53	20.07	—		20.21	20.54	—	—	21.24		—	—	—		21.52	—		—	22.30	—	—	—	着	にしかわだ
	19.57	20.10	—		20.24	20.57	—	—	21.28		—	—	—		21.55	—		—	22.34	—	—	—	着	えそじま
	20.03	20.16	—		20.30	21.03	—	—	21.34		—	—	—		22.02			—	22.40	—	—	—	着	とうぶうつのみや
20.10	—	浅草発は東武日光・東武宇都宮行新栃木で分割		19.54	—	—	—	—	—	20.49	21.15	—	—	22.03	—	—	—	—	—	—	—	—	発	しもいまいち
20.22	—			20.05	—	—	—	—	—	21.00	21.27	—	—	22.15	—	—	—	—	—	—	—	—	着	しんたかとく
20.31	—			20.12	—	—	—	—	—	21.07	21.34	—	—	22.24	—	—	—	—	—	—	—	—	着	きぬがわおんせん
20.35	—			═	—	—	—	—	—	21.12	21.39	—	—	═	—	—	—	—	—	—	—	—	着	きぬがわこうえん
20.39	—			—	—	—	—	—	—	═	21.43	—	—	—	—	—	—	—	—	—	—	—	着	しんふじわら
20.41	—	—	—	—	—	—	—	—	—	—	—	—	—	—	—	—	—	—	—	—	—	—	発	しんふじわら
20.43	—	—	—	—	—	—	—	—	—	—	—	—	—	—	—	—	—	—	—	—	—	—	着	りゅうおうきょう
20.48	—	—	—	—	—	—	—	—	—	—	—	—	—	—	—	—	—	—	—	—	—	—	着	かわじおんせん
20.50	—	—	—	—	—	—	—	—	—	—	—	—	—	—	—	—	—	—	—	—	—	—	着	かわじゆもと
20.56	—	—	—	—	—	—	—	—	—	—	—	—	—	—	—	—	—	—	—	—	—	—	着	ゆにしがわおんせん
21.03	—	—	—	—	—	—	—	—	—	—	—	—										—	着	なかみより
21.09	—	—	—	—	—	—	—	—	—	—	—	—										—	着	かみみよりしおばら
21.21	—	—	—	—	—	—	—	—	—	—	—	—										—	着	あいづこうげん
—	—	—	—	—	—	—	—	—	—	—	—	—										—	発	あいづこうげん
—	—	—	—	—	—	—	—	—	—	—	—	—										—	着	あいづたじま
—	—	—	—	東武日光方面は下今市乗換え 新栃木で19・26発の東武宇都宮行に接続	—	—	—	—	—	東武日光方面は下今市乗換え 新栃木で20・31発の東武宇都宮行に接続	—	—										—	着	ゆのがみおんせん
—	—	—	—		—	—	—	—	—		—	—										—	着	あしのまきおんせん
—	—	—	—		—	—	—	—	—		—	—	—	—	—	—	—	—	—	—	—	—	着	にしわかまつ
—	—	—	—		—	—	—	—	—		—	—	—	—	—	—	—	—	—	—	—	—	着	あいづわかまつ
																							き	うんてんびにごちゅういください。
																							じ	れんらくあんない

凡例

← 直通　⌒ 接続電車
← 接続　◆ 不定期
←---- 臨電接続　✓ 全車両座席指定

（注）会津バスの桧枝岐　尾瀬方面の運行は下記のとおりです。
●桧枝岐⟺御池間は5 1〜10 31まで
●御池⟺沼山峠間は5 10〜10 31まで

Twenty-four hour time is used on train timetables

etc., are given this way and if you can't figure it out quickly your train may leave without you! Announcers on buses don't speak slowly for the benefit of foreigners and you must be ready to pick up the information you need and listen intently.

- Draw some digital or analogue clockfaces and write below them the time in Japanese.
- Make a timetable for a whole school day in one-hour time segments, e.g.
  kuji: eigo desu
  juuji: suugaku desu
- Ask what time someone has particular subjects, e.g.: *Eigo wa nanji desu ka*. Answer: (*niji*) *desu*, etc.
- Two teams. Each takes turns giving a time, a number, or a phrase that you all should know, in English. The other team has to give the Japanese equivalent.

Check your understanding

Test yourself on numbers and times by writing the English equivalent of the following:

1 *Niji han desu.*
2 *sanjuuichi*
3 *Ima nanji desu ka.*
4 *hyaku*
5 *yonjuugo*
6 *san hachi kyuu no go ichi ichi*
7 *Rokuji han desu ka.*
8 *nanajuuyon*
9 *Ima yoji desu.*
10 *Go tasu roku wa juuichi desu.*

Unit 6

なんじ　に　いきます　か
nanji ni ikimasu ka
What time will you go?

NEW WORDS

うち	*uchi*	my house (home)
いえ	*ie*	someone else's house
えき	*eki*	station
みせ	*mise*	shop
どこ	*doko*	where (used in questions)
いきます	*ikimasu*	go
きます	*kimasu*	come
かえります	*kaerimasu*	return home
がっこう	*gakkoo*	school
みます	*mimasu*	see/look
じかん　が　あります	*jikan ga arimasu*	I have time
じかん　が　ありません	*jikan ga arimasen*	I don't have time
に	*ni*	to/at (particle)

STUDY

- Learn the last two phrases above by heart – they are very useful. We'll look at the grammar involved later.
- The new verbs listed above function the same way as the ones you already know. (By replacing the *masu* ending with *masen* you make the negative.)
- Read the dialogue below.

Ichiroo:
おはよう、　あした　どこ　に
いきます　か。
Ohayoo, ashita doko ni ikimasu ka.

Kenichi:
あした　がっこう　に　いきます。
まいにち　がっこう　に　いきます。
Ashita gakkoo ni ikimasu.
Mainichi gakkoo ni ikimasu.

Ichiroo:
じゃ　はちじ　はん　に　いきます
か。
Ja hachiji han ni ikimasu ka.

Kenichi:

そう です。 はちじ はん に いきます。 じゃ また。	*Soo desu. Hachiji han ni ikimasu. Ja mata.*

- Remind yourself of the verbs you know. Check that you remember the negative too:

yomimasu	*renshuu shimasu*
kikimasu	*ikimasu*
mimasu	*kimasu*
shimasu	*kaerimasu*
benkyoo shimasu	*hanashimasu*

- The new **particle** in this unit is ***ni*** **に**.
  Ni is the particle for "to" or "at". ***Ni*** is used with places and time. In a sentence, *ni* goes **after** the **place** or very **particular time** that you are talking about, and also after ***doko*** (question word for "where").
  e.g.: *Gakkoo* ***ni*** *ikimasu.*
  I go to school.
  Ashita doko ni ikimasu ka.
  Where will you go tomorrow?
  JAN san wa uchi ni kaerimasu.
  Jan returns home to her house.
  Sanji ni uchi ni kaerimasu.
  At three o'clock we will go home.

ACTIVITY

- Practice reading aloud the conversation between Kenichi and Ichiroo. You will probably understand perfectly. Check with the translation on p. 120 to see if you are correct.

STUDY

Previously you learned how to say things like:
"Mondays we study Japanese."
"I study English every day."
Now you can state a particular time for your activities and where you go to do them.
Kuji ni kyooshitsu ni ikimasu.
I'll go to the classroom at nine o'clock.

- **Using *ni* with times**
  Ni must be used when you are stating a **particular time**. It should not be used when you are talking generally. It is the same in English. We say: "On Mondays I practice piano." "I study every day."

When you say "at" or "on" in English you need to use ***ni*** in Japanese.

On Monday I'll ...
The sentences above need *ni* because they are stating a particular time.

- **Using *ni* with places**
  Ni can also mean **to** and is used to signal the place to which you will go: "I'll go **to** school."
  It is used in exactly the same way as the English "to" but is put after the name of the place instead of before.
  Gakkoo ***ni*** *ikimasu.* I will go to school.

ACTIVITIES

- Practice saying the following in Japanese:
  (Remember to put the time word first)
  A I go to school every day.
  B Bob comes today.
  C Keri will return home at 6 o'clock.
  D I won't study today.
  E I'll practice guitar at 4 o'clock.
  F On Tuesday I will study English.
  G This week I will see the cats.
  H Next week I will go to school.
  I I will come tomorrow.
  J Will you return home today?

- Match the sentences above with their Japanese equivalents below:
  1 *Kyoo kaerimasu ka.*
  2 *Raishuu gakkoo ni ikimasu.*
  3 *Yoji ni watashi wa GITAA o renshuu shimasu.*
  4 *Konshuu neko o mimasu.*
  5 *Mainichi gakkoo ni ikimasu.*
  6 *Rokuji ni KERI san wa kaerimasu.*
  7 *Kayoobi ni eigo o benkyoo shimasu.*
  8 *Kyoo BOBU san wa kimasu.*
  9 *Ashita kimasu.*
  10 *Kyoo benkyoo shimasen.*

- With a partner figure out what the following sentences mean:
  1 *Kyoo hon o yomimasen.*
  2 *Ashita FURANSUgo no REKOODO o kikimasu.*
  3 *Raishuu gakkoo ni ikimasen.*
  4 *Shichiji ni rekishi o benkyoo shimasu.*
  5 *Kyoo REKOODO o kikimasen.*
  6 *MAAKU san wa kimasen.*

- Discuss which sentences needed *ni* and why.

> There is a time difference between the U.S. and Japan of 14 hours on the East Coast and 17 hours on the West Coast. Hawaii is 19 hours behind Japan. It is important to know what the particular time difference is if you are traveling or if you want to make or receive phone calls. The reception you get from people when you phone in the middle of the night is not always what you would wish, even if you are only phoning to wish them well!

- Below is a translation of the conversation on p. 117.
  I: Good morning, where will you go tomorrow?
  K: I'll go to school tomorrow. I go to school every day.
  I: Well, will you be going at eight thirty?
  K: That's so. I'll be going at eight thirty. See you!

Writing practice

You know enough *hiragana* now to write much of the new vocabulary that you have learned.

- Try writing these words:
  shimasu *kimasu*
  ikimasu *kikimasu*

- The new syllables to practice are:

よ	き		を	で	す
yo	**ki**	(particle)	**o**	**de**	**su**

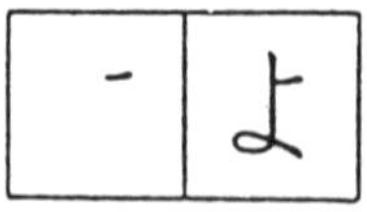

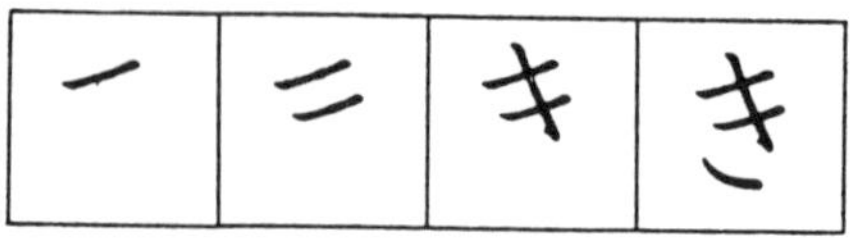

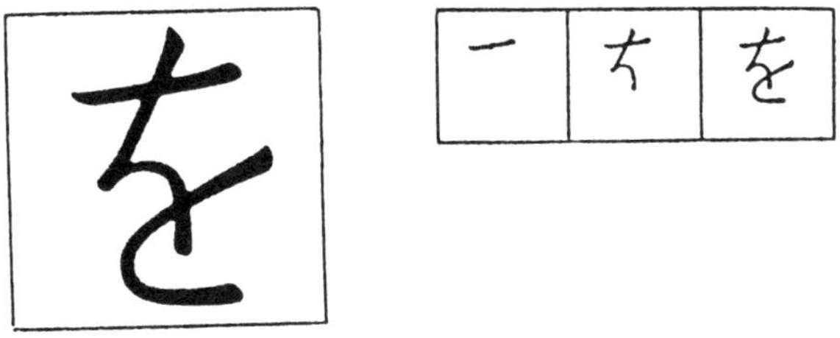

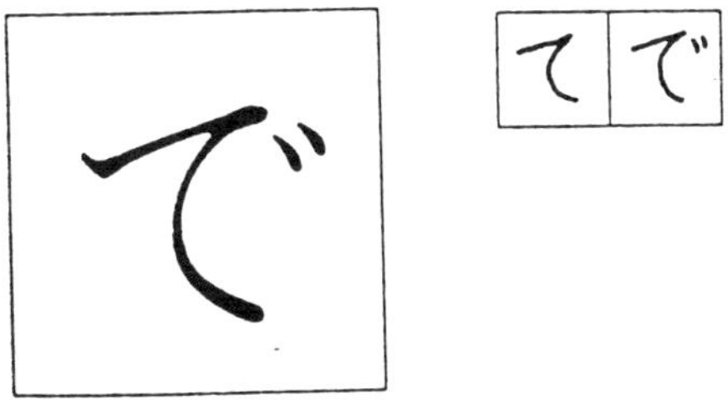

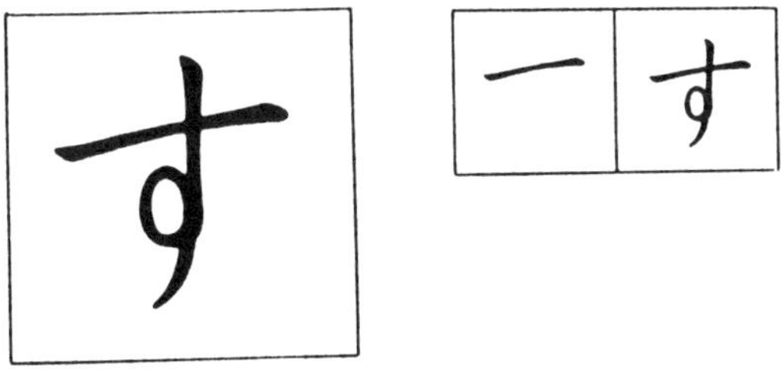

The ***o*** above is used only for the particle *o*, never for the ordinary *o* (お).

- Here are some sentences to write:

Hon o yomimasu.	I'll read the book.
E o mimasu.	I'll look at the picture.
Anata no e o mimasu.	I'll look at your picture.
Watashi no hon o yomimasu.	I'll read my book.
Kore o mimasu.	I'll look at this.
Sore o kikimasu.	I'll listen to that.
Are o yomimasu.	I'll read that (over there).

- You can write negatives of verbs, too. Write the negatives of five verbs of your choice in *hiragana*.

- After you have read the sentences below, write them in English. Compare your version with that of a friend. Discuss the reason for any differences in interpretation.

  Note: by adding two small strokes to *ta*, you make *da*: た → だ

  You make *do* from *to* in the same way: と → ど

  Now read and understand the following sentences.
  1 あした なに を します か。
  2 れきし を します。
  3 わたし に でんわ を します か。

4 あなた の なまえ を かいて ください。
5 わたし の かみ を みて ください。
6 どこ の かた です か。
7 ほん を よみます。
8 これ を しません。
9 かさ を みました。
10 にほん に かえります。

- Note: from *te*, you can make *de*: て → で

  And from *ko*, you can make *go*: こ → ご

- Look at the sentences below and then match them with the translations that follow.

  1 あした なに を します か。
  2 ほん を よみます か。
  3 どこ の かた です か。
  4 せいと です か。
  5 にほんご を します か。

  a Do you read books?
  b Where do you come from?
  c Are you a student?
  d What are you going to do tomorrow?
  e Do you do Japanese?

SOME STUDY TIPS
As with all your Japanese, don't worry about the things you can't do yet but practice the things you ***CAN*** do, frequently; and gradually absorb the rest. The more you practice in small, concentrated segments, the easier they become.

Unit 7

にじ　に　こうえん　に いきましょう
niji ni kooen ni ikimashoo
Let's go to the park at two o'clock

NEW WORDS

ビデオ　ゲーム	*BIDEO GEEMU*	video games
えいが	*eiga*	movies
いきましょう	*ikimashoo*	let's go
かえりましょう	*kaerimashoo*	let's go home
ききましょう	*kikimashoo*	let's listen
きましょう	*kimashoo*	let's come
こうえん	*kooen*	park
まち	*machi*	town
ハイキング	*HAIKINGU*	hiking
みましょう	*mimashoo*	let's look at/watch
ホノルル	*HONORURU*	Honolulu
ピクニック	*PIKUNIKKU*	picnic
プール	*PUURU*	swimming pool
ロサンゼルス	*ROSANZERUSU*	Los Angeles
しましょう	*shimashoo*	let's do/play
としょかん	*toshokan*	library
うみ	*umi*	sea/seaside
ニューヨーク	*NYUUYOOKU*	New York
よみましょう	*yomimashoo*	let's read

STUDY

- Read through the following conversation.

Sachiko:
ゆみこ　さん、こんにち　は。
Yumiko san, konnichi wa.

Yumiko:
さちこ　さん、　おひさしぶり です　ね。
Sachiko san, Ohisashiburi desu ne.

Sachiko:
すみません　が……きょう すいようび　です。いま　がっこう に　いきます。にじ　に　こうえん に　いきましょう　か。
Sumimasen ga . . . kyoo suiyoobi desu. Ima gakkoo ni ikimasu. Niji ni kooen ni ikimashoo ka.

Yumiko:
はい、　にじ　に　いきましょう。　*Hai, niji ni ikimashoo.*
じゃ　また。　*Ja mata.*

Wednesday is usually a half day in Japanese schools but they go to school on Saturday mornings to compensate. Wednesday afternoon is often a club activity time or time to get extra help from teachers. Sometimes it is free.

- The new verb form in this unit allows you to suggest activities to your friends: **Let's . . . .**
  Take off the ***masu*** from the verb and replace it with ***mashoo*** to say **Let's . . . .**
  For example:
  ikimasu → *ikimashoo*

- If you want to ask "Shall we go?" Just add ***ka*** to the end:
  ikimashoo → *ikimashoo ka*
  For example:
  Eiga ni ikimashoo ka. Shall we go to a movie?

ACTIVITIES

- Practice the following with a friend:
  A *Eiga ni ikimashoo ka.*
  B *Hai, eiga ni ikimashoo.*

  A *PUURU ni ikimashoo ka.*
  B *Hai, ikimashoo.*

  A *Mise ni ikimashoo ka.*
  B *Ee, ikimashoo.*
  (Remember, *ee* is an alternative for *hai.*)

- Practice making suggestions to your friends using all the verbs you now know:
  e.g. *yomimasu* *yomimashoo*
  Manga o yomimashoo ka.
  REKOODO o kikimashoo ka.
  Eiga ni ikimashoo ka.

  (*Manga* and *REKOODO* are objects, so they take the particle ***o***; *eiga* is a place to go to, so it has the particle ***ni*** after it.)

- Have a competition to see who can make the longest list of suggestions, preferably with a time included.

- Update your card collection by making cards with all the verbs you know. Make one set of the *masu* form, one set with *masen* and another set with *mashoo* endings.

- With a friend or a group, practice what you know. Set up piles of cards face down on a desk. Put them in this order:
  Time words/activities/verbs.
  Spread the particles out where you can easily see them. Make sure you have at least two *ni* cards. Leave object cards in another pile at the side. The aim is to turn up one card from each pile and make a sentence by inserting the correct particle in the correct place. If you need an object card instead of an activity to be able to make a sensible sentence, that is fine. Just take one from the side.

- With a small group, put on a role play. Decide on the situation and use as much of what you know as possible.

- With a partner, see how good you are at responding spontaneously to what someone says to you. Student *1*, out of the blue, says e.g. *Kyoo hon o yomimasu ka.* Student *2* replies with no hesitation: *Hai, kyoo hon o yomimasu* or *Iie, kyoo hon o yomimasen* etc. Take turns asking five questions each.

- Without practicing first, have a conversation with a friend. Greet each other appropriately for the time of day. Say what you plan to do today. Suggest an activity to do together at a particular time. If you learn to respond spontaneously to what people say to you, you are well on the way to real communication. After all, you don't usually plan what you are going to say in English before you speak, do you? So practice as much as you can, saying things to each other and answering in Japanese without planning it first.

Unit 8

きのう　なに　を　しました　か
kinoo nani o shimashita ka
What did you do yesterday?

NEW WORDS

きのう	*kinoo*	yesterday
せんしゅう	*senshuu*	last week
さくばん	*sakuban*	last night
しゅくだい	*shukudai*	homework
やきゅう	*yakyuu*	baseball
テレビ	*TEREBI*	television
パーティー	*PAATII*	party
ダンス	*DANSU*	dance
よる	*yoru*	in the evening
あさ	*asa*	in the morning

STUDY

- *Yoru* and *asa* have "in the" incorporated as part of their meaning. Never add *ni* with these words.

- It is Monday. Two friends meet after the weekend.

Sumiko:
きのう　なに　を　しました　か。　*Kinoo nani o shimashita ka.*

Kaeru:
べんきょう　しました　テニス　を　しました。　あなた　は。　*Benkyoo shimashita, TENISU o shimashita. Anata wa.*

Sumiko:
しゅくだい　を　しました。えいご　の　ほん　を　よみました。ピアノ　を　れんしゅう　しました。　やきゅう　を　しました。　*Shukudai o shimashita. Eigo no hon o yomimashita. PIANO o renshuu shimashita. Yakyuu o shimashita.*

Kaeru:
テープ　を　ききました　か。　*TEEPU o kikimashita ka.*

Sumiko:
ええ、ききました。　*Ee, kikimashita.*

- The **past** form of verbs in Japanese (which allows you to say what you **did**) is made by using another verb ending. Use the **stem** of the verb and add ***mashita***.
  For example:
  ikimasu → *ikimashita* いきます → いきました
  yomimasu → *yomimashita* よみます → よみました
  (If you find it hard to remember *mashita*, think of it as 'mashed up' or finished; and remember to say *mashita* as if it has no "i".)

- The past tense of ***desu*** is ***deshita***.
  Now you can answer questions like "When was the party?"
  Sakuban deshita. It was last night.
  Senshuu deshita. It was last week.

  Now you know how to say:
  Sakuban Hanako san no hon o yomimashita.
  I read Hanako's book last night.

  Senshuu NYUUYOOKU ni ikimashita.
  I went to New York last week.

  Kyoo sensei ni hanashimashita.
  I talked to the teacher today.

- The following phrases are very useful.
  じかん が ありました。
  Jikan ga arimashita. I had time.
  じかん が ありました か。
  Jikan ga arimashita ka. Did you have time?

Yakyuu, or baseball, is very popular in Japan. It is played everywhere and people are vitally interested in major competitions or local ones. It was introduced from America but very soon became a Japanese national sport and had its own name label (written in *hiragana*) given to it: **やきゅう**

- You can now say the following:

Yakyuu o mimashita.	I watched baseball.
TEREBI o mimashita.	I watched TV.
Yoru TEREBI o mimashita.	In the evening I watched TV.
Mokuyoobi no yoru TEREBI o mimashita.	Thursday evening I watched TV.

ACTIVITIES

- Practice using all the verb forms that you know for activities, in good sentences. Extend yourself to put as much in each sentence as you can. Don't be satisfied with only the verb. (Remember to put the particle *o* after activities you did, and the particle *ni* after places you went to, and particular times, e.g. four o'clock.)

- Joanne was asked what she did yesterday. She answered:
  "I went to the beach."
  "I read a book."
  "At five o'clock I went home."
  "I watched TV."
  Write Joanne's answers in your book. Under them write the *roomaji* translation. Under that write any words that you can write in *hiragana*. Under that leave a line free for your teacher to correct any mistakes.

- Make up five or more sentences of your own that tell what someone did yesterday. They are bound to sound a bit stilted, but until you have been learning Japanese for some time, anyone's language sounds a bit formal.

- Read your sentences to a neighbor.

- Ask your neighbor to tell you what you said, in English.

Unit 9

えいが に いきません でした
eiga ni ikimasen deshita
I didn't go to the movies

STUDY

- **The past negative of verbs**

  The past negative of verbs is formed by changing the ending added to the stem to …ません でした(. . . ***masen deshita***).

  For example:

iki* + *masen deshita	did not go
yomimasen deshita	did not read
mimasen deshita	did not see
kikimasen deshita	did not listen
Doyoobi ni eiga ni ikimasen deshita.	I did not go the the movies on Saturday.
Anata no inu o mimasen deshita.	I did not see your dog./I have not seen your dog.
Nihongo no hon o yomimasen deshita.	I did not (have not) read the Japanese language book.

ACTIVITIES

- Take turns asking your partner what he/she did yesterday. Answer what you did and what you didn't do, e.g. "I went to the beach. I did not study".

- Around the class. Tell everyone something that you did or did not do yesterday. Listen carefully so that you don't repeat what someone has already said. You may like to add to things you did not do, "I didn't have time".

- Write down what you did on each day of last week. To say "On Monday at one o'clock" etc. say: *Getsuyoobi no ichiji ni . . .* (Literally, "At one o'clock belonging to Monday . .")

- Around the class go through activities that Naomi did on a certain day. Start at 9 o'clock and go through until 9 o'clock at night.

- With a partner make a board game for other people to play. Rule a sheet of paper into squares. Number the squares. Each square should be given an activity, e.g. *Hon o yomimashita.* (A leisure activity or a study activity.)

  Use a spinner to move around the board, award three points for arriving on a leisure activity, and five points for a study activity (or the other way around!) and see which of you wins the most points. Four people at a time could perhaps play each other's games.

- Have a board game competition within your class to make games that would be fun to play (or at least help you to learn things in an easier way).

Writing practice

- There is so much that you can now write in *hiragana*. With a friend make up ten sentences that you can write entirely in *hiragana*. Write them carefully on paper and use them to test other people. Pass them to another two students and see if they can give you a *roomaji* version of what you have written.

- Next, try some more sentences off the top of your head. (If there are any syllables that you don't yet know, or any that have to be written in *katakana*, just write them in *roomaji* for the present.)

SOME STUDY TIPS

If you feel disappointed because you've been working hard and still don't really know the syllables, don't worry. Some people learn them easily and some take a bit longer. Just keep practicing **daily** and they'll eventually sink in!

Remember, you are in fact programming a computer (your brain) to take in all this new and very different information. It has only been partially trained to switch into Japanese. It has to learn how to take in the information, to store it, and to give it back to you at your command.

Daily practice is the key, even if it is only five minutes at a time. The more you go over vocabulary and writing in small doses, the more likely it is that your "computer" will pick up the information and become more receptive to new material because it has learned **how** to learn.

Ganbatte kudasai **Keep on trying!**

- Below are sentences that you are now able to write in *hiragana*. Try writing them and see how many you can do before checking with the translations that follow.

Note: 1) *ka* can be changed to *ga*: か → が
2) particle *wa* is written with the *ha* syllable は
(If you choose to use *watashi wa*)

1 I read the book. (past)
2 I am going to look at the dog.
3 I like books.

4 I saw the umbrellas.
5 I'm going to go to Japan tomorrow.
6 Are you going to go to Los Angeles?
7 I went home in the morning.
8 Tomorrow I'll read the book.
9 I'll look at your picture now.
10 Did you go to New York?

1 ほん を よみました。
2 いぬ を みます。
3 ほん が すき です。
4 かさ を みました。
5 あした にほん に いきます。
6 ロサンゼルス に いきます か。
7 あさ かえりました。
8 あした ほん を よみます。
9 いま あなた の え を みます。
10 ニューヨーク に いきました か。

- Match the following *roomaji* words with their *hiragana* equivalents.

1 *katakana*
2 *rekishi*
3 *kasa*
4 *kudasai*
5 *ikimasu*
6 *kore*
7 *kimasu*
8 *sore*
9 *kikimasu*
10 *nani*
11 *ano*
12 *ki*
13 *anata*
14 *san*
15 *ashita*
16 *ni*
17 *minasan*
18 *hon*
19 *kun*
20 *sensei*

a ください
b いきます
c れきし
d これ
e ききます
f なに
g さん
h あの
i きます
j かたかな
k くん
l みなさん
m あした
n き
o せんせい
p ほん
q に
r かさ
s あなた
t それ

Vocabulary checklist (Topic Four)

List One
Unit 1

なんばん	*nanban*	what number?
たす	*tasu*	added to

Unit 2

でんわ　ばんごう	*denwa bangoo*	telephone number
どう　いたしまして	*doo itashimashite*	Don't mention it

Unit 3

なんようび　です　か	*nanyoobi desu ka*	What day is it?
げつようび	*getsuyoobi*	Monday
かようび	*kayoobi*	Tuesday
すいようび	*suiyoobi*	Wednesday
もくようび	*mokuyoobi*	Thursday
きんようび	*kinyoobi*	Friday
どようび	*doyoobi*	Saturday
にちようび	*nichiyoobi*	Sunday

Unit 4

あした	*ashita*	tomorrow
いつ	*itsu*	when?
いつも	*itsumo*	always
こんしゅう	*konshuu*	this week
きょう	*kyoo*	today
まいにち	*mainichi*	every day
らいしゅう	*raishuu*	next week

Unit 5

ええ	*ee*	yes (alternative for *hai*)
はん	*han*	half
いま	*ima*	now
じ	*–ji*	(hour o'clock)
くじ	*kuji*	nine o'clock
よじ	*yoji*	four o'clock

Unit 6

どこ	*doko*	where?
いきます	*ikimasu*	go
じかん　が　あります	*jikan ga arimasu*	I have time
じかん　が　ありません	*jikan ga arimasen*	I don't have time
がっこう	*gakkoo*	school
きます	*kimasu*	come
かえります	*kaerimasu*	return home
みます	*mimasu*	see/look
えき	*eki*	station
みせ	*mise*	shop/store
うち	*uchi*	my house
いえ	*ie*	someone else's house

Unit 7

こうえん	*kooen*	park
ビデオ　ゲーム	*BIDEO GEEMU*	video games
えいが	*eiga*	films/movies
ホノルル	*HONORURU*	Honolulu
（いき）　ましょう	*(iki) mashoo*	let's (go)

まち	*machi*	town
ハイキング	*HAIKINGU*	hiking
ニューヨーク	*NYUUYOOKU*	New York
ピクニック	*PIKUNIKKU*	picnic
プール	*PUURU*	swimming pool
ロサンゼルス	*ROSANZERUSU*	Los Angeles
としょかん	*toshokan*	library
うみ	*umi*	sea

Unit 8

せんしゅう	*senshuu*	last week
きのう	*kinoo*	yesterday
しゅくだい	*shukudai*	homework
やきゅう	*yakyuu*	baseball
→ました	*–mashita*	(past tense ending)
→ません　でした	*–masen deshita*	(past negative ending)

List Two

へいせい	*heisei*	"Accomplishment of peace" (name of current Emperor's reign)
しょうわ	*shoowa*	(name of previous Emperor's reign)
がんばって　ください	*ganbatte kudasai*	Do your best!/Keep on trying!

TOPIC FIVE
the weather

Introduction

ACHIEVEMENTS

By the end of this unit you will be able to:
- describe the weather;
- ask and say what the weather may be like in the future.

Extension material will teach you how to:
- ask "why";
- give a reason;
- tell someone you will meet him/her.

おてんき　　Otenki

Otenki means "weather". Because the weather is so important in people's lives, the Japanese treat it with respect and give it the honorific *O* **お**. Until this century, Japan's economy was agricultural, so weather was even more important to the people in their working lives.

Comment on the weather in Japan is a common part of most introduction and greeting-type conversations and features in most people's ordinary daily conversation.

The climate of Japan is quite varied with great differences between north and south. It is affected by being only 200 kms. (125 miles) from the continental land mass of Eurasia. From Eurasia in summer it receives warm moist air currents and in winter cold dry ones. It is also affected by two major sea currents – one which warms southern Japan and one which cools northern Japan.

Japan has a mountain "backbone". Rain falls on the windward side and the other side is comparatively dry. Most of the country gets at least 100 cms. (40 inches) of rain a year. In June there is a "rainy season" called ***tsuyu*** or ***baiu***, and there are often typhoons in October. In winter Hokkaidoo has a lot of snow while Kyuushuu in the south is relatively warm and can grow semi-tropical fruits.

The Japanese are very conscious of having four distinctly separate seasons and are quite surprised to find that some other nations have clearly defined seasons, too. Consciousness and celebration of the seasons is probably greater in Japan, though, than anywhere else. As soon as the plum and cherry trees are in blossom in spring (***haru***), people take picnics and go out to admire the blossoms, eating under the cherry trees. This celebration is called ***hanami*** (flower viewing).

Winter in Kyuushuu is mild

Summer (***natsu***) is celebrated by making trips to the beaches and national parks and by letting off fireworks in special festival spectaculars while people enjoy firework-watching parties from vantage points. It is hot and often humid and people like to go outside in the evening.

Autumn (***aki***) is noted for its change of foliage color, and people take the opportunity for leaf and moon viewing parties.

Winter (***fuyu***) has, of course, its snow viewing, wherever there is snow, and people go to see the snow from less cold areas. Sapporo has its famous ice sculpture festival in February and other places have their special festivals too. All of these occasions are marked by special foods only eaten at that time of the year – a little bit like the way others have Easter eggs and Christmas cake.

The *kanji* for *tenki* is 天気.The kanji 天 (*ten*) looks like clouds over the *kanji* for "person", and means "sky" or "heaven". *Ki* means "anima" or "spirit".

天気

Japanese people usually watch weather forecasts carefully and carry umbrellas if there is any chance of rain. More umbrellas are sold yearly in Japan than anywhere else in the world.

Teru teru boozu
A *teru teru boozu* is a good weather charm which may be hung in the window to wish for fine weather the following day. It always works (they say!).

To make one:
Take a square of fabric or soft paper like a paper tissue. Into the center put a crumpled up ball of tissue or cloth. Turn it over, holding the ball firmly and tie a string around its "neck".

Decorate the head with a suitable smiling face to make the weather happy, and hang it in your window by the end of its neck thread. Good luck!

Unit 1

あつい　です　ね
atsui desu ne
It's hot, isn't it?

NEW WORDS

あき	*aki*	autumn
あめ	*ame*	rain/rainy
あつい	*atsui*	hot
あつくない	*atsukunai*	not hot
あたたかい	*atatakai*	warm
ふゆ	*fuyu*	winter
はなみ	*hanami*	flower viewing
はる	*haru*	spring
いい	*ii*	good
むし　あつい	*mushi atsui*	humid
なつ	*natsu*	summer
ね	*ne*	isn't it?
おてんき	*Otenki*	the weather
さむい	*samui*	cold
すずしい	*suzushii*	cool
わるい	*warui*	bad
いい　おてんき　です	*ii Otenki desu*	it's good weather

STUDY

- Study the following phrases:

いい　おてんき　です　ね。　*Ii Otenki desu ne.*
It's good weather, isn't it?

はい、　あつい　です　ね。　*Hai, atsui desu ne.*
Yes, isn't it hot?

In this unit you will learn some adjectives used to describe the weather, and some names (nouns) of different elements.

Adjectives tell you more information about nouns and pronouns, e.g. "warm weather". In a sentence like "It is warm", "warm" tells you about "it", which in this case is the weather. The pronoun "it" stands in place of a noun.

- **いい** *Ii* is an adjective and means "good".
Atsui, samui, warui are also adjectives.

The adjectives in Japanese go in front of the noun, the same as in English. Japanese true adjectives always end in *ai, ii, ui, ei,* or *oi.*

- *Atsui Otenki desu.* It's hot weather.
  Substitute any of the adjectives for *atsui* and you can describe the present weather.
  samui Otenki
  atatakai Otenki
  suzushii Otenki
  mushi atsui Otenki
  All of these are followed by *desu.*

> ***Mushi atsui***
> *Mushi* means "steam" but it has a synonym which means "worm" or "insect". (*Mushi atsui* may be easier to memorize if you remember that worms and insects multiply rapidly in humid weather!)
>
> In Japanese it is difficult to sort out which meaning is intended when the word is written in *roomaji* or *hiragana*. However, in *kanji* it is very clear because even if words sound the same, the *kanji* will be different, coming from different picture ideas.

- Here is a rule to use with adjectives:
  (Notice *ii* is not on the list. Use *warui* as an alternative way of saying "not good" for the present.)
  To make an adjective into the negative: take off the *i* and add *kunai*.
  あつい → あつくない です ***atsui*** ⟶ ***atsukunai desu***

  さむい → さむくない です ***samui*** ⟶ ***samukunai desu***
  Practice with all the adjectives you know.

- Add a time word to the beginning and that's all you need to describe temperature: *Kyoo atsui desu ne.* It's hot today, isn't it?

  Kyoo atsukunai desu ne.
  It's not hot today, is it?

  Ima suzushikunai desu.
  It's not cool now.

- There is a special way to put adjectives into the past tense. You will learn how to do that later. You can, however, say *atsui Otenki deshita.* "It was hot weather". Look at the following examples:

  Samui Otenki deshita.
  It was cold weather.

Ii Otenki deshita.
It was good weather.

So you can say it **was** good weather by putting the adjective ***ii*** in front of the noun. But **you cannot put an adjective in front of *deshita.*** You cannot say ***atsui deshita.***

ACTIVITIES

Match the sentences in the two columns:

1	*Mainichi samui desu.*	It's cool, isn't it?
2	*Kyoo atatakai desu.*	It's bad weather, isn't it?
3	*Suzushii desu ne.*	It's cold every day.
4	*Ii Otenki desu.*	It's good weather.
5	*Warui Otenki desu ne.*	It's warm today.
6	*Atsukunai desu.*	It's not cool, is it?
7	*Atatakakunai desu.*	The weather is not bad.
8	*Suzushikunai desu ne.*	It's not cold.
9	*Otenki wa warukunai desu.*	It's not hot.
10	*Samukunai desu.*	It's not warm.

Check your understanding

Kyoo doyoobi desu. Suzuki san to Yamazaki san wa kooen ni ikimasu.

Suzuki:
やまざき　さん、　おはよう。　いい　おてんき　です　ね。 — *Yamazaki san, Ohayoo. Ii Otenki desu ne.*

Yamazaki:
はい、いい　おてんき　です。　あつい　です　ね。　こうえん　に　いきましょう　か。 — *Hai, ii Otenki desu. Atsui desu ne. Kooen ni ikimashoo ka.*

Suzuki:
ええ、　なに　を　しましょう　か。 — *Ee, nani o shimashoo ka.*

Yamazaki:
テニス　を　しましょう　か。 — *TENISU o shimashoo ka.*

Suzuki:
いいえ、　きのう　テニス　を　しました。　きょう　はなみ　に　いきましょう。 — *Iie, kinoo TENISU o shimashita. Kyoo hanami ni ikimashoo.*

Yamazaki:
そう　しましょう。　なんじ　に　いきましょう　か。 — *Soo shimashoo. Nanji ni ikimashoo ka.*

Suzuki:

いま　いきましょう。 — *Ima ikimashoo.*

Yamazaki:

なんじ　に　かえります　か。 — *Nanji ni kaerimasu ka.*

Suzuki:

ろくじ　に　かえりましょう。 — *Rokuji ni kaerimashoo.*
いきましょう。 — *Ikimashoo!*

How well did you understand? Check with the translation below.

Today is Saturday. Mr. Suzuki and Mr. Yamazaki are going to go to the park.

Suzuki: Hello, Yamazaki. It's lovely weather isn't it?
Yamazaki: Yes, it's lovely. It's hot, isn't it?
Shall we go to the park?
Suzuki: Yes, what shall we do?
Yamazaki: Shall we play tennis?
Suzuki: No, I played tennis yesterday.
Let's go flower viewing today.
Yamazaki: Let's do that. What time shall we go?
Suzuki: Let's go now.
Yamazaki: What time will we come home?
Suzuki: Let's return at six o'clock.
Let's go!

Unit 2

きょう あめ です
kyoo ame desu
Today is rainy

STUDY

雨

- To say "Today is rain(y)", you need to use a noun ***ame*** (rain).
  The *kanji* for rain looks like an umbrella and rain drops 雨

- あめ です ね *Ame desu ne.* It's rainy, isn't it?
  There is rain, isn't there?

  In English we often put "isn't it?" on the end of sentences expecting that the person to whom we are speaking will agree with us. The Japanese use *ne* to do that. They feel that by using *ne* and assuming agreement from someone, you create a feeling of oneness between two people – something they see as being very important. If you think about it, we get pleasure from feeling that others agree with us, too.

ACTIVITIES

- Work in small groups and use the table below. Student A chooses one word from row **1** and one word from row **2** and makes a sentence. Student B chooses in the same way as Student A and so on.

1	***ame***	***atsukunai***	***samui***	***suzushii***	***atatakai***
2	***getsuyoobi***	***ashita***	***kyoo***	***kinoo***	***mokuyoobi***
1	***ii Otenki***	***ame***	***samukunai***	***atatakakunai***	***samui***
2	***kayoobi***	***suiyoobi***	***kinyoobi***	***senshuu***	***konshuu***
1	***atatakai***	***ame***	***atsui***	***suzushii***	***mushi atsui***
2	***mainichi***	***kyoo***	***kinyoobi***	***ashita***	***suiyoobi***

- Work out a role play in which you talk to someone about an activity for today and mention the weather. The role play can be as long as you choose, using any material from the five topics in this book.

- Make a weather chart for each day of a fictitious month by dividing a sheet of paper or card into 30 squares. On each square put the state of the weather and the day. With a friend throw dice to move from the beginning to the end of the month.

  First, each time you land you must tell your friend what day it is, what the weather is like, what you plan to do, and what you won't do.

  Then, using the chart again, imagine that the month is over, so everything you say will refer to the past. Say what day it **was**, what the weather **was** like, what you **did**, and what you **did not** do.

- Make an accurate weather chart for the present month and remember to update it every day.

- Write sentences using one word from each row of the above table. Write as much as you can in *hiragana*. Use *roomaji* for the syllables you can't write in *hiragana*.

Unit 3

さむい　でしょう
samui deshoo
It will probably be cold

NEW WORDS

シカゴ	*SHIKAGO*	Chicago
ボストン	*BOSUTON*	Boston
でしょう	*deshoo*	probably
なぜ　です　か	*naze desu ka*	Why?
から	*kara*	because
か	*ka*	or
あした　あつい でしょう　か。	*Ashita atsui deshoo ka.*	Do you think tomorrow will be hot or rainy?
あめ でしょう　か。	*Ame deshoo ka.*	
あいます	*aimasu*	meet

STUDY

- The sentences ***Ashita atsui deshoo ka. Ame deshoo ka*** literally mean "Tomorrow hot probably? Rainy probably?" The two separate sentences may be used to say "**or**". For example:
  SHIKAGO ni ikimasu ka. BOSUTON ni ikimasu ka.
  Will you go to Chicago? (**or**) Will you go to Boston?

  Atsui desu ka. Samui desu ka.
  Is it hot? (**or**) Is it cold?

- *Samui deshoo ka.* — Do you think it will be cold?
  Samui deshoo. — It will probably be cold.

  Don't use *deshoo* in any other situation than the weather because you have only learned this context so far. You should not apply it elsewhere at this stage as it needs verb forms different from the ones you have learned.

ACTIVITIES

- Make a conversation with a partner in which you discuss the weather yesterday and say what you did because of it; say what the weather is today and what you will do because of it; say what the weather may be like tomorrow; and make a suggestion about what you could do.

- Check your understanding in conversation with a partner, with the whole class, or as a written exercise.

- Answer the following questions in Japanese with truthful answers:
  1 *Kyoo atsui desu ka. Samui desu ka.*
  2 *Ashita atatakai deshoo ka.*
  3 *Kinoo ame deshita ka.*
  4 *Raishuu atsui deshoo ka.*
  5 *Doyoobi ame deshoo ka.*
  6 *Getsuyoobi wa ame deshita ka.*
  7 *Ima Otenki wa nan desu ka.*
  8 *Kyoo no hachiji ni samui Otenki deshita ka.*
  9 *Konshuu no nichiyoobi wa warui Otenki deshita ka.*
  10 *Atatakai desu ka. Suzushii desu ka.*

Winter song

Yuki

Yuki ya konko
Arare ya konko
Futte wa Futte wa
Zunzun tsumoru
Yama mo nohara mo
Wataboooshi kaburi
Kareki no korazu
Hana ga saku

Extension Unit

なぜ　です　か
naze desu ka
why?

STUDY

- It is possible to ask "Why?" (or "Why not?") with the phrase ***"Naze desu ka".*** Study the following examples:

A: きょう　テニス　を　しません。	*Kyoo TENISU o shimasen.*	I won't play tennis today.
B: なぜ　です　か。	*Naze desu ka.*	Why (not)?
A: あつい　です。	*Atsui desu.*	It's hot.

A: あした　プール　に　いきません。	*Ashita PUURU ni ikimasen.*	I won't go to the pool tomorrow.
B: なぜ　です　か。	*Naze desu ka.*	Why (not)?
A: あめ　でしょう。	*Ame deshoo.*	I think it will rain. (It will probably rain.)

A: ビル　さん、　おはよう。きょう　うみ　に　いきます　か。	*BIRU san, Ohayoo. Kyoo umi ni ikimasu ka.*	Hi, Bill. Are you going to go to the beach today?
B: いいえ。	*Iie.*	No.
A: なぜ　です　か。	*Naze desu ka.*	Why (not)?
B: あめ　でしょう。	*Ame deshoo.*	It's probably going to rain.

あつい　です　から
atsui desu kara
because it's hot

STUDY

- A simple way to give a reason for your actions is to use ***kara*** in the following way.

あつい　です　から　シカゴ　に　いきません。	*Atsui desu kara SHIKAGO ni ikimasen.*	Because it's hot, I won't go to Chicago.

さむい　です　から うち　に　かえります。	*Samui desu kara* *uchi ni kaerimasu.*	Because it's cold, I will go home.

- In Japanese you always put **the reason for your action first**.

- For the moment, use *kara* with weather or time words only. Later you will learn how to say that you **want** to do something – a fuller use of *kara* will be explained then.
  Be content to stay within the framework of the course. It offers you a lot of opportunities for extension and you may make serious mistakes that will consolidate incorrect patterns if you try to be too clever!

ACTIVITY

- How would you say the following in Japanese?
  (Remember: 1) The reason goes first
  2) In English we often say "so" instead of "because").

1 I won't play tennis, because it's hot today.
2 Haruko is going to read a book, because it is rainy.
3 Because it is cold today, I will watch TV; I won't go to town.
4 I did not do my homework yesterday, because it was fine weather.
5 I will go flower viewing, because it is warm today.
6 It's not warm today, so I will play netball.

ベン　さん　に　あいます
BEN san ni aimasu
I'll meet Ben

STUDY

- Here is another extension opportunity:
  Perhaps you want to say things like:
  "I'll meet you at three thirty"
  or "I went to the pictures with Felise"

あいます **aimasu** **meet**

In English we often say "I **saw** Ben" when we really mean "I **met** Ben". The Japanese are more specific. If they had only seen Ben across the road, they would say:
BEN san o mimashita.
He was an object they had seen. If they had actually come face to face with Ben or had spoken to him they would have said:
BEN san ni aimashita. I met (to) Ben.
The meaning is "I went up **to** Ben or he came up **to** me."
Always use *ni* in front of *aimasu*.

ACTIVITY

- *Sanji ni aimasu*. We'll meet at three o'clock. You know that *ni* means **at** when used with time. So it will help you remember to use *ni* with *aimasu* if you practice using different times with *aimasu*.

  How would you say the following in Japanese?
  1. I'll meet you at four o'clock.
  2. Because it's hot, let's meet Hisako at two o'clock.
  3. Akiko is going to go home at one o'clock, because she is cold. She will not meet Kenji.
  4. You will not meet Masamu at ten o'clock today, because it is rainy. He doesn't like the rain.
  5. It will probably be cold tomorrow, because it is cold today. Let's meet at eleven o'clock.
  6. Let's meet on Thursday at nine o'clock.

EXTENSION ACTIVITIES

- Turn to your neighbor. Greet him or her. Ask about health, and add an expression about the weather and tell him or her about your activities. Arrange to meet again before saying goodbye.

- Practice changing *atatakai* and *suzushii* into the negative. It takes a while for most people to get their tongues around them!

- Here are some words to extend your vocabulary.

yuki	snow
kiri	fog
shimo	frost
kaze	wind
akarui	bright
kaminari	thunder (*kami* means "god" or "gods"; *kami kaze* means "wind of the gods"; *kaminari* "anger of the gods")

Which of the words above is an adjective? How can you tell?

- With a partner construct sentences about what you are **not** going to do, and give your reason – remember it will only be because of the weather.

- Practice using *kara* in sentences like:
  "Because it's three o'clock now, I'll go home."
  (*Ima sanji desu kara uchi ni kaerimasu.*)
  "Because it's six o'clock, I'll watch TV."
  (*Rokuji desu kara TEREBI o mimasu.*)

- Have fun with your friends making up your own play from the material you have learned so far. It will help you in many ways. Writing it, you will review all your vocabulary and grammar structures. Practicing it, you will become fluent in the sentences you have included. Performing it, you will improve your speaking skills, because you will need to check your pronunciation so that everyone else can easily understand you. And listening to others, you will realize that you really can understand what is being said. Congratulations!

Round up time

Around the class, try to give cultural background information that you have learned so far. See how many times you can go around the class with everyone contributing something.

Keep a tally of the number. You may be surprised how much knowledge you have collectively!

Do a similar thing with sentence patterns and vocabulary.

Vocabulary checklist (Topic Five)

List One
Introduction

あき	*aki*	autumn
ふゆ	*fuyu*	winter
はなみ	*hanami*	flower viewing
はる	*haru*	spring
なつ	*natsu*	summer
おてんき	*Otenki*	weather

Unit 1

あめ	*ame*	rain(y)
あたたかい	*atatakai*	warm
あたたかくない	*atatakakunai*	not warm
あつい	*atsui*	hot

あつくない	*atsukunai*	not hot
いい	*ii*	good
いい　おてんき　です	*ii Otenki desu*	It's good weather
むし　あつい	*mushi atsui*	humid
ね	*ne*	isn't it?
さむい	*samui*	cold
さむくない	*samukunai*	not cold
すずしい	*suzushii*	cool
すずしくない	*suzushikunai*	not cool
わるい	*warui*	bad

Unit 3

あいます	*aimasu*	meet
あつい　でしょう　か。 あめ　でしょう　か。	*Atsui deshoo ka. Ame deshoo ka.*	Do you think it will be hot or rainy?
か	*ka*	or
から	*kara*	because
なぜ　でしょう　か。	*naze deshoo ka*	why (not)?

Extension

あかるい	*akarui*	bright
かみなり	*kaminari*	thunder
きり	*kiri*	fog
かぜ	*kaze*	wind
しも	*shimo*	frost
ゆき	*yuki*	snow

List Two

ばいう	*baiu*	rainy season
ボストン	*BOSUTON*	Boston
シカゴ	*SHIKAGO*	Chicago
つゆ	*tsuyu*	rainy season

TOPIC SIX myself and others

Introduction

ACHIEVEMENTS

By the end of this topic you will be able to introduce yourself to others more fully by:

- saying how old you are;
- saying what day and month your birthday is;
- giving more information about your likes and dislikes;
- giving more information about what you do, don't do, did and didn't do;

and you will be able to find out the same information from others.

You will also be able to write all the *hiragana* syllables plus some combined sounds, and you will have made a start on writing *katakana*.

Note:
In this topic you will notice that most of the personal names are not Japanese. This topic is about yourself and your ordinary life and you are therefore more likely to be using names which originate in countries outside Japan. They will therefore be written in *katakana*.

Special birthdays in Japan
Shortly after birth, children are taken to Shinto shrines for a blessing. (Shinto is one of the major religions in Japan.) Most people attend Shinto ceremonies throughout their lives but funerals are conducted according to Buddhist ritual. (Buddhism is the other major religion.)

しち ご さん ***Shichi go san*** **(Seven-five-three festival)**
This festival is for boys and girls aged three, boys of five, and girls of seven. On November 15 each year children of these ages are dressed in colorful *kimono* or their best clothes and are taken to various shrines to give thanks for good health and to receive a blessing. Shrines are crowded on this day with family groups.

The children will be bought a long bag containing ***chitose ame***, which means "thousand year candy" and which symbolizes long life and happiness.

Long ago there were religious ceremonies to mark children's stages of growth. Children under seven were called "children of God" and if a child under this age died, people believed that it would be reborn. The parents had to be ready to receive it again, so the child was not given full funeral rites.

After the age of seven children were assumed to have left infancy behind and to be entering childhood. This is why, when the Emperor Meiji made education compulsory in the 1860s, children started school at seven.

In those days, there were two ways of calculating age. In one system, called ***kazoedoshi***, a child born even on December 31 became one year old on January 1. This meant they were actually starting school at six years old. When the old system was abolished all Japanese people became one year younger!

せいじん の ひ *Seijin no hi* (Adults' day)

The old way of calculating age still lingers in this ceremony, which is held every year on January 15, a national holiday. On this day, all those who have reached the age of twenty during the previous year have their official "Coming of Age" ceremony. They go en masse to local council offices or the City Hall to be welcomed into adulthood – with its legal and social responsibilities – by the mayor and council.

This is another occasion for wearing *kimono*, though young men tend to prefer a suit.

At twenty, young people gain the right to vote officially.

Another birthday that many Japanese await eagerly is their eighteenth. From that day, after very strict training and having passed a stringent driving test, they may hold a driver's license.

Men are allowed to marry at eighteen and women at sixteen, as long as they have their parents' consent.

Writing practice

- し じ じゅう
  shi → *ji* → *juu*

  To make *juu*, a small, half-sized *yu* plus *u* is added to *ji*.
  Practice writing these syllables:

  じ ゆ ゅ う
  ji *yu* *yu* (half-size) *u*

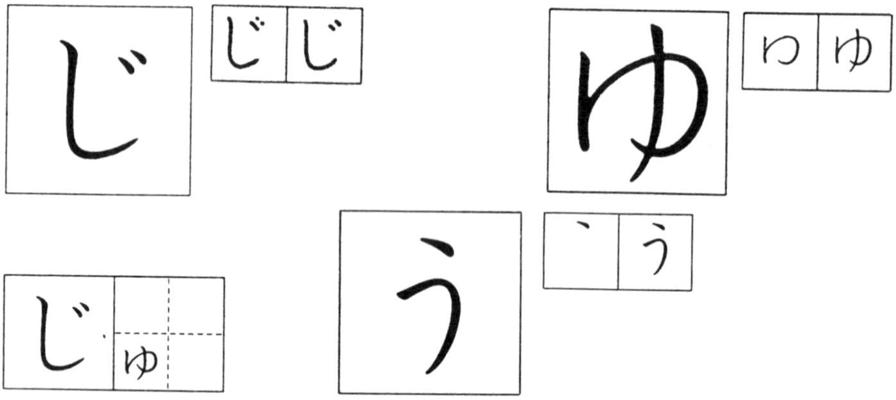

- To double the *u* sound, *u* is added to other combinations, e.g. *kyuu, shuu.*

  き きゅ きゅう
  ki → *kyu* → *kyuu*

  し しゅ しゅう
  shi → *shu* → *shuu*

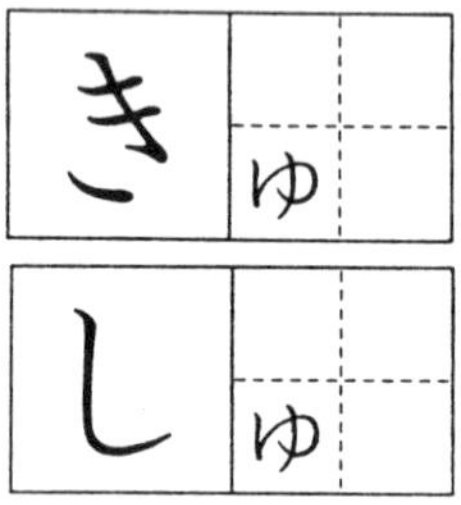

- To double a consonant (i.e. everything other than the vowels *a, i, u, e, o*) a half-sized *tsu* syllable is put before the consonant. For example:

  は はっさい
  ha → *hassai*

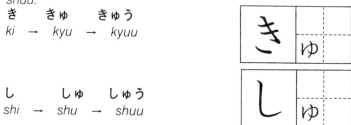

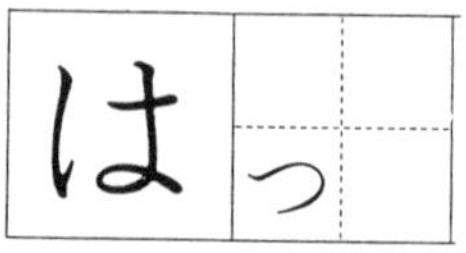

The syllable *tsu* is quite difficult to master. Practice until you are sure you have the balance right.

Practice writing the following.

いっさい	*issai*	one year old
はっさい	*hassai*	eight years old
じゅっさい	*jussai*	ten years old

- A *hiragana* syllable is a consonant plus a vowel or a single vowel (except for the syllable *n*). Let's look at those syllables which end in the vowel *o*. These are *ko, so, to, no, ho, mo, ro, yo.* (You have learned to write all of these except *ro* and *mo*.)

  To double the *o* on these syllables use the *u* syllable you have just learned. (This may seem strange but it is the way it is done!) For example:

  こ　　こう
  ko → *koo*

  そ　　そう
  so → *soo*

  Practice the following:

こう	そう	とう	のう	ほう	よう
koo	*soo*	too	noo	*hoo*	*yoo*

- Practice the two syllables *ro* and *mo*.
  ろ　も
  ro　*mo*

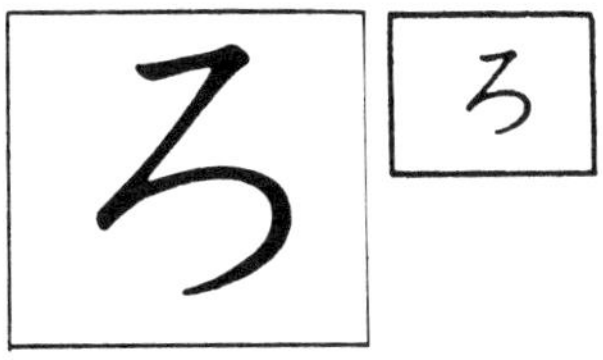

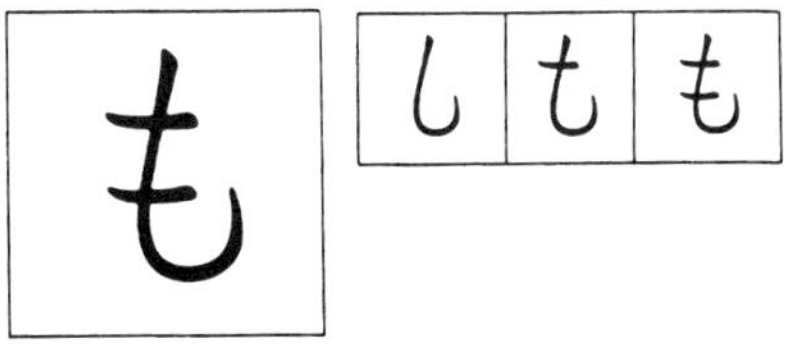

Now practice writing *roo* and *moo*.

- Practice writing the following words:

きのう	*kinoo*
がっこう	*gakkoo*
すうがく	*suugaku*
きゅうしゅう	*kyuushuu*
れんしゅう	*renshuu*
そう　です	*soo desu*

- Practice the following syllables:

  そ　　ぞ
  so → *zo*

  て　　で
  te → *de*

  さ　　ざ
  sa → *za*

  は　　ば
  ha → *ba*

- Practice the following words:

ぞう	zoo	(elephant)
ざっし	zasshi	
ばん	ban	

Unit 1

なんさい です か
nansai desu ka
How old are you?

(Review numbers before you begin.)

Kenichi has brought a friend along to Kimiko's party.

Kenichi:

きみこ　ちゃん、こちら　は わたし　の　ともだち　の ゆみこ　ちゃん　です。	*Kimiko chan, kochira wa* *watashi no tomodachi no* *Yumiko chan desu.*

Kimiko:

こんばん　は。はじめまして。	*Konban wa. Hajimemashite.*

Yumiko:

はじめまして。きょう　は あなた　の　たんじょうび　です　か。	*Hajimemashite. Kyoo wa* *anata no tanjoobi desu ka.*

Kimiko:

ええ、そう　です。	*Ee, soo desu.*

Yumiko:

なんさい　です　か。	*Nansai desu ka.*

Kimiko:

じゅうろくさい　です。 ゆみこ　さん　は。	*Juurokusai desu.* *Yumiko san wa.*

Yumiko:

じゅうななさい　です。 けんいち　くん、なんさい　です か。	*Juunanasai desu.* *Kenichi kun, nansai desu ka.*

Kenichi:

わたし　は　じゅうはっさい　です。	*Watashi wa juuhassai desu.*

NEW WORDS

ともだち	*tomodachi*	friend
こちら	*kochira*	this is (very polite)
ちゃん	*chan*	friendly way to speak of your girlfriends — used after first names only
おいくつ　です　か	*Oikutsu desu ka*	How old are you? (formal)
なんさい　です　か	*nansai desu ka*	How old are you? (informal)

さい	*sai*	counter for age
いっさい	*issai*	one year old
にさい	*nisai*	two years old
さんさい	*sansai*	three years old
よんさい	*yonsai*	four years old
ごさい	*gosai*	five years old
ろくさい	*rokusai*	six years old
ななさい	*nanasai*	seven years old
はっさい	*hassai*	eight years old
きゅうさい	*kyuusai*	nine years old
じゅっさい	*jussai*	ten years old
じゅういっさい	*juuissai*	eleven years old
じゅうにさい	*juunisai*	twelve years old
じゅうさんさい	*juusansai*	thirteen years old, etc
はたち	*hatachi*	twenty years old

STUDY

- You will notice that there are three exceptions to the pattern:

いっさい	***issai***	not	*ichisai*
はっさい	***hassai***	not	*hachisai*
じゅっさい	***jussai***	not	*juusai*

  (Eleven years old becomes *juuissai*, eighteen becomes *juuhassai*.)

- Note that when talking about age you use ***yon*** not ***shi*** for four. Learn the exceptions carefully.

- ***Sai*** is the counter for age. Counters have been mentioned before — they are special suffixes for counting different things. You already know that ***jin*** is a suffix used as a counter for people, and ***ji*** is a counter for hours. As you progress through the course you will be introduced to the special ways of counting that you are likely to need in basic conversation.

- ***Oikutsu desu ka*** can be answered using *issai, nisai*, etc, but there is an alternative way of answering, which will be taught later.

- ***Hatachi*** is a special word used for being twenty years old.

- In the dialogue, Kimiko says "***Yumiko san wa***" to ask "How about you (Yumiko)?" It is more common to use people's names and titles instead of *anata* ("you"), even when speaking directly to people.

- *Watashi no tomodachi no Yumiko chan wa . . .*
  "My friend Yumiko . . ."
  Learn this pattern well.

- *Watashi no tomodachi no KEN kun wa hatachi desu.*
  "My friend Ken is twenty."

Watashi no tomodachi no Hiroko chan wa juuhassai desu.
"My friend Hiroko is eighteen."

Remember, use ***kun*** after boys' names and ***chan*** after girls' names if you are talking about young people you know well.

Check your understanding

Did you understand the conversation above? Before you read the English equivalent, read over the Japanese version again while your teacher or other students read it aloud. Don't actually translate it word for word, just read and listen to it, and let your mind absorb what it means.

Now check that your understanding was correct.

Kenichi:	Kimiko, this is my friend Yumiko.
Kimiko:	It's nice to meet you.
Yumiko:	I'm pleased to meet you, too. Is it your birthday today?
Kimiko:	Yes, that's right.
Yumiko:	How old are you?
Kimiko:	Sixteen. What about you?
Yumiko:	Seventeen. How old are you Kenichi?
Kenichi:	I'm eighteen.

ACTIVITIES

- Practice telling your partner the ages of all your friends, using the following pattern:
  Watashi no tomodachi no (PAMU) chan wa (juusansai) desu.
  Watashi no tomodachi no (BEN) kun wa (juuyonsai) desu.

- Practice asking your partner about the age of his/her friends, using the following pattern:
  Anata no tomodachi no (JON) san wa nansai desu ka.
  Anata no tomodachi no (RIN) san wa nansai desu ka.

Reading practice

Read the following sentences aloud.

1 わたし は にほんご が すき です。
2 いま なんじ です か。
3 じゅうじ に あいます。
4 はな が すき です か。
5 みちこ さん は はっさい です。

6 かさ　です。
7 ざっし　です。
8 ゆみこ　さん　は　じゅうはっさい　です。
9 それ　は　き　です。
10 きょう　うみ　に　いきます。

Unit 2

あたらしい せいと です か
atarashii seito desu ka
Are you a new student?

Listen carefully to the following conversation between two new visiting pupils at a *kootoogakkoo* (High School) who are determined to try to speak only Japanese at school. Next read it aloud, paying particular attention to pronunciation.

Robert:

こんにち は。わたし の なまえ は ロバート です。はじめまして。

Konnichi wa. Watashi no namae wa ROBAATO desu. Hajimemashite.

Chris:

はじめまして どうぞ よろしく。わたし の なまえ は クリス です。あたらしい せいと です か。

Hajimemashite doozo yoroshiku. Watashi no namae wa KURISU desu. Atarashii seito desu ka.

Robert:

はい、あたらしい せいと です。なんさい です か。

Hai, atarashii seito desu. Nansai desu ka.

Chris:

じゅうろくさい です。あなた は。

Juurokusai desu. Anata wa.

Robert:

じゅうごさい です。こうとうがっこう の いちねんせい です。

Juugosai desu. Kootoogakkoo no ichinensei desu.

Chris:

そう です か。わたし は にねんせい です。

Soo desu ka. Watashi wa ninensei desu.

Robert:

なにじん です か。

Nanijin desu ka.

Chris:

アメリカじん です。あなた は。

AMERIKAjin desu. Anata wa.

Robert:

カナダじん です。トロント に すんで います。

KANADAjin desu. TORONTO ni sunde imasu.

Chris:	
なに　を　べんきょう　します か。	*Nani o benkyoo shimasu ka.*
Robert:	
すうがく　と　えいご　と にほんご　と　かがく　と しゃかい　を　べんきょう します。	*Suugaku to eigo to nihongo to kagaku to shakai o benkyoo shimasu.*
(The bell rings.) そろそろ　しつれい します…また あいましょう　ね。	 *Sorosoro shitsurei shimasu . . . mata aimashoo ne.*
Chris:	
はい、また　あいましょう。	*Hai, mata aimashoo.*

NEW WORDS

と	*to*	and (in a defined list)
あたらしい	*atarashii*	new
また	*mata*	again
いちねんせい	*ichinensei*	first-year student
にねんせい	*ninensei*	second-year student
トロント	*TORONTO*	Toronto
そろそろ　しつれい　します	*Sorosoro shitsurei shimasu*	Sorry, I must be going
…に　すんで　います	*. . . ni sunde imasu*	I live in . . .
(Review)		
ニュージーランド	*NYUUJIIRANDO*	New Zealand
オーストラリア	*OOSUTORARIA*	Australia

STUDY

- ***Sorosoro shitsurei shimasu*** takes a bit of practice to say easily but it is very useful as it means "I apologize for my rudeness but I must be going". ***Shitsurei shimasu*** on its own is used to say "I apologize for my rudeness". It is used a great deal in situations where we would say "Sorry". It is not used for apologizing in situations where you have broken someone's plate or knocked something over, but only where you are saying sorry for an action that could be considered impolite.

  Practice saying *shitsurei shimasu* if you are late for class, accidentally bump into someone, or butt into a conversation without thinking.

  Use *sorosoro shitsurei shimasu* as a way of taking leave of people in your role plays and in real life.

- ***Mata aimashoo*** means "Let's meet again". *Mata* means "again" and you will remember *aimashoo* as "Let's meet".

- ***TORONTO ni sunde imasu.***
  I live in Toronto.
  Learn this phrase as a lexical item at the moment, the grammar construction will be taught later.
  Substitute the name of your town/city and learn this phrase by heart.

- You will have noticed by now that European names are altered a little in Japanese to fit the syllable patterns that the Japanese feel comfortable with. A name like Mike becomes *MAIKU*, Chris becomes *KURISU*, Pam becomes *PAMU*. And names that have an "l" in them, use "r" in its place, for example Lisa and Lynn become *RISA* and *RIN*.
  If you haven't already worked out the sound of your friends' names in Japanese, practice them now so that you feel comfortable with the sounds too and can recognize the intended name if it is used in conversation.

Check your understanding

Did you understand the whole conversation? Review any vocabulary that you had forgotten, then read the translated conversation below. Discuss anything you are not sure about.

Robert: Hello (Good morning). My name is Robert.
Nice to meet you.
Chris: I'm pleased to meet you. My name is Chris.
Are you a new student?
Robert: Yes I am. How old are you?
Chris: I'm sixteen. How about you?
Robert: I'm fifteen. I'm a first-year High School student.
Chris: Is that so? I'm a second-year student.
Robert: Where are you from?
Chris: I'm American. What about you?
Robert: I'm Canadian. I live in Toronto.
Chris: What are you going to study?
Robert: Math, English, Japanese, Science, and Social Studies.
(The bell rings.) Sorry, I have to go. Let's meet again, shall we?
Chris: Yes, let's.

STUDY

- Practice explaining that you are a first-year student or a second-year student.
  e.g. *Watashi wa ichinensei desu.*
  Practice saying that your friend (Bill) is a first- or second-year student.
  e.g. *Watashi no tomodachi no BIRU san wa ninensei desu.*
  Practice saying that you are a first- or second-year High School student.
  Practice saying that your friend (*MARIO*) is a first- or second-year High School student.

- Review the use of the ***no*** particle. For example:
  Watashi no desu. Watashi no hon desu, etc.

- When you learned the adjectives in the weather unit you learned to make an adjective negative by taking off the last "*i*" and adding "*kunai*". You can do this with *atarashii* to say you are not a new student or your book is ***not*** new: *atarashii* (new) *atarashikunai* (not new)
  eg: *Watashi no hon wa atarashikunai desu.*
  Make sentences like:
  My book is new.
  My book is not new.
  The car is new/not new.
  Jane's umbrella is new/not new.
  My friend Jim's notebook is new/not new etc.
  Ask if someone's (pen) is new.

- Test each other on the sound of European names in Japanese.

- Learn to write your own name and your best friend's name in *katakana*.

ACTIVITIES

- Without looking again at the Japanese version of the conversation that you have just studied, write the conversation in *roomaji*.

- With a partner act out a similar conversation, in which you greet someone for the first time, ask their age and nationality, and find out at least one more thing about them before saying goodbye.
  Don't plan it out first. Just start the conversation and let it happen! It is important to listen to what someone says to you and respond intelligently. It is what happens in normal conversation – you don't have time to plan your sentences before you reply!

- With a partner, or brainstorming from the whole group, make a list of all the questions you are now able to ask someone.
  Write the questions on cards. Put the cards face down on a table. Each person in turn takes one from the top of the pile, calls out a name followed by *san*, and asks the question written on that card. If the person called cannot think of an answer, someone else may reply.
  Take the pile of question cards and work through them, writing an answer for each, or answering orally.

- Make a list of all the things you can now tell someone about yourself.

- Interview each other and write down the answers to your questions. You may like to follow this up by reporting to the class, telling them all about the person you interviewed, or making a poster to put on the wall giving all the information you have gleaned.

- Work in a small group and tell each other about your friends.

Learning a language

In Topic 7 you will extend your knowledge of the use of *san, chan,* and *kun*. You have already learned a lot of basic, polite expressions used when meeting and speaking with Japanese people. However, in situations where students are talking to each other, we need to learn the colloquial, everyday way of addressing people we know well, and also learn how foreigners are addressed by Japanese.

The Japanese, just like people everywhere, have more relaxed language for everyday use among people they know well. This more relaxed way of speaking is called "the plain form". You will gradually be able to learn more of it as your knowledge of Japan, its people and its language grows.

In the early stages of learning Japanese, we need to learn patterns that are polite at any time so, inevitably, we are going to sound rather formal. Japanese people learning English find it very difficult to understand our everyday language because they too learn polite forms first. When they visit us, they worry because they can't understand us, despite years of study.

When we visit Japan, we feel the same frustration. But don't worry – the people who are hosting you, or to whom you have gone for help, will modify their language when they speak to you, just as we try to do when speaking to people of other nationalities.

Remember that learning to speak another language fluently takes a very long time, even though you may get very good at it with lots of study and practice with native speakers. But this doesn't mean that you can't communicate – far from it. Even now there is a great deal that you can say and every day you will add to your competency.

Children are often able to communicate well in a new language because their attitude is quite different from older people. Younger children are less afraid to make errors, they are less inhibited, and they are less worried about their cultural identity. Being aware of this may help you when studying Japanese. Keep in mind that progress can be made if you practice new language, constantly review what you have learned, and use the language you know for communication without worrying too much about making mistakes.

Accept a "pat on the back" for all that you have learned so far in Japanese. Remember that phrase *Ganbatte kudasai* – and keep on trying! Each day is another step forward to easier communication and better understanding of this fascinating language and culture.

Unit 3

Writing practice

- You know し ***shi***, じ ***ji***, and ***juu*** じゅう
  Now learn ***shoo*** and ***joo***.

  しょう　　じょう
  shoo　　***joo***

  Practice the half-size ***yo***.

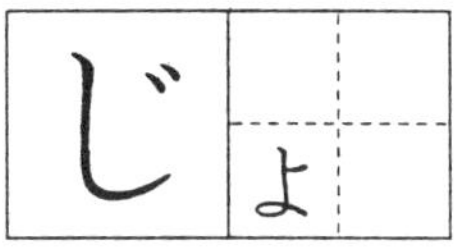

Use a half-size ***yo*** with ***shi*** to make ***sho***, and use a half-sized ***yo*** with ***ji*** to make ***jo***. Add ***u*** う to double the "o" sound.

- Review ***shuu***: しゅう
- Learn the syllable ***ra*** ら

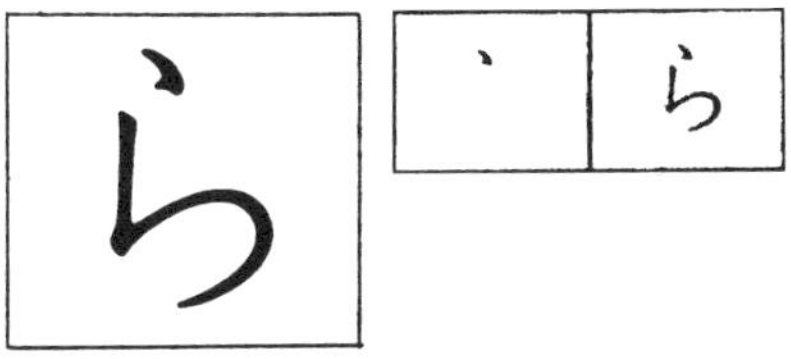

- You are now equipped to read the *hiragana* in the next dialogue, and quite a lot of the words in the vocabulary list that follows the dialogue. Try reading the *hiragana* without looking at the *roomaji*.

あなた の たんじょうび です か
anata no tanjoobi desu ka
Is it your birthday?

Two students are talking about Julie's party.

Rosemary:
きょう　パーティー　に　いきます。　*Kyoo PAATII ni ikimasu.*

Daniel:
だれ　の　パーティー　です　か。　*Dare no PAATII desu ka.*

Rosemary:

ジューリ　さん　の　パーティー　です。 | *JUURI san no PAATII desu.*

Daniel:

ジューリ　さん　の　たんじょうび　です　か。たんじょうび　の　パーティー　です　か。 | *JUURI san no tanjoobi desu ka. Tanjoobi no PAATII desu ka.*

Rosemary:

はい、きょう　ジューリ　さん　の　たんじょうび　です。 | *Hai, kyoo JUURI san no tanjoobi desu.*

Review this vocabulary:

たんじょうび	*tanjoobi*	birthday
きょう	*kyoo*	today
あした	*ashita*	tomorrow
きのう	*kinoo*	yesterday
こんしゅう	*konshuu*	this week
せんしゅう	*senshuu*	last week
らいしゅう	*raishuu*	next week
せんしゅう　の　どようび	*senshuu no doyoobi*	last Saturday
らいしゅう　の　げつようび	*raishuu no getsuyoobi*	next Monday
いつ	*itsu*	when
げつようび	*getsuyoobi*	Monday
かようび	*kayoobi*	Tuesday
すいようび	*suiyoobi*	Wednesday
もくようび	*mokuyoobi*	Thursday
きんようび	*kinyoobi*	Friday
どようび	*doyoobi*	Saturday
にちようび	*nichiyoobi*	Sunday
ジューリ	*JUURI*	Julie

Check the dialogue above with the translation below.

R: I'm going to a party today.
D: Whose party?
R: Julie's party.
D: Is it Julie's birthday? Is it a birthday party?
R: Yes, today is Julie's birthday.

STUDY

- To avoid repeating the word "party", the third line of the dialogue could read:
  JUURI san no desu.
  It's Julie's.

- For "Saturday's party" say "the party belonging to Saturday", i.e.: *Doyoobi no PAATII.*

If "Saturday's party" is the topic of the sentence, it must be followed by ***wa***:
Doyoobi no PAATII wa . . .
(Talking about) Saturday's party .

- There are not usually any particles between nouns or adjectives and *desu, dewa arimasen, deshita*, and *dewa arimasen deshita*.
  For example:
  Watashi no PAATII desu.
  It is my party.
  "Party" is a noun and goes right in front of *desu*.
  Atsui desu.
  It is hot.
  Atsui is an adjective and goes right in front of *desu*.
  However, if you leave out the noun to say, for example, "It is mine", it is *Watashi no desu*, because the noun is understood – mentally it is still there.

- *Anata no wa* (Talking about yours) is short for
  Anata no tanjoobi wa.
  "How about your birthday?"

- It may help if you think of ***no*** in this context as the first two letters in the English word, *noun*. Remember: ***no*** replaces a *noun*.
  The other particles you know (***wa***, ***o***, ***ni***) will never be used in front of *desu, dewa arimasen, deshita*, or *dewa arimasen deshita*.

あなた の たんじょうび は いつ です か

Anata no tanjoobi wa itsu desu ka
When is your birthday?

Will:
あなた の たんじょうび は いつ です か。 — *Anata no tanjoobi wa itsu desu ka.*

Nicole:
あした です。あなた の は。 — *Ashita desu Anata no wa.*

Will:
わたし の たんじょうび は げつようび です。 — *Watashi no tanjoobi wa getsuyoobi desu.*

Nicole:
そう です ね。 — *Soo desu ne.*

Look at the English version below to check your understanding:
W: When is your birthday?
N: It's tomorrow. How about yours?
W: My birthday is on Monday.
N: Oh, that's right.

ACTIVITIES

Practice asking each other "When is your birthday?" and give different (false) answers according to the following suggestions:
Monday/Thursday/tomorrow/next week/this week/next Tuesday/next Friday/today.

Now try some in the past tense, for example:
Anata no tanjoobi wa itsu deshita ka.
When **was** your birthday?
Senshuu no suiyoobi deshita.
Last Wednesday.
Use the following suggestions: last Wednesday/yesterday/last Saturday/last Monday/last Sunday.

Check your understanding

What do the following mean in English?
1 *Getsuyoobi wa watashi no tanjoobi desu.*
2 *Anata no tanjoobi wa suiyoobi desu ka.*
3 *JUURI san no tanjoobi wa itsu desu ka.*
4 *RIN san no tanjoobi wa doyoobi desu.*
5 *Kyoo wa dare no tanjoobi desu ka.*
6 *Kayoobi no PAATII wa dare no desu ka.*
7 *Kinyoobi wa PAATII desu ka.*
8 *Getsuyoobi no rokuji wa MEERI san no PAATII desu.*
9 *Tanjoobi ga suki desu.*
10 *Tanjoobi no PAATII ga suki desu ka.*

Check whether you understood correctly by looking at the answers below:
1 Monday is my birthday.
2 Is your birthday on Wednesday?
3 Julie's birthday, when is it?/When is Julie's birthday?
4 Lyn's birthday is Saturday.
5 Whose birthday is it today?
6 Whose is Tuesday's party?
7 (Talking about) Friday, is it a party?
8 (Talking about) Six o'clock on Monday, it's Mary's party.
9 I like birthdays.
10 Do you like birthday parties?

Writing practice

- You know ***he*** へ
  From ***he*** you can make ***be***:

  へ → べ
  he → ***be***

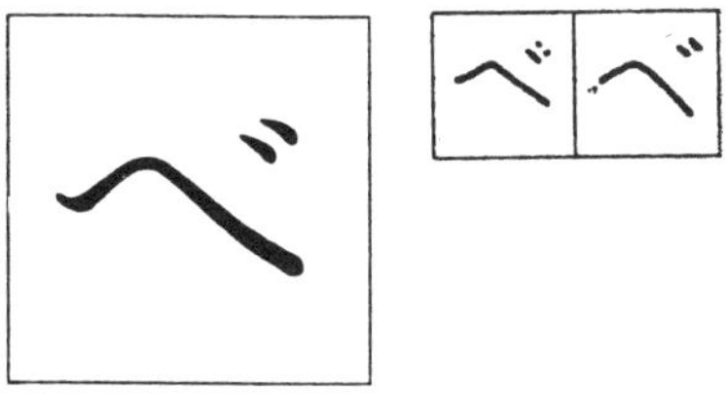

- Practice the syllable ***ri*** り

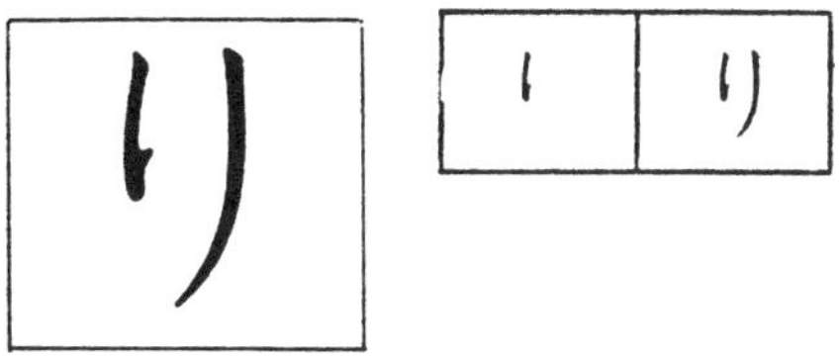

- You know **se** せ
  From **se** you can make **ze**:

  せ → ぜ
  se → **ze**

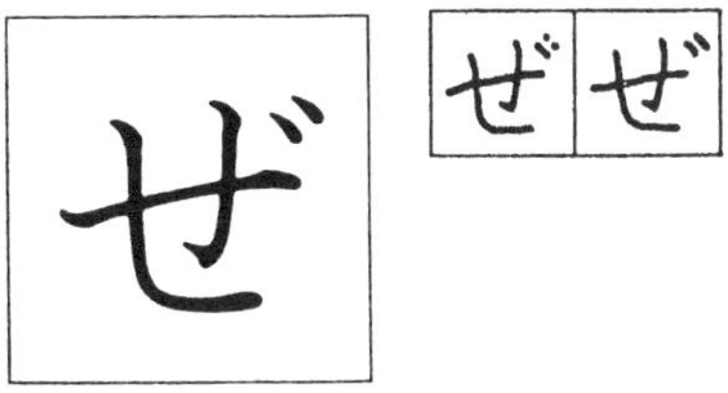

- Learn ***o*** お

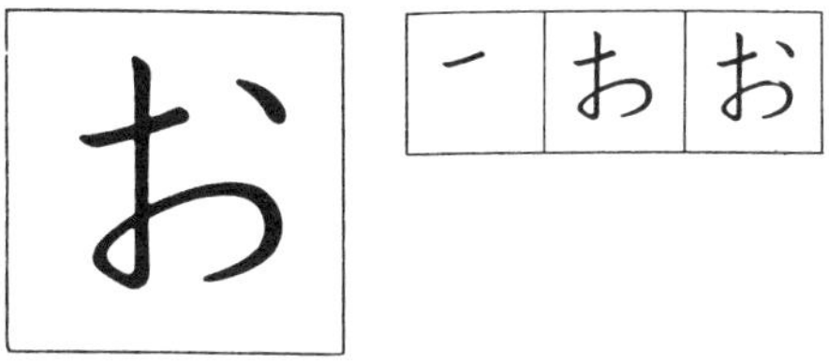

This writing practice will help you with the review exercises that follow.

Review

How do you ask . . .
1 . . . someone's name?
2 . . . someone's age?
3 . . . someone's nationality?
4 . . . if something belongs to someone?
5 . . . when something will be?
6 . . . what something is?
7 . . . what something is called in Japanese?
8 . . . if someone is well?

9 . . . what someone studies?
10 . . . what someone likes/dislikes?
11 . . . what someone did yesterday?
12 . . . what someone is going to do today?
13 . . . what someone will do tomorrow?
14 . . . where someone will go?
15 . . . where someone has been?
16 . . . if someone has returned home?
17 . . . someone to meet you on a particular day?
18 . . . someone to meet you at a particular time?
19 . . . what the time is?
20 . . . why?

Answers (Cover the *roomaji* while you practice reading the *hiragana*).

1 お なまえ は なん です か。/ あなた の なまえ は なん です か。
O namae wa nan desu ka/Anata no namae wa nan desu ka.

2 おいくつ です か。/ なんさい です か。
Oikutsu desu ka./Nansai desu ka.

3 どこ の かた です か。/ なにじん です か。
Doko no kata desu ka./Nanijin desu ka.

4 あなた の です か。/ これ は あなた の です か。
Anata no desu ka./Kore wa anata no desu ka.

5 (パーティー)は いつ です か。/ いつ です か。
(PAATII) wa itsu desu ka./Itsu desu ka.

6 なん です か。/ これ は (それ は/あれ は) なん です か。
Nan desu ka./Kore wa (sore wa/are wa) nan desu ka.

7 にほんご の なまえ は なん です か。
Nihongo no namae wa nan desu ka.

8 おげんき です か。
Ogenki desu ka.

9 なに を べんきょう します か。
Nani o benkyoo shimasu ka.

10 なに が すき です か。/ なに が きらい です か。
Nani ga suki desu ka./Nani ga kirai desu ka.

11 きのう なに を しました か。
Kinoo nani o shimashita ka.

12 きょう なに を します か。
Kyoo nani o shimasu ka.

13 あした なに を します か。
Ashita nani o shimasu ka.

14 どこ に いきます か。
Doko ni ikimasu ka.

15 どこ に いきました か。
Doko ni ikimashita ka.

16 (サラ) さん は かえりました か。
(SARA) san wa kaerimashita ka.

17 (げつようび) に あいましょう か。
(Getsuyoobi) ni aimashoo ka.

18 (よじ)に　あいましょう　か。
(Yoji) ni aimashoo ka.
19 いま　なんじ　です　か。
Ima nanji desu ka.
20 なぜ　です　か。
Naze desu ka.

Note
If some of these questions were difficult for you, it would be sensible to solve the problems before you continue.
Look back in your notes or in the textbook and see if you can solve your own problem. If you still can't understand why it is done that way, ask your teacher for help.

Writing practice

- Practice ***ke***: け

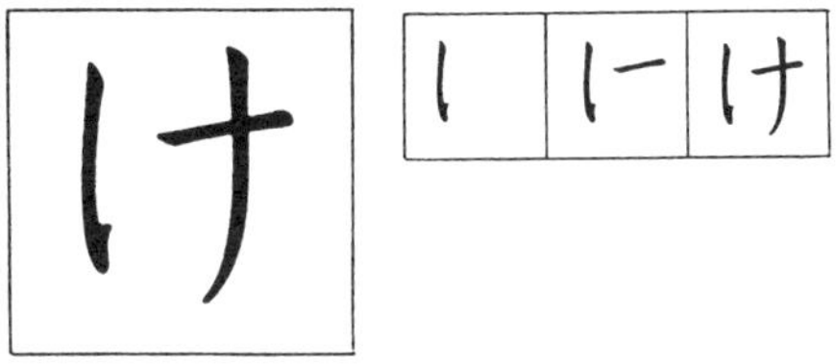

From **ke** you can make **ge**:

け　げ
ke → **ge**

- From **ka** you can make **ga**:
か　が
ka → **ga**

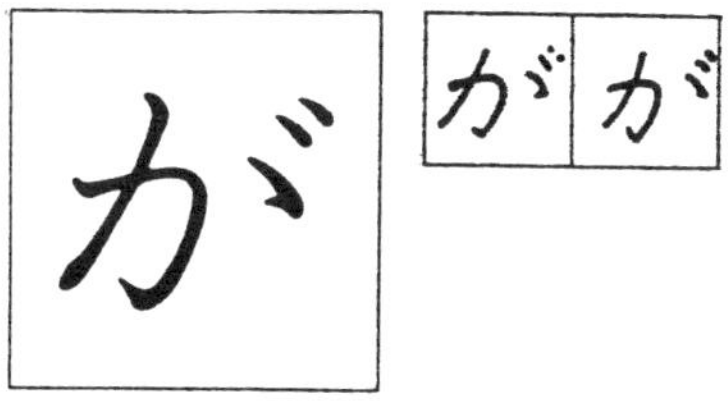

- Practice ***ru***: る

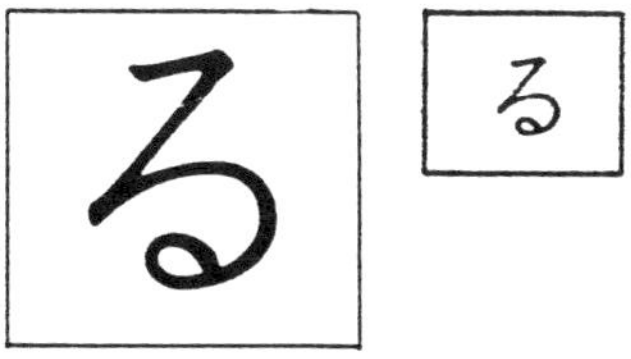

- Practice ***chi***: ち

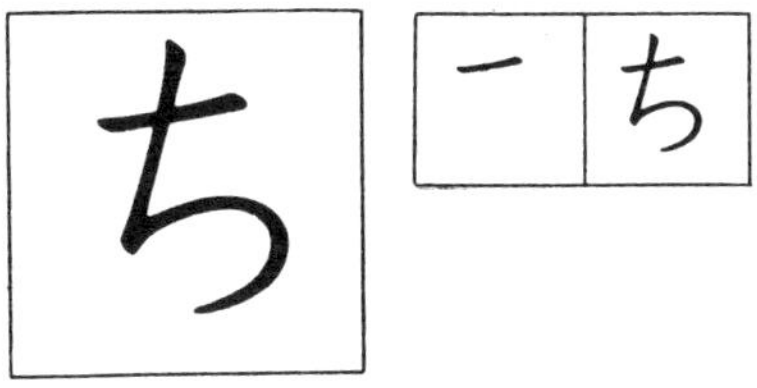

From ***chi*** you can make ***choo***:
ち　ちょう
chi → ***choo***

ACTIVITIES

- Look at the *hiragana* version of the questions on p. 19-20. How many of the questions can you read?

- Look at the chart of information about people below. Take turns going around the class to make a profile of each person in Japanese sentences.
  For example: (Your information)
  Sam/14 years old/American/birthday — tomorrow/weather tomorrow — probably fine/party next Saturday at seven o'clock.
  (You can say)
  SAMU san wa juuyonsai desu. AMERIKA jin desu. Ashita wa SAMU san no tanjoobi desu. Ashita ii Otenki deshoo. SAMU san no tanjoobi no PAATII wa doyoobi no shichiji desu.

Chris • 17 years old. • New Zealander. • Birthday tomorrow. • Party tomorrow 7 p.m. • Weather probably good. • Will play baseball.	**Heidi** • 16 years old. • German. • Birthday today. • Party today 12 noon. • Weather good. • Will go to a movie.
Shaun • 15 years old. • Australian. • Birthday yesterday. • Party today 4 p.m. • Weather warm. • Will play video games.	**Guy** • 15 years old. • English. • Birthday yesterday. • Party today 5 p.m. • Weather bad. • Will play video games.
Mark • 14 years old. • Australian. • Birthday tomorrow. • Party tomorrow 6 p.m. • Weather probably hot. • Will play tennis.	**Donna** • 15 years old. • Canadian. • Birthday yesterday. • Party yesterday. • Weather was good. • Went to the beach.
Katy • 15 years old. • American. • Party last Wednesday. • Weather was good. • Went to a movie.	**Tim** • 16 years old. • American. • Birthday tomorrow. • Party today 8 p.m. • Weather is hot. • Will go to a movie.

Nicole
- 16 years old.
- French.
- Birthday on Friday.
- Party tomorrow 7 p.m.
- Weather probably good.
- Will go to the beach.

Suzette
- 16 years old.
- Canadian.
- Birthday on Thursday.
- Party on Saturday 8 p.m.
- Weather probably cold.
- Will go to a movie.

Bridget
- 17 years old.
- Australian.
- Birthday today.
- Party tomorrow 5 p.m.
- Weather probably rainy.
- Will go to the beach.

Sam
- 15 years old.
- English.
- Birthday tomorrow.
- Party next Sunday at 6 p.m.
- Weather probably fine.
- They will go to town.

Japanese festivals

Japanese festivals (***matsuri***) are many and varied and differ from one part of the country to another. Wherever they are and whatever the time of year they are always colorful and interesting to watch.

The festivals celebrate historical events, religious ceremonies, and folk tales in a lively way, and the Japanese take great pleasure in participating in them. There are literally thousands of festivals every year but the ones discussed below are some of the most widely enjoyed.

Shoogatsu

Shoogatsu literally means "the first month of the year", but usually refers to the first three days or the first week of the New Year, starting January 1 (***ichigatsu tsuitachi***). It is customary to take a holiday at this time and practically everyone has the first three days off work and school – these days are called ***sanganichi***.

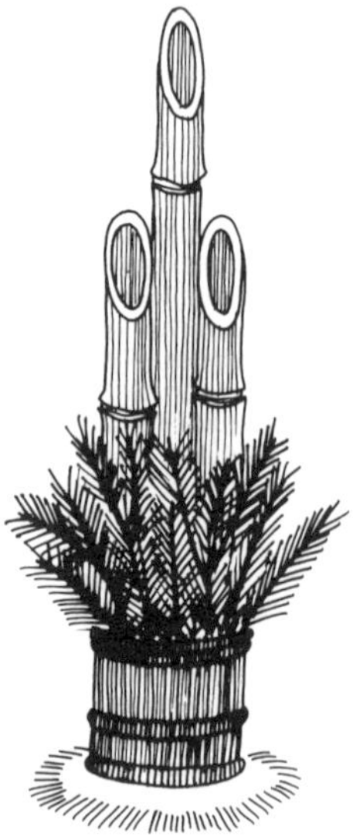

Shoogatsu welcomes in the New Year and people make fresh resolutions. The Japanese have a saying – "***Ichinen no kei wa gantan ni ari***" – which means that you should make your plans on New Year's Day.

People wish each other a Happy New Year by saying ***Akemashite Omedetoo gozaimasu*** or ***Yoi Otoshi o***.

There are a great many customs, special foods, games, and traditional decorations associated with *shoogatsu*. Some people get up before dawn to see the year's first sunrise — mountaintops are popular vantage points! On one day before the end of the first week, most people will visit a shrine or temple to pray for health and happiness. This visit is called ***hatsumoode***, and vast crowds file into the more famous shrines.

Children are given good luck gifts and pocket money. One of the special games they enjoy playing during *shoogatsu* is ***hanetsuki***, a form of badminton played with brightly colored shuttlecocks and wooden bats. It's played inside because it is very cold in Japan in January.

The house is prepared with special decorations. Pine branches and bamboo bound with sacred straw are placed at the door or gate. The pine tree symbolizes long life.

Hatsumoode

Setsubun

On February 3 (***nigatsu mikka***) roasted beans (*mame*) are scattered around the house to expel the devils that have crept in during the winter. People shout *Oni wa soto, Fuku wa uchi* – "Devils get out". "Good luck come in."

Some say that it is a good excuse for cleaning the house thoroughly after the winter. Others say that the "devils" are symbolic of the irritations that people have felt, cooped up in their homes during the long winter. It is the eve of the official beginning of spring – so take whichever story you prefer! The person who throws the beans should traditionally be someone born in that particular animal year.

Ne (rat)	1948	1960	1972	1984
Ushi (ox)	1949	1961	1973	1985
Tora (tiger)	1950	1962	1974	1986
U (hare)	1951	1963	1975	1987
Tatsu (dragon)	1952	1964	1976	1988
Mi (serpent)	1953	1965	1977	1989
Uma (horse)	1954	1966	1978	1990
Hitsuji (sheep)	1955	1967	1979	1991
Saru (monkey)	1956	1968	1980	1992
Tori (cock)	1957	1969	1981	1993
Inu (dog)	1958	1970	1982	1994
I (boar)	1959	1971	1983	1995

▲ **Find out which animal year was your year of birth.**

Hinamatsuri

The third day of the third month (***sangatsu mikka***) is when girls traditionally bring out sets of about fifteen dolls to show their friends.

The dolls represent members of the ancient imperial court and are displayed on seven tiers of shelves. The Emperor and Empress dolls are displayed on the top shelf and beneath them are lords, ladies, musicians, servants, and miniature furniture.

After two or three weeks the dolls are put away and kept in storage for the rest of the year.

Hanami

April has local festivals but probably the most important occasion in the month is the Entrance Ceremony for the beginning of the school year.

April is also the month for ***hanami*** (flower viewing, usually cherry blossom viewing) and people picnic under cherry trees in bloom. This event varies in date across the country as the cherry trees bloom at different times, starting in the warmer southern regions.

Hanami

Kodomo no hi

May the fifth (***gogatsu itsuka***) is Children's Day — *kodomo no hi*. On this day homes with children have a tall bamboo pole outside, from which carp streamers (***koinobori***) fly. For the Japanese, the carp represents strength, determination, and courage. They hope that their children will grow up to have the same characteristics. In homes, models of *samurai* warriors (another symbol of strength) are displayed.

This day used to be called Boys' Day, but has been renamed to include girls as well.

Taue matsuri

The sixth day of the sixth month (***rokugatsu muika***) was traditionally Rice-Planting Day. Young rice plants were transplanted into flooded rice paddies by women wearing new *kimono*. The children were kept busy running to and fro, keeping the women supplied with the delicate rice plants, which can only survive a few minutes out of the water.

While the women and children worked away, the men stood on the sides of the field beating drums to provide a rhythm and singing folk songs. Naturally they got very dry and had to lubricate their throats and keep up their energy by drinking lots of **sake** (rice wine). At the end of the day, the women (who had spent the day up to their knees in water with backs bent) went home to produce a delectable meal of rice cakes and special festival food for their families!

This festival is in June because that's when the rainy season (***tsuyu***) begins and the rice fields can be easily irrigated. The *taue matsuri* is held only in some areas now as mechanical planting has taken over the job.

Carrying a portable shrine (*mikoshi*)

Tanabata

On the seventh day of the seventh month (***shichigatsu nanoka***) is *tanabata*, the Star Festival. Originally introduced from China, this festival celebrates the annual meeting of the stars Altair and Vega, popularly known as a pair of unfortunate lovers — the weaver princess and the cowherd — who were banished to the sky because of their unsuitable liaison.

Obon

This festival takes place between the thirteenth and sixteenth of August Japanese people retain very strong emotional links with their ancestors and believe that at this time the spirits of the ancestors return to this world, to their old homes and families.

This isn't an occasion for feelings of sadness — families like to show respect for their dead and remind them that they are still part of the family emotionally and are not forgotten. It is realized that whatever a family has now, or is like now, is very dependent on the way its belongings, beliefs, and traditions have been built up by previous generations.

Everyone tries to return to their home towns for *Obon* and public transport is even more crowded than usual.

At this time there are also special festivals to remember those who died in war or at sea. On Tokyo's Sumida River on August 15, people release lanterns with the names of dead relatives written on them into the river at night. Thousands of glowing lanterns can be seen floating down the river.

(O) Tsukimi

September has magnificent harvest moons and is the time for moon-viewing parties (***tsukimi***). In country districts at this time, the rice harvest is offered to the local shrines in thanksgiving. Japanese children look for a rabbit in the moon, and fifteen special rice dumplings called ***odango*** are put in people's windows, along with fruit and pampas grass, as an offering to the rabbit in the moon.

Dressing for a festival day

October has local festivals but no major national ones. This month, though, is a popular time for weddings, as is the spring, so many people have personal anniversaries.

November 15 is the time for the *shichi go san* festival that you have already learned about.

In December, people are caught up in preparations for the New Year celebrations and it is also very cold. Maybe that is why there are no major festivals held in this month.

ACTIVITIES

- Ask at your local library for more information on these and other festivals and Japanese folklore:
  1 Find Japanese stories to tell to the class (in English).
  2 Research a particular festival and put the information on a poster to display in your classroom so that others can share and enjoy the information.

- Learn the greetings for New Year by heart.

Potato digging festival

Unit 4

あなた の たんじょうび は なんがつ です か

Anata no tanjoobi wa nangatsu desu ka

What month is your birthday?

NEW WORDS

なんがつ	*nangatsu*	What month?
いちがつ	*ichigatsu*	January
にがつ	*nigatsu*	February
さんがつ	*sangatsu*	March
しがつ	*shigatsu*	April
ごがつ	*gogatsu*	May
ろくがつ	*rokugatsu*	June
しちがつ	*shichigatsu*	July
はちがつ	*hachigatsu*	August
くがつ	*kugatsu*	September
じゅうがつ	*juugatsu*	October
じゅういちがつ	*juuichigatsu*	November
じゅうにがつ	*juunigatsu*	December
はる	*haru*	spring
なつ	*natsu*	summer
あき	*aki*	autumn
ふゆ	*fuyu*	winter
おたんじょうび おめでとう ございます	*O tanjoobi Omedetoo gozaimasu*	Happy Birthday

STUDY

- Note that ***shi*** is used for the fourth month, not ***yon***; ***shichi*** is used for the seventh month, not ***nana***; ***ku*** is used for the ninth month, not ***kyuu***.

- The pattern for asking "What month is your birthday?" or "What month is it?" is as follows:
  Talking about your birthday *Anata no tanjoobi wa*
  what month is it? *nangatsu desu ka.*
  This is reversed from the English pattern. As you will have already noticed, this is the normal pattern for a Japanese sentence. Pick out what you are talking about (the topic), follow it with *wa*, then say what you want to say about the topic, or ask your question.

  It's the same when you talk about yourself: *Watashi wa juusansai desu.* Or when you want to talk about your dog: *Inu wa watashi no desu.* Or when you want to talk about your teacher: *Sensei wa watashi no PAATII ni ikimasen.*

- When answering the question: *Anata no tanjoobi wa nangatsu desu ka*, you can either say *Watashi no tanjoobi wa (sangatsu) desu*, or just *(Sangatsu) desu*.

- You can wish someone a Happy Birthday by saying: *O tanjoobi Omedetoo gozaimasu.*

ACTIVITIES

- Take turns going around the class asking:
  Anata no tanjoobi wa nangatsu desu ka.
  Reply: *Watashi no tanjoobi wa (ichigatsu) desu,* etc.

- A student or the teacher calls out a number between one and twelve. You must give the English month as fast as you can.
  Extend this by calling out either the English month or the Japanese month name and students give the equivalent as quickly as possible.

- Make a chart of the class's birthday months.
  Label the months in Japanese, of course!

- Seasons in Japan are very clearly defined. If you had been born in Japan, in which season would your birthday fall?

Haru	spring	March, April, May
Natsu	summer	June, July, August
Aki	autumn	September, October, November
Fuyu	winter	December, January, February

  You may remember that *Haruko* means "Spring child". Can you figure out how you would name a baby a summer, fall or winter child?

- Ask each other the following questions:
  1 *Setsubun wa nangatsu desu ka.*
  (Answer, e.g. *Setsubun wa nigatsu desu.*)
  2 *Setsubun wa itsu desu ka.*
  3 *Shoogatsu wa nangatsu desu ka.*
  4 *Hinamatsuri wa nangatsu desu ka.*
  5 *Obon wa nangatsu desu ka.*
  6 *Kodomo no hi wa nangatsu desu ka.*
  7 *Shichi go san wa nangatsu desu ka.*
  Look back to check that you were correct.

Nigatsu

In February plum blossoms open and people rejoice that spring is on its way after the cold of winter.

Sangatsu

During March the cherry trees bloom and people take advantage of the warming days to go out and look at the cherry blossoms. They make parties out of the occasion, taking picnics to eat under the cherry trees. It is a time for drinking *sake* and enjoying getting together with friends in the open air.

These excursions are called *hanami* (flower viewing). *Hana* means flower, *mi* comes from *mimasu* (see/look).

The school year in Japan begins in April so the beginning of *hanami* signals that the end of the school year is approaching.

SONG

Sakura Sakura

Cherry blossoms in the spring sky
As far as the eye can see
They're like a mist or floating clouds
So fragrantly wafting
Come, Oh come, come, Oh come
Let us go to see the cherries!

Check your understanding

Match the following sentences:

1 *Anata no tanjoobi wa itsu desu ka.*
2 *Haru desu.*
3 *Watashi no tanjoobi wa shichigatsu desu.*
4 *Nangatsu desu ka.*
5 *Hachigatsu desu.*
6 *Shoogatsu wa ichigatsu desu.*
7 *Hachigatsu wa Obon desu.*
8 *Kodomo no hi wa gogatsu desu.*
9 *Otsukimi wa kugatsu desu.*
10 *Taue matsuri wa rokugatsu desu.*

a It's August.
b My birthday is in July.
c When is your birthday?
d It's spring/It's in spring.
e What month is it?
f Children's Day is May.
g Moon viewing is September.
h August is *Obon*.
i The rice planting festival is in June.
j *Shoogatsu* is January.

Quiz

What do you remember about the special festivals? See how many correct answers you can give without looking back at the information.

1 What happens at *Obon*?
2 What does *shoogatsu* celebrate?
3 At *setsubun*, what is the traditional shout? Why is this shouted?
4 What is the special food eaten at *Otsukimi*?
5 If you were invited to *hanami*, what would you be going to do?
6 The poor separated star lovers meet on only one night of the year. Which night?
7 If you saw carp streamers fluttering in the breeze outside houses, what date would it probably be?
8 You are invited to visit a family and upon arrival are taken to see a doll collection. What is the festival?
9 You watch a TV program on June 6 about old customs in Japan. Which festival would it be about?
10 What would you say to wish your friends "Happy New Year"?

Writing practice

- Make ***ji*** and ***joo***:

  し　じ　じょう
  shi → ***ji*** → ***joo***

- From ***hi*** you can make ***bi***:

  ひ　び
  hi → ***bi***

- Make **do** from **to**:

  と　ど
  to → **do**

- Make ***da*** from ***ta***:

  た　だ
  ta → ***da***

- Make ***zu*** from ***su***:

  す　ず
  su → ***zu***

- Practice writing the following:
  たんじょうび
  げつようび
  かようび
  すいようび
  もくようび
  きんようび
  どようび
  こども　の　ひ
  どう　いたしまして
  どうぞ　よろしく

- Practice using the half-size ***tsu*** to double the consonant:
  mikka　みっか
  yokka　よっか
  You will need to look carefully to see where the syllable is a full-size ***tsu*** and where it is a half-size ***tsu*** being used to double a consonant.

Unit 5

あなた の たんじょうび は なんがつ なんにち です か
Anata no tanjoobi wa nangatsu nannichi desu ka
What date is your birthday?

Kara wants to know Dean's birth date and can't resist showing off her knowledge of Japan and its festivals at the same time. Not to be outdone, Dean shows off his knowledge, too.

Kara:
あなた の たんじょうび は なんがつ なんにち です か。 — *Anata no tanjoobi wa nangatsu nannichi desu ka.*

Dean:
ごがつ いつか です。 — *Gogatsu itsuka desu.*

Kara:
そう です か。ごがつ いつか は にほん の こども の ひ です。 — *Soo desu ka. Gogatsu itsuka wa nihon no kodomo no hi desu.*

Dean:
あなた の たんじょうび は なんがつ なんにち です か。 — *Anata no tanjoobi wa nangatsu nannichi desu ka.*

Kara:
わたし の たんじょうび は しがつ にじゅうさんにち です。 — *Watashi no tanjoobi wa shigatsu nijuusannichi desu.*

Dean:
シェクスピア の たんじょうび でした。 — *SHEKUSUPIA* (Shakespeare) *no tanjoobi deshita.*

Kara:
そう です か。じょうず です ね。 — *Soo desu ka. Joozu desu ne.*

NEW WORDS

じょうず です ね	*joozu desu ne*	You're clever aren't you!
こども の ひ	*kodomo no hi*	Children's Day
なんにち	*nannichi*	what date?
なんがつ	*nangatsu*	what month?

The following dates are for reference only at this point:

ついたち	*tsuitachi*	first of a month
ふつか	*futsuka*	second of a month

みっか	*mikka*	third of a month
よっか	*yokka*	fourth of a month
いつか	*itsuka*	fifth of a month
むいか	*muika*	sixth of a month
なのか	*nanoka*	seventh of a month
ようか	*yooka*	eighth of a month
ここのか	*kokonoka*	ninth of a month
とおか	*tooka*	tenth of a month
じゅういちにち	*juuichinichi*	eleventh
じゅうににち	*juuninichi*	twelfth
じゅうさんにち	*juusannichi*	thirteenth
じゅうよっか	*juuyokka*	fourteenth
じゅうごにち	*juugonichi*	fifteenth
じゅうろくにち	*juurokunichi*	sixteenth
じゅうななにち	*juushichinichi*	seventeenth
じゅうはちにち	*juuhachinichi*	eighteenth
じゅうくにち	*juukunichi*	nineteenth
はつか	*hatsuka*	twentieth
にじゅういちにち	*nijuuichinichi*	twenty-first
にじゅうににち	*nijuuninichi*	twenty-second
にじゅうさんにち	*nijuusannichi*	twenty-third
にじゅうよっか	*nijuuyokka*	twenty-fourth
にじゅうごにち	*nijuugonichi*	twenty-fifth
にじゅうろくにち	*nijuurokunichi*	twenty-sixth
にじゅうななにち	*nijuushichinichi*	twenty-seventh
にじゅうはちにち	*nijuuhachinichi*	twenty-eighth
にじゅうくにち	*nijuukunichi*	twenty-ninth
さんじゅうにち	*sanjuunichi*	thirtieth
さんじゅういちにち	*sanjuuichinichi*	thirty-first

STUDY

- The list of dates above is a formidable one! Use it for reference only at this point and learn it gradually as you get used to using dates in your conversations.

  Be particularly careful to get the spelling of the dates right. You can see how easy it would be to mix up some of them. Look carefully at the spelling of the following ones: ***mikka***, ***yokka***, ***muika***, ***yooka***, ***juuyokka***, ***hatsuka***, ***nijuuyokka***.

  These dates appear very complicated but just as you have learned with other things in Japanese, you have to accept them and gradually absorb them. When you want to find a particular date refer to the list here. It is also repeated at the back of the book for easy reference.

- This is how you tell someone your birth date:
  Watashi no tanjoobi wa sangatsu juuyokka desu.
  Notice that the month is put first, followed immediately by the date. No particles go between the words of the date.

  Learn your own birth date by heart. Learn the phrase *Joozu desu ne* and add it to future conversation.

Writing practice

- Review the syllable ***ro***: ろ
- Review ***nu***: ぬ
- Write the following in *hiragana*:
  juurokunichi
  rokugatsu
  nijuuroku
  inu
- Practice writing out in *hiragana* other dates shown on the preceding page.

STUDY

- Look at the following patterns:
  "I went to Australia on the twelfth of June."
  Watashi wa rokugatsu juuninichi ni OOSUTORARIA ni ikimashita.
  "I returned home on July the sixth."
  Shichigatsu muika ni kaerimashita.
  Notice that, just as with other time words you know like "today", "tomorrow", etc., the time word here goes after the topic in your sentence. Often the topic will not be spoken so the time or phrase will appear to be the first thing in the sentence.

- Look at the calendar page on the next page for a fictitious thirty-one day month.
  1 Go through the calendar carefully, saying the date for each day, i.e: *tsuitachi, futsuka, mikka . . .*
  2 Practice giving the day as well as the date: For example: *Hachigatsu futsuka getsuyoobi desu.*
  It's Monday the second of August.

日ようび nichiyoobi	月ようび getsuyoobi	火ようび kayoobi	水ようび suiyoobi	木ようび mokuyoobi	金ようび kinyoobi	土ようび doyoobi
1	2	3	4	5	6	7
8	9	10	11	12	13	14
15	16	17	18	19	20	21
22	23	24	25	26	27	28
29	30	31				

いちがつ

ACTIVITIES

- Draw up a similar calendar on a separate sheet of paper. Decide which month it is to be and give it the appropriate number of days.
  Label each day with its name and date in Japanese.

- With a partner, referring to only one of your books at a time, ask each other: "What is the month? What is the date?" pointing to different days.
  Your question will be:
  Nangatsu nannichi desu ka.
  Your answer:
  (Shigatsu nanoka) desu.

- Now try a different question, for example:
  What day is the fourth of December?
  Juunigatsu yokka wa nanyoobi desu ka.
  It's (a) Tuesday.
  Kayoobi desu.
  Notice the order of the sentence and where you have to put ***wa***, because in this sentence you are talking about that particular date — the fourth of December.
  Don't get confused between day and date:
  nannichi what date?
  nanyoobi what day?

Check your understanding

First, figure out the dates for the past week to today, and for the week ahead of today.

What do the following sentences mean? For each question, write out the question in a notebook and under it write the *roomaji* equivalent. Also write out the *roomaji* answer and under it write the English equivalent. If you want to do it in *hiragana* too that would be fantastic! (You can do most of it now from your own accumulated store of knowledge. The words you don't know can be picked out from the Japanese script vocabulary list.)

1 What date is next Monday?
2 What date is next Friday?
3 What date is next Wednesday?
4 What date is next Saturday?
5 What date was last Sunday?
6 What date was last Thursday?

7 What date is next Tuesday?
8 What date is next Sunday?
9 What date was last Monday?
10 What date was last Friday?

Did you remember that to say "Last Monday" you have to say *Senshuu no getsuyoobi* and follow it with ***wa***, because that is your topic? ("Next Monday" would be *Raishuu no getsuyoobi wa . . .*)
Did you remember to use the past tense *deshita* for "was"?

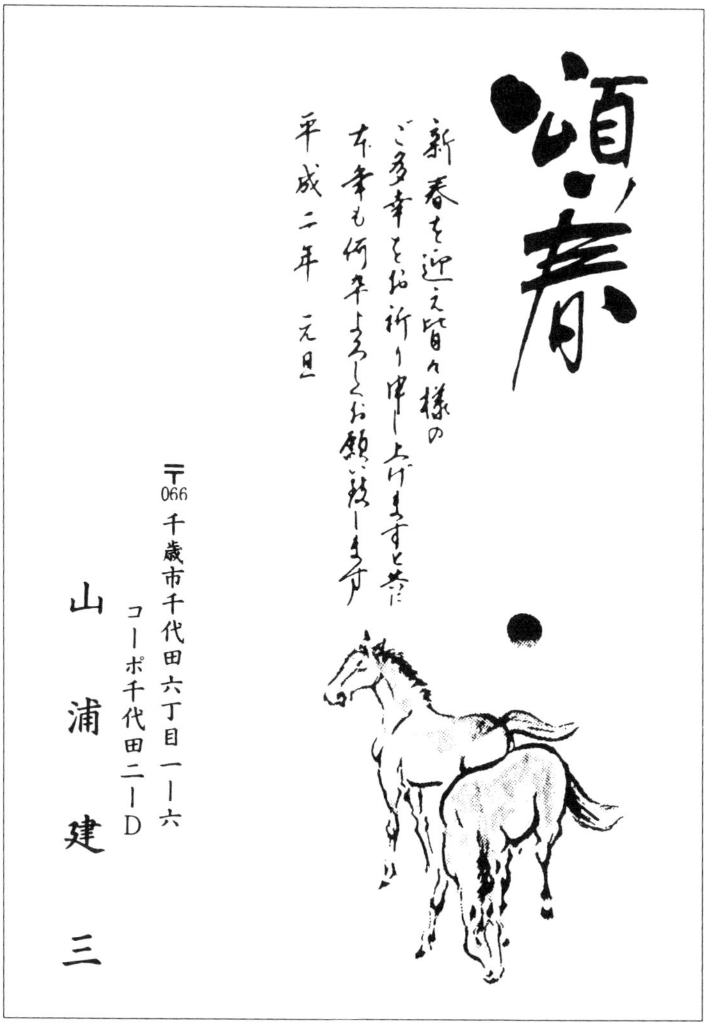

New Year's card

Unit 6

わたし　も　アメリカじん　です
Watashi mo AMERIKAjin desu
I'm American, too

Ms. Jones, a teacher of Japanese, enters the classroom at the beginning of a new school year. She asks her students some questions.

Jones:
こんにち　は。 — *Konnichi wa.*
はじめまして　どうぞ　よろしく。わたし　の　なまえ　は　ジョンス　です。 — *Hajimemashite doozo yoroshiku. Watashi no namae wa JONSU* (Jones) *desu.*

New pupils:
はじめまして。 — *Hajimemashite.*

Jones (to a new student):
あなた　の　なまえ　は　なん　です　か。 — *Anata no namae wa nan desu ka.*

Ann:
わたし　の　なまえ　は　アン　グリーン　です。 — *Watashi no namae wa AN GURIIN* (Ann Green) *desu.*

Jones:
なんさい　です　か。 — *Nansai desu ka.*

Ann:
じゅうごさい　です。 — *Juugosai desu.*

Jones:
どこ　の　かた　です　か。 — *Doko no kata desu ka.*

Ann:
カナダじん　です。 — *KANADAjin desu.*

Jones:
ありがとう。 — *Arigatoo.*

(She asks another student)
おなまえ　は　なん　です　か。 — *Onamae wa nan desu ka.*

James:
ジェムス　スコット　です。 — *JEMUSU SUKOTTO* (James Scott) *desu.*
わたし　は　じゅうろくさい　です。 — *Watashi wa juurokusai desu.*
アメリカじん　です。 — *AMERIKAjin desu.*

Jones:

わたし　も　アメリカじん　です。さあ、にほんご　を　べんきょう　しましょう。きょう　は　なんがつ　なんにち　です　か。	*Watashi mo AMERIKAjin desu. Saa, nihongo o benkyoo shimashoo. Kyoo wa nangatsu nannichi desu ka.*

Pupils:

きょう　は　しがつ　いつか　です。	*Kyoo wa shigatsu itsuka desu.*

Jones:

よくできました。	*Yoku dekimashita.*

NEW WORDS

も	*mo*	too/also/as well (particle)
さあ	*saa*	Well then/Now . . . (an utterance expressing this meaning)
よく できました	*yoku dekimashita*	Well Done!

STUDY

- *Watashi mo AMERIKAjin desu.* The particle ***mo*** introduced in this unit allows you to tell people that you like the same things or are the same age, or that you went to the same place or are going to the same place. Useful, isn't it?

  Look at the following sentences:
  RISA san wa juugosai desu. ROBAATO kun mo juugosai desu, Lisa is fifteen. My friend Robert is fifteen too. (*Kun* is only used for males as you learned previously.)

  Watashi wa juusansai desu. Anato mo juusansai desu ka.
  I'm thirteen. Are you thirteen too?

  You can now extend your greetings conversations considerably.

Check your understanding of the dialogue.

Jones: Good afternoon/Hello. I'm pleased to meet you. My name is Jones.
Pupils: We're pleased to meet you.
Jones: What is your name?
Ann: My name is Ann Green.
Jones: How old are you?
Ann: I'm fifteen.
Jones: What nationality are you?
Ann: I'm Canadian.
Jones: Thank you.
What's your name?

James: James Scott. I'm sixteen. I'm American.
Jones: I'm American too. Now . . . let's study Japanese. What's the date today?
Pupils: The fifth of April.
Jones: Well done! (for being able to give the date in Japanese)

ACTIVITY

With two friends perform a roleplay in which you introduce yourselves as fully as possible to a new teacher and help her to find out what subjects you study and the things you like to do (Don't forget to have one person saying things like "I like it too" or "I do it too" at intervals to make sure everyone is involved.)

Ask the teacher some questions too, to get to know her.

STUDY

Below is a list of verbs that you know, to refresh your memory. Check that you are certain of the meaning of each before you continue.

Verb	**Present/future**	**Negative**	**Past**	**Past negative**	**Suggestion**
is	*desu*	*dewa arimasen*	*deshita*	*dewa arimasen deshita*	*deshoo*
go	*ikimasu*	*ikimasen*	*ikimashita*	*ikimasen deshita*	*ikimashoo*
come	*kimasu*	*kimasen*	*kimashita*	*kimasen deshita*	*kimashoo*
return	*kaerimasu*	*kaerimasen*	*kaerimashita*	*kaerimasen deshita*	*kaerimashoo*
look/see	*mimasu*	*mimasen*	*mimashita*	*mimasen deshita*	*mimashoo*
read	*yomimasu*	*yomimasen*	*yomimashita*	*yomimasen deshita*	*yomimashoo*
speak	*hanashimasu*	*hanashimasen*	*hanashimashita*	*hanashimasen deshita*	*hanashimashoo*
study	*benkyoo shimasu*	*benkyoo shimasen*	*benkyoo shimashita*	*benkyoo shimasen deshita*	*benkyoo shimashoo*
do	*shimasu*	*shimasen*	*shimashita*	*shimasen deshita*	*shimashoo*
meet	*aimasu*	*aimasen*	*aimashita*	*aimasen deshita*	*aimashoo*
practice	*renshuu shimasu*	*renshuu shimasen*	*renshuu shimashita*	*renshuu shimasen deshita*	*renshuu shimashoo*

ACTIVITY

Write a story about your life to read to other students. Practice it until you are sure that you are achieving the very best Japanese sound you can. Use as many of the above verb forms as possible.

You may like to offer it to your teacher for checking to be sure that you have everything, particularly particles, in the right place.

Writing practice

- Practice the syllable ***me***: め

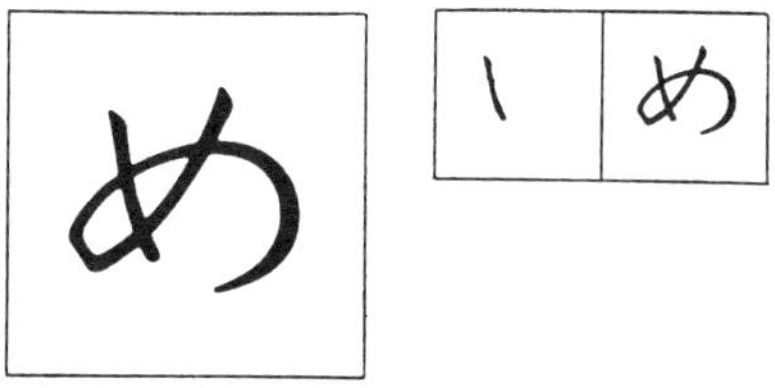

- Review ***mo***: も

- Practice writing words with the ***mashoo*** or ***shoo*** ending. Write the following words and put the English equivalent beside them.

でしょう
いきましょう
きましょう
かえりましょう
みましょう
よみましょう
はなしましょう
べんきょう　しましょう
れんしゅう　しましょう

Reading practice

Read aloud the conversation at the beginning of this unit. Below are some of the *katakana* words used:

カナダ	*KANADA*	Canada
アメリカ	*AMERIKA*	America
ジョンス	*JONSU*	Jones
ジェムス	*JEMUSU*	James
スコット	*SUKOTTO*	Scott

Practice reading them until you recognize them.

STUDY

You can now say things like:
"I'll go too."
"Shall we go too?"
"Are you going to go as well?"

Look at these examples:

Watashi mo ikimasu.	I will go too.
Anata mo ikimashita ka.	Did you go too?
AN san mo ikimasu.	Anne is going to go as well.
Hon mo yomimasu.	I'll read the book too.
REKOODO mo kikimashita.	I listened to the record too.
Doyoobi mo ikimashita.	I went on Saturday as well.

Note: the particle ***mo*** has taken the place of any other particle.

Unit 7

せ　が　たかい　です
Se ga takai desu
I'm tall

In this unit you will learn how to tell people about your physical characteristics, and how to describe others.

Brenda tells us about herself:

わたし　は　ブレンダ　です。	*Watashi wa BURENDA desu.*
オーストラリアじん　です。	*OOSUTORARIAjin desu.*
せ　が　たかい　です。	*Se ga takai desu.*
め　が　あおい　です。	*Me ga aoi desu.*
かみ　の　け　が　くろい　です。	*Kami no ke ga kuroi desu.*
あし　が　ながい　です。	*Ashi ga nagai desu.*
じゅうさんさい　です。	*Juusansai desu.*
わたし　の　たんじょうび　は	*Watashi no tanjoobi wa*
さんがつ　いつか　です。	*sangatsu itsuka desu.*

Study the new vocabulary carefully and figure out what Brenda is saying about herself.

NEW WORDS

せ　せい	*se* (or *sei*)	height
たかい	*takai*	tall/high/expensive
ひくい	*hikui*	short in height/low
め	*me*	eyes
かみ　の　け	*kami no ke*	hair
あし	*ashi*	legs or feet
あおい	*aoi*	blue (adjective)
くろい	*kuroi*	black (adj)
あかい	*akai*	red (adj)
きいろい	*kiiroi*	yellow (adj)
ながい	*nagai*	long (adj)
みじかい	*mijikai*	short (adj)
ちゃいろ	**chairo*	brown color (Noun)
みどりいろ	**midoriiro*	green color (Noun)
いろ	*iro*	color (Noun)
おとこ　の　こ	*otoko no kc*	boy
おんな　の　こ	*onna no ko*	girl
しょうがくせい	*shoogakusei*	elementary school pupil

ちゅうがくせい	*chuugakusei*	junior high school student (Japan: age 13-15)
こうこうせい	*kookoosei*	high school student (Japan: age 16-18)
めがね を かけます	*megane o kakemasu*	I wear glasses
めがね を かけません	*megane o kakemasen*	I don't wear glasses
(Interest only) いちにちじゅう	*ichinichijuu*	all day long

STUDY

- ***Ga*** is another particle. You will notice that Brenda uses the ***ga*** particle after the thing about herself that she particularly wants you to focus on.
  The complete sentence would be:
  Watashi wa se ga takai desu.
  "(Talking about me) the thing I really want to tell you about is that I'm tall." It is the one thing about yourself that you want to mention in the sentence, and which you want your listener to focus on. That is why you use the ***ga*** particle because ***ga*** signals to people to take particular note of the thing in front of it.
  If you think about it, it's much the same with the other use of ***ga*** that you have learned already:
  Watashi wa inu ga suki desu.
  "(Talking about me)/(As for me) I like **dogs**."
  Watashi wa kuruma ga kirai desu.
  "(Talking about me)/(As for me) I dislike **cars**."
  The meaning is: "There may be lots of other things I could tell you about myself but at the moment I want you to focus on this particular bit of information."
  So, whenever you want to talk about one particular thing about yourself, you must put ***ga*** after that part.

- The word for "height" can be spelled two ways. Both are correct: ***se*** or ***sei***.

- Two words in the word list have been marked with an asterisk (*): ***chairo*** and ***midoriiro***. The reason is that you have to keep these color words separated from the adjectives red, blue, etc., even though they do describe colors. **They are not adjectives and cannot behave like adjectives**. They are actually nouns: "brown color" and "green color". That seems peculiar from an English viewpoint because we can say "green eyes", "brown eyes", using our adjectives "green" and "brown". Japanese does not have adjectives for "green", "brown", and several other colors. It has nouns which have ***iro*** on the end.
  You learned previously that true adjectives have *ai, ii, ui, ei*, or *oi* on the end. Therefore it is easy to see that *chairo* and *midoriiro* do not fit that rule — so they cannot be adjectives.

The Japanese language is very consistent. When you have learned a rule it always stays the same. English, of course, delights in exceptions to its rules!

- ***Iro*** means "color". So you can ask "What color?" with
  Nani iro desu ka.
  Or you can ask "What color eyes?" with
  Me ga nani iro desu ka.
  (Remember to put ***ga*** after the part of the body that you want specifically to talk about.)
  Practice these patterns with all the appropriate words in the vocabulary list.

- If you want to say "My eyes are not blue", remember the rule for turning a positive adjective into a negative one: **take off the *i* and add *kunai*.** Learn the following rule carefully: **use *wa* with negatives**. For example:
  Me wa aokunai desu.
  "My eyes are not blue."
  Imagine you are answering questions (in a letter or on the telephone) about your appearance. The person has never met you, and they ask: "Are your eyes blue?" with *Me ga aoi desu ka.* ("The thing I want you to talk about is your eyes".) What we are talking about has been established. Therefore, in your reply, you answer with *Me wa* . . . You don't need to force people to know what you are talking about because they are the ones who brought up the subject. For example:

Ashi ga nagai desu ka.	Are your legs long?
Ashi wa nagakunai desu.	My legs are not long.
Se ga takai desu ka.	Are you tall?
Se wa takakunai desu.	I'm not tall.

  (This last sentence gives you the opportunity for expressing a height between tall and short.)
  Practice changing all the adjectives in the vocabulary list into the negative. Remember to say ***wa*** with negatives, not ***ga***. Also remember that you can never change the ***iro*** words into the negative in the same way as you change adjectives. The ***iro*** words are nouns and so have their own rule. So for the moment don't attempt to say "not green", "not brown". We'll leave those for later so you won't get them confused.

- ***Otoko*** means "male", ***onna*** means "female". ***Otoko no ko*** is therefore "a male child" (a boy) and ***onna no ko*** is "a female child" (a girl). Here is the *kanji* for your interest:
  otoko 男
  onna 女
  ko 子
  Otoko is a stylized picture of a ricefield on a man's shoulders. This symbolizes the fact that it is a man's responsibility to feed his family. Rice is of course the staple food in Japan. This is also one *kanji* that males need to know if they wish to find the appropriate toilet.
  Onna is a stylized figure of a woman in a sitting position. This may have its origins in the fact that the traditional role of the woman was to

男
女
子

take care of the more sedentary tasks of the home and family, while the man's work more often took him outside the home.

- ***Ko*** is the beginning of the word ***kodomo***, "child" こども
  When you put the *kanji* together you get:
  otoko no ko 男の子 (boy)
  onna no ko 女の子 (girl)

Check your understanding

A

Here are three descriptions of people. Read them carefully. After you have read them through, be prepared to answer the questions in either English or Japanese.
(*tsuitachi* = first of the month)
Find *katakana* words in the *roomaji* text.

1

ジョン さん
ジョン さん は おとこ の こ です。
せ が ひくい です。
じゅうごさい です。
たんじょうび は じゅうがつ ついたち です。
ジョン さん は ニュージーランド の こうとうがっこう の にねんせい です。
め が ちゃいろ です。かみ の け が ながい です。
あし が みじかい です。
ジョン さん は サッカー が すき です。
がっこう が すき です。
ともだち が すき です。
おんな の こ が きらい です。
らいしゅう は ジョン さん の たんじょうび です。

JON san (John)
JON san wa otoko no ko desu. Se ga hikui desu. Juugosai desu. Tanjoobi wa juugatsu tsuitachi desu.
JON san wa NYUUJIIRANDO no kootoogakkoo no ninensei desu. Me ga chairo desu. Kami no ke ga nagai desu. Ashi ga mijikai desu.
JON san wa SAKKAA ga suki desu. Gakkoo ga suki desu. Tomodachi ga suki desu. Onna no ko ga kirai desu.
Raishuu wa JON san no tanjoobi desu.

2

レー さん
レー さん は おんな の こ です。
じゅうさんさい です。
たんじょうび は じゅうがつ ついたち です。
せ が たかい です。

め　が　あおい　です。
かみ　の　け　が　ながい　です。
レー　さん　は　いい　せいと　です。
べんきょう　が　すき　です。
ほん　が　すき　です。
どようび　と　にちようび　に　としょかん　に　いきます。
いちにちじゅう　ほん　を　よみます。しゅくだい　を　します。
よる　レー　さん　は　べんきょう　します。
ピアノ　を　れんしゅう　します。

REE san (Rae)
REE san wa onna no ko desu. Juusansai desu. Tanjoobi wa juugatsu tsuitachi desu.
Se ga takai desu. Me ga aoi desu.
Kami no ke ga nagai desu.
REE san wa ii seito desu.
Benkyoo ga suki desu.
Hon ga suki desu.
Doyoobi to nichiyoobi ni toshokan ni ikimasu.
Ichinichijuu hon o yomimasu. Shukudai o shimasu.
Yoru REE san wa benkyoo shimasu. PIANO o renshuu shimasu.

3
デビド　さん
デビド　さん　は　オーストラリアじん　の　おとこ　の　こ　です。
せ　が　たかい　です。
たんじょうび　は　しちがつ　いつか　です。
じゅうななさい　です。
にほんご　の　にねんせい　です。
オーストラリア　の　こうとうがっこう　の　よねんせい　です。
まいにち　デビド　さん　は　フルート　を　れんしゅう　します。
テニス　を　れんしゅう　します。
しゅくだい　を　しません。しゅくだい　が　きらい　です。
テレビ　が　すき　です。
よる　テレビ　を　みます。
デビド　さん　は　せんしゅう　オーストラリアじん
の　ともだち　と　まち　に
いきました。　えいが　に　いきました。

DEBIDO san (David)
DEBIDO san wa OOSUTORARIAjin no otoko no ko desu.
Se ga takai desu.
Tanjoobi wa shichigatsu itsuka desu.
Juunanasai desu.
Nihongo no ninensei desu.
OOSUTORARIA no kootoogakkoo no yonensei desu.
Mainichi DEBIDO san wa FURUUTO o renshuu shimasu.
TENISU o renshuu shimasu.
Shukudai o shimasen. Shukudai ga kirai desu. TEREBI ga suki desu.

Yoru TEREBI o mimasu.
DEBIDO san wa senshuu OOSUTORARIAjin no tomodachi to machi ni ikimashita. Eiga ni ikimashita.

1 What do Rae and John have in common?
2 What does John dislike?
3 What do John and David have in common?
4 What musical instrument does Rae play?
5 Who is tall and who is short?
6 What does David do in the evenings?
7 Who doesn't like homework?
8 Who likes sports?
9 Who is the oldest?
10 Who went to a film in town last week, and who did he/she go with?

B

Think of ten more questions you can ask your partner in English about these people. You must, of course, figure out the answers yourself first!
Question each other. Answer in English.

C

Translate the descriptions into English.

Megane o kakemasu

D

Divide the class into small groups. Each group of students imagine they are private detectives who have been following one of the described people for the past week and have a complete file on his/her movements. Work out a rough idea in each group of what the character did and did not do each day, with times in case they are asked for. Write it down so you don't give conflicting evidence! Each group takes turns answering questions from the rest of the class in Japanese.

For example:

What did he/she do last Thursday?
Did he/she go to town last Monday?
What did he/she do?
What time did he/she do that?
What date was it?

Ask for more personal descriptions. When you have discovered ten things, change detectives.

Unit 8

Here is a labeled illustration that will help you describe other parts of the body.

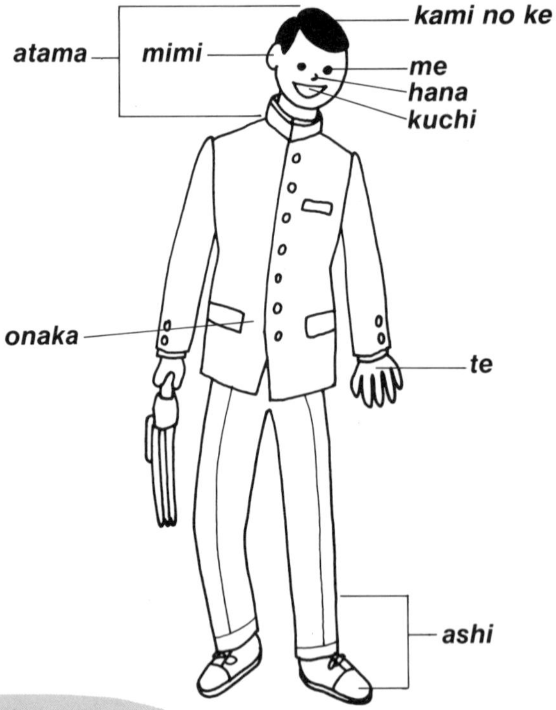

NEW WORDS

はな	*hana*	nose
くち	*kuchi*	mouth
みみ	*mimi*	ear(s)
め	*me*	eye(s)
あたま	*atama*	head
おなか	*onaka*	stomach
て	*te*	hand
トロント	*TORONTO*	Toronto
そうじ　します	*sooji shimasu*	to clean (do the cleaning)

STUDY

Learn how to write the name of your own town or city in *katakana*.

Now you can put all that you have learned together, to describe yourself.

For example:

Watashi wa se ga hikui desu. Otoko no ko desu.

Watashi no namae wa HENRI desu.

TORONTO ni sunde imasu.
Juugosai desu.
TORONTO no kookoosei desu.
Kami no ke ga kuroi desu. Me ga kuroi desu.
Mimi ga chiisai desu. Ashi ga mijikai desu.
Watashi wa mainichi GITAA o renshuu shimasu.
Kayoobi to mokuyoobi wa karate o shimasu.
Senshuu machi ni ikimashita. Karate o mimashita.
Tomodachi to karate no eiga ni ikimashita.
Karate ga suki desu kara karate no hon o yomimasu.

Now check your understanding

I am short (in height). I am a boy.
My name is Henry.
I live in Toronto.
I'm fifteen.
I'm a student at a Toronto high school.
My hair is black. My eyes are black.
My ears are small. My legs are short.
I practice guitar every day.
Tuesdays and Thursdays I do karate.
Last week I went to town. I watched karate.
I went with my friend to a film about karate (a karate film).
Because I like karate, I read karate books.

Note: Japanese people refer to the color of eyes as being "black", where in English "black eyes" has a totally different meaning! We can translate *me ga kuroi desu* as "dark eyes".

ACTIVITIES

- Now try interviewing people, using the chart on the next page. Work in groups of three or five. Copy and cut up the chart.

  Each person will take one of the names on the chart, will have the basic information, and will answer the questions. The questioner has to try to get all the information possible.

  The other members of the group are responsible for checking the information and for listening carefully to the two who are directly involved. They should note the number of questions involved.

  The person who has just been interviewed becomes the next questioner.

- Make posters of the people in the chart. Write all the information about them on the chart in *roomaji* or *hiragana*. Any words you are not sure about can be carefully copied from the vocabulary list.

Maria Olivetti
- Female.
- Italian.
- 17 years old.
- Lives in Rome.
- Tall
- Long, black hair.
- Studies English, Italian, Math, Science, History and Physical Education.
- Likes music and sports.
- Will go to Germany in May.

Philip Smith
- Male.
- English.
- 18 years old.
- Lives in London.
- Tall.
- Brown hair.
- Studies French, English, Geography, Math and History.
- Likes movies.
- Went to France last year on vacation.

Dirk Vanderpoel
- Male.
- Dutch.
- 14 years old.
- Lives in Amsterdam.
- Tall.
- Blond.
- Likes school. A good student.
- Calls friends every day. Plays tennis on Saturday. Dislikes TV.

Lin Cheung
- Female.
- Chinese.
- 15 years old.
- Lives in Beijing.
- Short.
- Black hair. Wears glasses.
- Very good student. Studies English, French, Chinese, Math, and History.
- Likes music. Practices the piano every day.
- Dislikes apples.

Paolo De Vega
- Male.
- Spanish.
- 15 years old.
- Lives in Madrid.
- Short.
- Black hair, brown eyes.
- Dislikes school.
- Likes girls.
- Went to the movies on Saturday with his friend.

Jessie Nalatu
- Female.
- 15 years old.
- Hawaiian.
- Lives in Honolulu.
- Likes the beach and mountains.
- Likes fish.
- Will not go to the mainland because her mother is ill.

Susan Lemesurier
- Female.
- 15 years old.
- Canadian.
- Lives in Toronto.
- Short.
- Brown eyes. Wears glasses.
- Studies guitar.
- Likes magazines and music.
- Doesn't like boys very much.

Paul Carter
- Male.
- American.
- 16 years old.
- Lives in New York.
- Short.
- Black hair.
- Dislikes studying.
- Likes the guitar. Practices daily.
- Went to Boston last month.

Wi Henare
- Male.
- 14 years old.
- New Zealander.
- Lives in Wellington.
- Studies English, Science, Math, and History.
- Tall.
- Likes sports. Plays soccer.
- Dislikes books.

Liew Wah
- Male.
- Taiwanese.
- 18 years old.
- Lives in Taipei with his mother.
- Likes newspapers and movies.
- Reads English every day.
- Plays music every day.
- Will go to Australia in December.

Hans Strese
- Male.
- 16 years old.
- German.
- Lives in Hamburg.
- Tall.
- Blond hair, blue eyes.
- Likes cars and sports. Dislikes History.
- Will go to America in August.

Tazuko Higashi
- Female.
- 16 years old.
- Japanese.
- Lives in Nagasaki.
- Tall.
- Likes basketball. Dislikes dogs and hot weather.
- Went to the mountains last week.
- Will go to Tokyo in March.

Minerva Garera
- Female.
- 15 years old.
- Mexican.
- Lives in Cuernavaca.
- Has one younger sister (Maria) and two older brothers.
- Likes swimming. Plays volleyball.
- Will go to Boston in October.

Susan Mill
- Female.
- 14 years old.
- Australian.
- Lives in Sydney.
- Short.
- Blue eyes.
- Reads books every day.
- Likes cats and dogs. Dislikes sports.
- Went to New York in July.

Writing practice

- Learn the syllable ***fu*** ふ

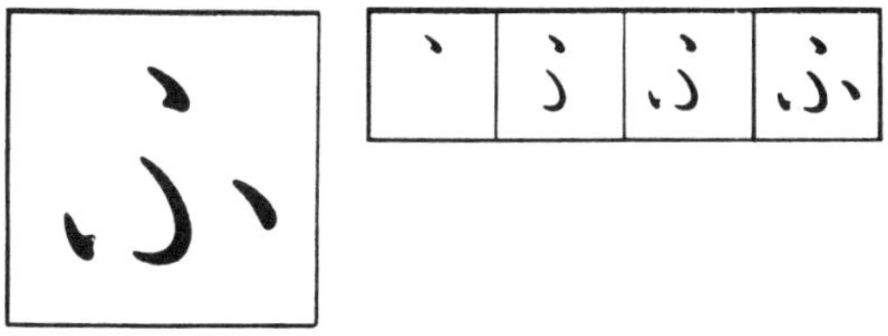

From ***fu*** you can make ***bu*** ふ → ぶ

Write: *fuyu*
fudebako

- Learn the syllable ***ya*** や

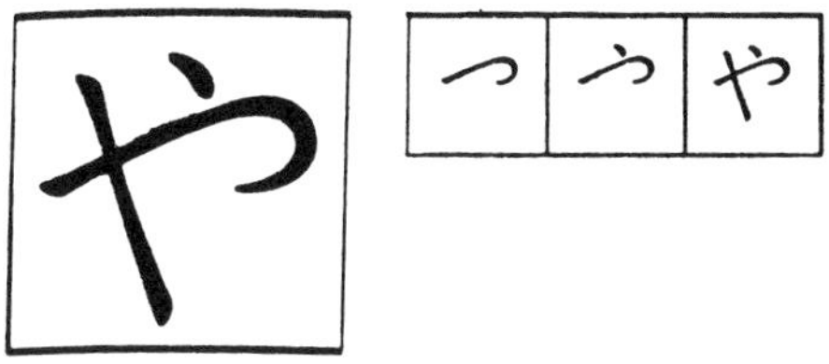

Use the half-size **ya** to make combined sounds, like **cha** and **ja**
ちゃ じゃ

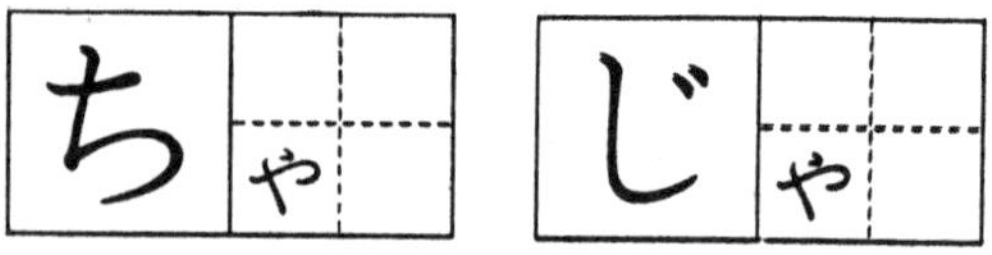

Write: *chan*
janken

- Learn the syllable **mu** む

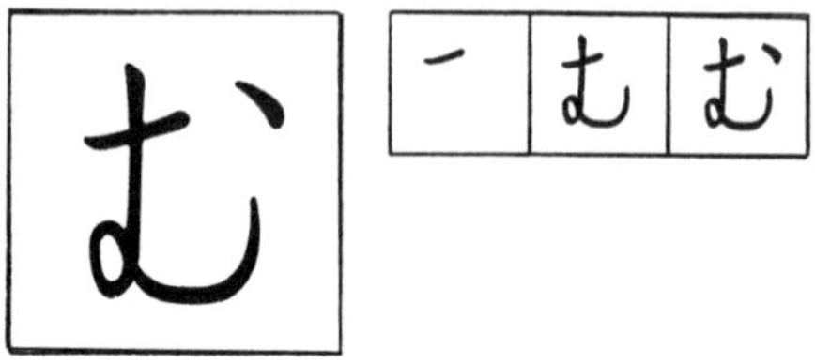

Write: *murasaki iro*

- Review **su** and **zu**:
す → ず

ACTIVITIES

- Divide into two teams. Draw two rectangular frames on the board. The teacher calls out a part of the body and Student One of each team rushes out to be the first to draw that part of the body in an appropriate place. A mark is given to the first team who drew the correct part. Student Two of each team draws the next part of the body and so on until you run out of vocabulary. At that point the next student must give a sentence about the figure. (Both teams' representatives need to be given time to tell their sentence at this point, instead of racing to be first, and if their sentence is correct that team wins a point.)
  Comment on a physical characteristic or say what he/she does, until each person in each team has had a turn.

- The same sort of game may be played either on the board or on paper using only faces, in which case smaller groups work best.

- Extend this activity by preparing a short story about your finished portrait to tell other groups.

- For interest and to give you practice in describing people and animals the following vocabulary is included to allow you to describe an imaginary or mythical animal of your choice.

どうぶつ	*doobutsu*	animal
さくばん	*sakuban*	yesterday evening

(For interest only)

むらさきいろ	*murasakiiro*	purple
だいだいいろ	*daidaiiro*	orange
ももいろ	*momoiro*	peach-pink
ねずみいろ	*nezumiiro*	gray

Note: These colors are more of the ***iro*** group that you learned about before. They are **not** adjectives. They are **nouns**.

STUDY

- The color words used in the following sentences are from the noun group.

  Murasakiiro desu. It is purple.
  Murasakiiro dewa arimasen. It is not purple.
  Me ga daidaiiro desu. The eyes are orange.
  Me wa daidaiiro dewa arimasen./
  Me wa daidaiiro janai desu. The eyes are not orange.
  (*Janai desu* is a familiar or short form of *dewa arimasen*. It is some time since you have reviewed *dewa arimasen, deshita,* and *dewa arimasen deshita*. You may need to take a few minutes to refresh your memory.)
  Te ga murasakiiro deshita.
  The hands were purple.
  Te wa nezumiiro dewa arimasen deshita.
  The hands were not gray.
  You have already learned how to say the following:
  Hon desu. It is a book.
  Hon dewa arimasen. It is not a book.
  Inu deshita. It was a dog.
  Kasa dewa arimasen deshita. It was not an umbrella.

- Learn the new vocabulary and then read about the strange creature:
  せ　が　たかい　です。
  Se ga takai desu.
  あたま　が　おおきい　です。
  Atama ga ookii desu.
  かみ　の　け　が　みじかい　です。
  Kami no ke ga mijikai desu.
  め　が　ちいさい　です。くろい　です。
  Me ga chiisai desu. Kuroi desu.
  みみ　が　むらさきいろ　です。
  Mimi ga murasakiiro desu.
  はな　が　あかい　です。
  Hana ga akai desu.
  おなか　が　おおきい　です。
  Onaka ga ookii desu.
  あし　が　みじかい　です。
  Ashi ga mijikai desu.
  て　は　ありません。
  Te wa arimasen.

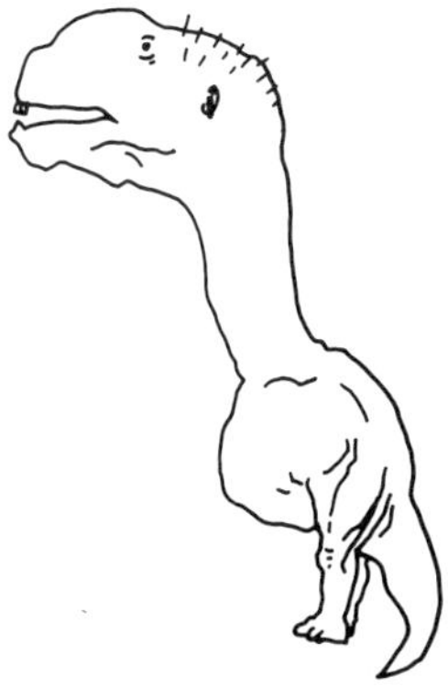

ACTIVITIES

- Draw this creature. Each person's drawing will be different but will have the same characteristics. Label the parts of the creature's body appropriately in Japanese.

- Draw creatures of your own design. Divide into small groups and put a selection of four or five pictures in front of each group. One person chooses a picture but doesn't tell the others which has been chosen. The other members of the group keep asking questions until they identify the chosen picture. The person who makes the final correct guess is given the next turn.

じゃんけん *Janken*

This simple hand game of "rock-paper-scissors" is used often by Japanese for deciding order or turns, or choosing who will do something. It quickly establishes a winner and a loser, and it is one of the first games Japanese children learn.

The two or more players shout *Jankenpon* and simultaneously use their hands to make a rock (*guu*) scissors (*choki*) or paper (*paa*).

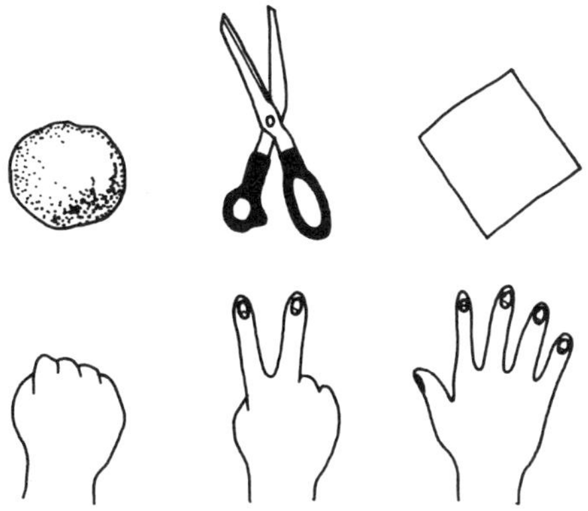

Rock beats scissors, paper beats rock, scissors beats paper.

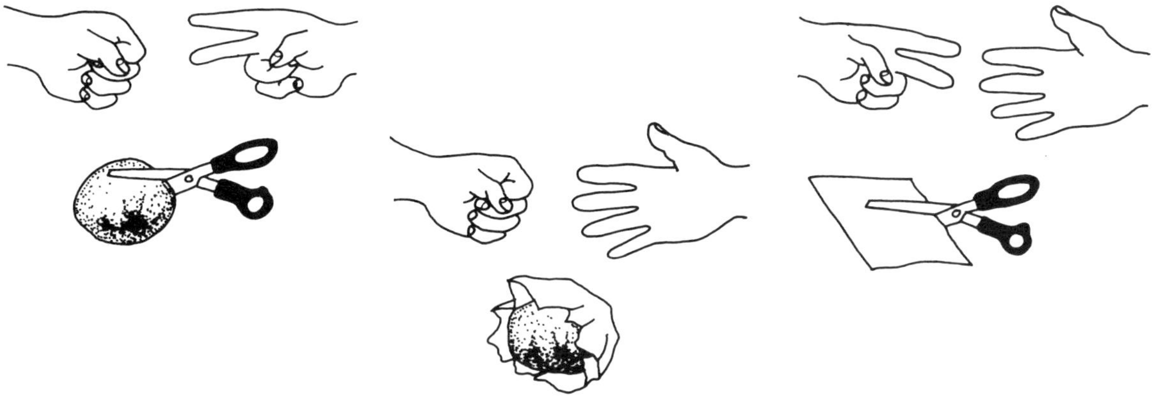

When the same sign is given by all the players, or when all three signs are given by some of them the round is called *aiko*, a draw. The players shout *aiko deshoo* and try again until someone wins.

Topic Six Review

The caption to this photo is in code. Use the code key provided to figure out what the caption says. Use the code key for other coded captions elsewhere in the book.

Coded caption 1
5. 31./11. 24./2.
16. 47. 31./46./47. 31./11. 24.
16. 47. 31. 21. 31./46./43. 41. 48./6./17. 9. 32. 5.
46./47. 31./20./49. 18. 7. 24./

Code Key

あ	1	い	12	う	22	え	33	お	42
か	2	き	13	く	23	け	34	こ	43
さ	3	し	14	す	24	せ	35	そ	44
た	4	ち	15	つ	25	て	36	と	45
な	5	に	16	ぬ	26	ね	37	の	46
は	6	ひ	17	ふ	27	へ	38	ほ	47
ま	7	み	18	む	28	め	39	も	48
や	8			ゆ	29			よ	49
ら	9	り	19	る	30	れ	40	ろ	50
わ	10	を	20	ん	31				
で	11	じ	21	が	32	ど	41	だ	51

CROSSWORD (TOPIC SIX REVIEW)

Try the following crossword. Write your answers in *roomaji*.

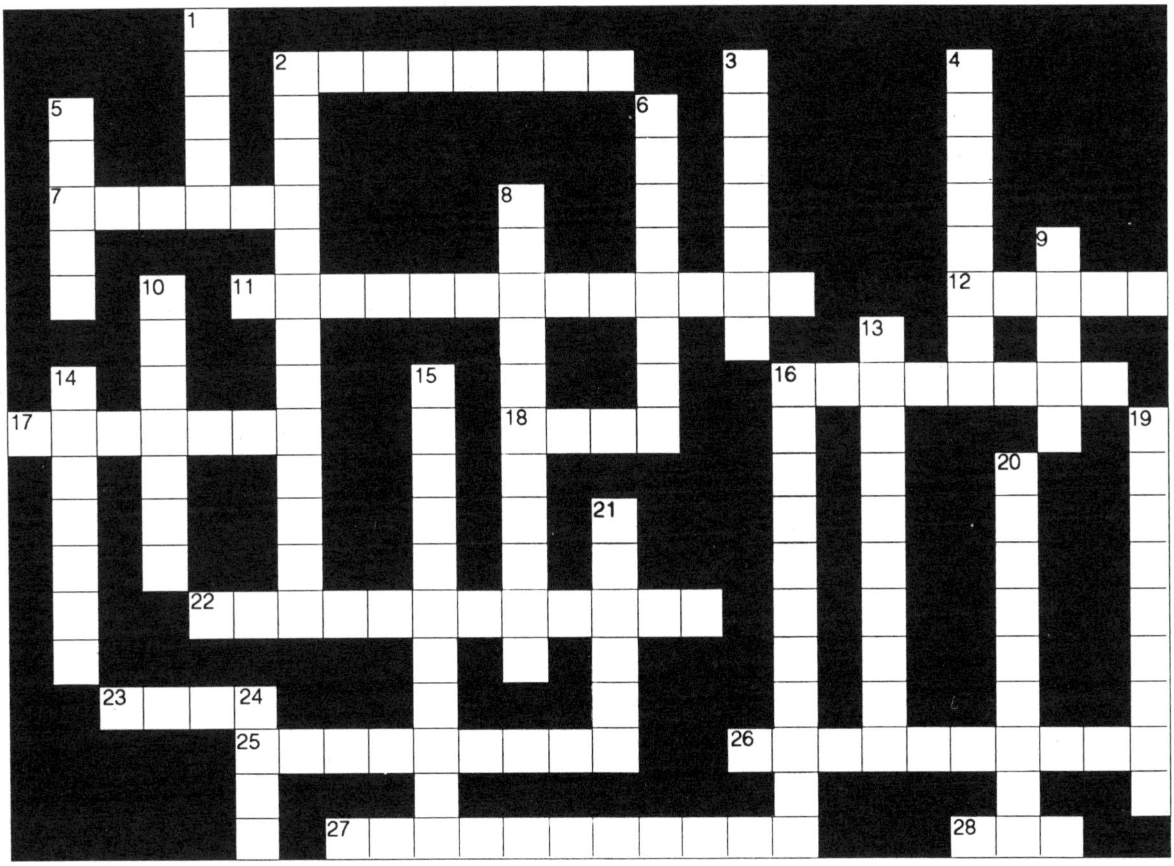

ACROSS

2 . . . . *shitsurei shimasu*
7 tomorrow
11 How old are you? (polite)
12 stomach
16 April
17 twenty years old
18 red
22 New Zealand
23 ears
25 first of a month
26 first year student
27 Junior high school student
28 blue

DOWN

1 mouth
2 (he) is short in height
3 twentieth of a month
4 ninth of a month
5 head
6 eleven years old
8 Rice planting Festival
9 summer
10 September
13 Sunday
14 Tuesday
15 July
16 thirtieth of a month
19 new
20 Auckland
21 Flower viewing Festival
24 when

TOPIC SEVEN families and friends

Introduction

ACHIEVEMENTS

By the end of this Topic, you will know how to:

- describe the composition of your family;
- describe individual family members in some detail;
- talk about other people's families;
- say someone does things too, doesn't do things either, or did things too;
- say neither A nor B does or did things, or both A and B do things, or did things.

You will also learn more *hiragana* combined sounds, and learn to recognize more *katakana* syllables.

Japanese families

The most honored family in Japan is the Imperial family. It consists of the Emperor and Empress and their children and grandchildren.

The Imperial family, according to tradition, are descendants of the goddess Amaterasu. She is the goddess who protects all Japan, and is the most important of all Japanese deities. Because the Emperor is descended from this goddess, emperors of Japan were traditionally revered as gods until the time of the Emperor Shoowa (Hirohito) who died in 1989. He disclaimed the label "god" and led his people as a figurehead only, leaving decisions of state to a democratically elected parliament. Nonetheless, many old Japanese still gave him the homage due to a god.

平成

The current emperor's actual name is Akihito. He has no surname (unlike the British Royal family, whose family name is Windsor Mountbatten). Upon assuming the title of Emperor, he chose the name *HEISEI* ("*accomplishment of peace*") as the name for his Imperial Era, and by which he would be known after his death. His subjects refer to him simply as *TENNOO HEIKA,* which means "His Majesty the Emperor."

His wife is Empress Michiko. They have three children.

Traditionally Japanese people have lived in extended family groups. It was the custom for the oldest son to take care of his aging parents. When he married, the new daughter-in-law moved into her husband's family home and took over the running of the household under the guidance of her mother-in-law. When

the children were born, the grandmother was always there to advise and look after them.

This was the accepted way of life. It was very desirable to have male children because they would look after the parents. Girls, when they married, would move to their husbands' homes and in many practical respects would be lost to their own parents. In practice of course, many girls without brothers ended up caring for their husbands' families and their own. Even today many families feel slightly disappointed if their firstborn is a girl.

Males in Japan have traditionally received very special treatment from females. Wives used to wait on husbands and children in every way. Husbands would arrive home to find welcoming wives waiting in the *genkan* (entrance hall) to help them to take off their shoes and exchange them for house slippers.

The husband was then ushered into the living room and handed food, drink and the newspapers while the wife went back into the kitchen to prepare food.

Nowadays there is a move away from this traditional lifestyle, but men still do not, on the whole, help as much in the home or with the family as their Western counterparts.

The small houses and apartments that people live in often do not have space for the extended family, and many people now work a long way away from their home towns and villages. In the country, the traditional ways still continue but in the towns people are having to adapt to new patterns. This is difficult for the older generation to accept. Recently some senior citizen homes have opened in Japan, for elderly people whose families cannot have them living with them. Senior retirement villages like those known in the U.S. and elsewhere, where there are support services close by, are also being discussed.

The family in Japan is a tight unit and family members will do everything possible to protect, support and encourage the other members. At Obon (in August) families gather together from all parts of the country, to have a total family time, to give presents and to catch up on each other's news in much the same way that other nationalities do at Christmas or Thanksgiving.

Manners

In Japan people are very proud of their families, but you might not notice that they are. They rarely praise their own families – sometimes they may even put them down. Husbands will tell you that their wives are not very good at cooking, that their children are mediocre students etc, when in fact they are convinced that their wife or child is the best! They put themselves down all the time, too, while praising other people, often undeservedly. Your job is to say "No, that's not so. Your wife is a wonderful cook. Your child is a fantastic student." They will deny it, but underneath really appreciate your praise.

Very quickly on meeting you they will ask you to excuse their poor English, apologize for their humble home, and generally try to make you feel good by putting themselves down. They will also compliment you on your Japanese, saying things like "*Nihongo ga joozu desu ne*" even when you are able to communicate very little. It is sincere because they are genuinely surprised to find foreigners learning their language, but even more than that is the desire to make you feel good.

You, of course, reply "*Watashi no nihongo wa mada heta desu*" or some such phrase to say that your Japanese is not yet very good.

Similar humbling of yourself happens when you go visiting and take a gift — the usual thing to do when you visit someone in Japan. As Japanese people hand over their gifts, which they may have taken endless trouble over, they say "*Tsumaranai mono desu ga . . .*", meaning "It's a worthless little thing . . . It's nothing much . . .".

When you meet a Japanese family you may be surprised that they don't look you in the eye, but stand with eyes cast down while you introduce yourselves. This is due to shyness. It used to be considered rude to look older people in the eye, but Western influence has changed that way of thinking. Another habit that many foreigners find strange is seeing Japanese women covering their mouths with their hands when they laugh. It is a habit built up over hundreds of years when it was considered bad form for a woman to show her teeth.

Blowing noses on handkerchiefs is a Western habit that Japanese people think very unhygienic and rude. They use tissues rather than handkerchiefs. Thousands and thousands of really beautiful handkerchiefs — even designer label handkerchiefs — are sold in Japan, but they are for delicate face mopping on humid days, not for blowing noses upon. We would turn away from the group if we had to blow our noses, but Japanese will often sniff until they get to a point where they can politely leave the room to clear their noses. For Westerners this can be as irritating as our use of handkerchiefs is to them!

In the last fifty years Japan has been very much influenced by the West and old established patterns have begun to change. From the days of warlords and samurai in Japan, Japanese people learned to hide their feelings because they were likely to be killed without hesitation if the samurai interpreted their expressions as being disloyal. You may have heard the expression "inscrutable". An inscrutable expression is one that gives nothing away. For hundreds of years, Japanese parents instilled this survival trait into their children and it became, according to some historians, a national habit.

Unit 1

ぼく の かぞく です
boku no kazoku desu
This is my family

Eric is an only child. He is showing one of his friends a photo of himself with his parents.

Eric:

ぼく の かぞく です。	*Boku no kazoku desu.*
はは です。ちち です。	*Haha desu. Chichi desu.*
ぼく です。	*Boku desu.*

Sam:

おとうさん は せ が たかい です ね。	*Otoosan wa se ga takai desu ne.*
ちち は せ が ひくい です。	*Chichi wa se ga hikui desu.*

NEW WORDS

ぼく	*boku*	me/I (males only)
おかあさん	*okaasan*	mother (Your own and other people's)
おとうさん	*otoosan*	father (Your own and other people's)
はは	*haha*	Mom (Your own)
ちち	*chichi*	Dad (Your own)
じゃ/では	*ja/dewa*	Well/Well then
おおきい	*ookii*	big
ちょっと まって ください	*chotto matte kudasai*	Please wait a minute/moment
おかえりなさい	*Okaerinasai*	Welcome home
ちいさい	*chiisai*	small
と	*to*	and
こちら	*kochira*	this is . . . (when introducing someone very politely)

Review

ともだち	*tomodachi*	friend
みて ください	*mite kudasai*	Please look
きいて ください	*kiite kudasai*	Please listen

(Review other similar commands)

Note how *otoosan* and *okaasan* are written.

Check your understanding of the conversation.

Eric: This is my family.
Mom. Dad. Me.

Sam: Your father's tall, isn't he?
My father's short.

STUDY

- ***To*** may be used to say "and" between nouns, only in a defined list. For example:
  Okaasan ***to*** *otoosan wa se ga takai desu.*
  My mother and father are tall.
  You have used ***to*** before to give a total list of school subjects. You used ***ya*** to give a general list that had the idea of "etcetera" or "and the like".
  You may also use ***to*** to say that you did something with someone, or that you are going to do something with someone. For example:
  Tomodachi to eiga ni ikimashita.
  I went to the movies with my friends.

- **Family**
  The fact that you use different words for your own family from those used for other people's families, may take a little more thought initially. For your own mother and father you can choose either the more formal *okaasan* and *otoosan* or the familiar *haha* and *chichi*. But you always use *okaasan* and *otoosan* for someone else's family. In the house you will call your own parents *okaasan/otoosan*, but when talking to others you may use *haha/chichi*.

- *haha* 母 *chichi* 父
  Here is the kanji for *haha*. The same *kanji* is used for *okaasan*.
  Chichi/otoosan is represented by two crossed swords, symbolizing a father protecting his family.

母

父

- Talking about your own mother, you can say:
  Haha no namae wa HANA desu.
  Or more formally: *Okaasan no namae wa HANA desu.*
  But someone who asks you what your mother's name is will ask: *Okaasan no namae wa nan desu ka.*
  You have to become very much at ease with these differences so that you answer comfortably with your own family labels when you are asked about your family by others who are using the more formal labels.
  Here is the pattern:
  You are asked: *Otoosan wa se ga takai desu ka.*
  You answer: *Hai, chichi wa se ga takai desu.*
  Or: *Hai, otoosan wa se ga takai desu.*
  You are asked: *Okaasan wa kami no ke ga nagai desu ka.*

You answer: *lie, haha wa kami no ke ga mijikai desu.*
Or; *lie, okaasan wa kami no ke ga mijikai desu.*

It is your choice which terms you use for your own parents just as in English some people call their parents Mother and Father and others call them Mom and Dad or other familiar names.

However, for other people's families you always use the formal terms.

ジェーン さん の かぞく
JEEN san no kazoku
Jane's family

Jane is showing a photo of her family to a Japanese friend.

haha **Jenny** ***watashi*** **Jane** ***chichi*** **Bob**

This is what Jane says. (Because she is female, she uses *watashi* when speaking of herself.)

Jane

これ は ちち です。	*Kore wa chichi desu.*
ちち の なまえ は	*Chichi no namae wa*
ボブ です。	*BOBU desu.*
これ は はは です。	*Kore wa haha desu.*
はは の なまえ は	*Haha no namae wa*
ジェニ です。	*JENI desu.*
これ は わたし です。	*Kore wa watashi desu.*

SONG

Kimigayo ("The reign of our Emperor" – the Japanese national anthem.)

Ten thousand years of happy reign be thine
Rule on, my lord, till what are pebbles now
By ages united to mighty rocks shall grow
Whose venerable sides the moss doth line.

Look at the photo above. How would you introduce the people to a Japanese friend? Imagine you are the girl in the middle, and that the adults are your own parents.

Reading practice

A Read and understand these sentences.

1 わたし は まいにち まち に いきます。
2 まりこ さん が きます。
3 わたし は うち に かえります。
4 しおり さん は きません。
5 うみ に いきません。
6 すずき さん は まち に いきません。
7 かえりません。
8 どこ に いきます か。
9 はなこ さん は きました。
10 うみ に いきません でした。
11 あなた は まいにち まち に いきました か。
12 よしこ さん は きません でした。
13 いきました か。
14 かえりません でした。
15 うち に いきません でした か。

B Match the *hiragana* sentences with their *roomaji* equivalents below. How many did you read correctly?

1 *Watashi wa mainichi machi ni ikimasu.*
2 *Mariko san ga kimasu.*
3 *Watashi wa uchi ni kaerimasu.*
4 *Shiori san wa kimasen.*
5 *Umi ni ikimasen.*
6 *Suzuki san wa machi ni ikimasen.*

7 *Kaerimasen.*
8 *Doko ni ikimasu ka.*
9 *Hanako san wa kimashita.*
10 *Umi ni ikimasen deshita.*
11 *Anata wa mainichi machi ni ikimashita ka.*
12 *Yoshiko san wa kimasen deshita.*
13 *Ikimashita ka.*
14 *Kaerimasen deshita.*
15 *Uchi ni ikimasen deshita ka.*

サイモン さん の かぞく
SAIMON san no kazoku
Simon's family

At school Simon has met a Japanese boy, Junji. Today, Simon is showing him a photo of his family.

boku	***haha***	***chichi***
Simon	**Kathy**	**Bert**

When Simon speaks of himself, he uses *boku* instead of *watashi*, because he is a male. He uses *kun* when talking about his male friend. There are many differences in Japanese between male and female language patterns. You will gradually become familiar with them as you continue your study.

Simon:
こちら は ぼく の かぞく です。 — *Kochira wa boku no kazoku desu.*

Junji:
そう です か。おとうさん です か。 — *Soo desu ka. Otoosan desu ka.*

Simon:
はい、ちち です。 — *Hai, chichi desu.*

Simon shows Junji another photo.

Junji:	
だれ　です　か。	*Dare desu ka.*
Simon:	
ちち　です。	*Chichi desu.*
Junji:	
おとうさん　の　なまえ　は　なん　です　か。	*Otoosan no namae wa nan desu ka.*
Simon:	
バート　です。	*BAATO* (Bert) *desu.*
Junji:	
おかあさん　です　か。	*Okaasan desu ka.*
Simon:	
ええ　そう　です。はは　の なまえ　は　キャシー　です。 これ　は　ぼく　です。	*Ee, soo desu. Haha no namae wa* *KYASHII* (Kathy) *desu.* *Kore wa boku desu.*
Junji:	
そう　です　ね。 あなた　の　ともだち　です　か。	*Soo desu ne.* *Anata no tomodachi desu ka.*
Simon:	
はい、ぼく　の　ともだち の　ケン　くん　です。 ケン　くん　は カナダじん　です。	*Hai, boku no tomodachi no KEN* (Ken) *kun desu.* *KEN kun wa* *KANADAjin desu.*
Junji:	
あなた　の　うち　です　か。	*Anata no uchi desu ka.*
Simon:	
はい、わたし　の　うち　です。	*Hai, watashi no uchi desu.*

Junji comes home from school with a photo of Simon and his family to show his mother. She is busy in the kitchen, but she calls out the standard reply to his shouted "*Tadaima*".

Junji:	
ただいま。	*Tadaima.*
Okaasan:	
おかえりなさい。	*Okaerinasai.*
Junji:	
おかあさん、みて　ください。	*Okaasan, mite kudasai.*
Okaasan:	
ちょっと　まって　ください… …なん　です　か。	*Chotto matte kudasai . . .* *. . . nan desu ka.*
(He shows her the photo)	
Junji:	
ぼく　の　ともだち　です。	*Boku no tomodachi desu.*

Okaasan:	
ともだち　の　なまえ　は　なん です　か。	*Tomodachi no namae wa nan desu ka.*
Junji:	
サイモン　です。こちら　は サイモン　さん　の　おかあさん です。	*SAIMON desu. Kochira wa SAIMON san no okaasan desu.*
こちら　は　サイモン　さん　の おとうさん　です。	*Kochira wa SAIMON san no otoosan desu.*
サイモン　さん　は アメリカじん　です。	*SAIMON san wa AMERIKAjin desu.*
サイモン　さん　の　うち　は おおきい　です　ね。	*SAIMON san no uchi wa ookii desu ne.*

Practice reading these conversations aloud. If a girl were speaking, how would you change the wording?

Learn the phrase *Tadaima* and its response *Okaerinasai*.

ACTIVITIES

- With a friend, talk in Japanese about the photos introduced in this unit. Try to say at least three things about each. Remember that the families shown are not your families, so say *BAATO san wa SAIMON san no otoosan desu*, etc.

- Describe each person in the photo in as much detail as possible.

Writing practice

- Practice ***otoosan*** and ***okaasan***:
  おとうさん　おかあさん
  otoosan　okaasan

- Review ***ho*** ほ
  and learn ***bo*** ぼ

  ぼ

  ぼぼ

- Review ***ta*** and ***da***: た　だ

  Review ***so*** and ***zo***: そ　ぞ

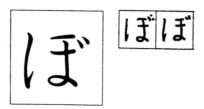

Unit 2

こちら　は　わたし　の　かぞく　です
kochira wa watashi no kazoku desu
Here is my family

NEW WORDS

あに	*ani*	older brother (your own)
いもうと	*imooto*	younger sister (your own)
こちら　へ　どうぞ	*kochira e doozo*	This way, please
Review		
そうじ　します	*sooji shimasu*	to clean (do the cleaning)
テレビ	*TEREBI*	TV
Interest only		
フィリッピン	*FIRIPPIN*	Philippines

Leila's little sister has just rushed in to tell her family that Leila is on her way with their exchange student – a visitor from the Philippines, called Cely. The whole family goes out to the gate. Leila moves along the line introducing them very politely.

Leila:
こちら　は　わたし　の　かぞく　です。 — *Kochira wa watashi no kazoku desu.*

Cely:
はじめまして　どうぞ　よろしく。 — *Hajimemashite doozo yoroshiku.*

Family:
はじめまして。 — *Hajimemashite.*

Leila:
はは　です。はは　の　なまえ　は　キャシー　です。 — *Haha desu. Haha no namae wa KYASHII* (Kathy) *desu.*

Haha:
おなまえ　は　なん　です　か。 — *Onamae wa nan desu ka.*

Cely:
セリ　です。フィリッピンじん　です。 — *SERI* (Cely) *desu. FIRIPPINjin desu.*

Haha:
そう　です　ね。フィリッピン　は　あつい　です　ね。 — *Soo desu ne. FIRIPPIN wa atsui desu ne.*

Cely:
はい、そう　です。 — *Hai, soo desu.*

Haha:
ふゆ　です　から　きょう　さむい　です。 — *Fuyu desu kara kyoo samui desu.*

Leila:	
ちち　です。ちち　の　なまえ　は　ビル　です。	*Chichi desu. Chichi no namae wa BIRU desu.*
Cely:	
こんにち　は。	*Konnichi wa.*
Leila:	
あに　です。じゅうろくさい　です。あに　の　なまえ　は　マイク　です。	*Ani desu. Juurokusai desu. Ani no namae wa MAIKU desu.*
Cely:	
こんにち　は。	*Konnichi wa.*
Mike:	
こんにち　は。	*Konnichi wa.*
Leila:	
サラ　です。いもうと　です。	*SARA desu. Imooto desu.*
(Pointing to Spot)	
わたし　の　いぬ　です。スポット　です。	*Watashi no inu desu. SUPOTTO desu.*
こちら　へ　どうぞ、うち　に　きて　ください。	*Kochira e doozo, uchi ni kite kudasai.*
Cely:	
ありがとう　ございます。	*Arigatoo gozaimasu.*

Check your understanding of the conversation. Answer in English.

1 How many people are there in Leila's family?
2 What is the mother's name?
3 What time of year is it?
4 How old is Leila's older brother?
5 Does Leila have a younger brother or younger sister?
6 What kind of pet does the family have?

STUDY

In Japanese, as you have seen, there are words for your own parents that are different from those you use for other people's families. There are also different words for the other members of a family too. (To avoid confusion they are introduced unit by unit, to give you time to absorb them.)

Get used to using *imooto* for your own younger sister and *ani* for your own older brother.

ACTIVITY

With a partner, imagine you both have an older brother and a younger sister and describe them as fully as you can, using *"Imooto wa. . . "* or *"Ani wa. . . "* Make sure that your pronunciation of *ani* is very clear.

STUDY

- ***Doozo*** is used in many ways: to tell people to go in front of you; to say "help yourself"; and in some situations where you want to say "please".
  Learn the phrase ***Kochira e doozo*** as a way of politely telling someone to "go this way".

- You will have noticed that **kochira** is the same very polite word you used to say "This is . . ." in polite introductions. It is often difficult to have direct translations for words and you really have to see what would fit best in the context. You will extend your use of *kochira* in later units.
  A similar thing happens in the translations of *Ohayoo gozaimasu, konnichi wa*, and *konban wa*. They can be adjusted to fit the situation or the person you are talking to, when you translate them into English. We have more variety in our greetings and tend to adjust them for different occasions and different people.

- ***Sooji shimasu*** is a compound verb that works the same way as *benkyoo shimasu* and *renshuu shimasu*. For example:
  Kuruma o sooji shimashita.
  I cleaned the car.
  Uchi o sooji shimasu.
  I'm going to clean the house.

ACTIVITIES

- Use the conversation above for a role play. Work hard to improve your pronunciation and to make the situation seem real. When you all know your lines really well, you may like to entertain your group.

- Update your vocabulary cards. Put them in a pile. In a group, take turns taking a card and making a sentence that includes that word.
  See if you can go through the whole pack without anyone in your group having to pass because they can't think of a sentence.
  Alternatively, just use the cards for a quick check through, each person picking one off the pile and giving the word in English. If you don't know a word, put it at the bottom of the pile. The one who ends with the most cards is the winner.

- Draw a picture of Leila's family to correspond with the information given and label it with the names.

Check your understanding of the dialogue at the beginning of this unit.

Leila: This is my family.
Cely: I'm pleased to meet you.

Family: We're pleased to meet you.
Leila: This is my mother. Her name is Kathy.
Mother: What is your name?
Cely: Cely. I'm from the Philippines.
Mother: So I believe. It's hot in the Philippines isn't it?
Cely: Yes, it is.
Mother: Because it's winter it's cold today.
Leila: This is my father. His name is Bill.
Cely: Hello.
Leila: This is my older brother. He is sixteen. His name is Mike.
Cely: Hi.
Mike: Hi.
Leila: This is Sarah, my younger sister.
(Pointing to Spot)
This is my dog. He's Spot. Please come this way. Come into the house.
Cely: Thank you.

STUDY

Practice talking about your family, yourself, and friends. Build up one profile together on the board and then develop your own to a similar pattern, e.g.

Haha no namae wa BERIRU (Beryl) *desu.*
Yonjuuissai desu.
AMERIKAjin desu.
Se ga takai desu.
Kami no ke ga nagai desu.
SUPOOTSU ga suki desu.
Doyoobi SAKKAA o shimasu.
Itsumo uchi o sooji shimasu.

Chichi no namae wa TOMU desu.
Yonjuugosai desu.
AMERIKAjin desu.
Se ga takai desu.
SUPOOTSU ga kirai desu.
Hon ga suki desu.
Doyoobi kuruma o sooji shimasu.
TEREBI o mimasu. Hon o yomimasu.
Itsumo uchi o sooji shimasen.
(Remember that *itsumo* means "always" but with a negative it means "never".)

ACTIVITY

Extend the descriptions as far as you can, giving activities for days of the week, and particular times.

Writing practice

- Look carefully at the way to write ***chotto matte***. You need to double consonants in both words.
  ちょっと　まって
  chotto matte
  Remember: double a consonant by putting a half-size *tsu* in front of it.
  Review ***cho***: ちょ
- Practice writing ***sooji***: そうじ
- Review ***juu***: じゅう
- Learn to recognize *TEREBI* in *katakana*: テレビ
  Learn ***TE*** テ

  Learn ***RE*** レ

  Learn ***HI*** ヒ → ***BI*** ビ

Reading practice

- Review these two hiragana: ち　は
  Remember that ***ha*** is used for the particle ***wa***, as well as for ***ha***.
  Read the information then answer the questions in *hiragana* that follow.

ちち　は　せ　が　たかい　です。
はは　は　せ　が　ひくい　です。
ちち　は　かみ　の　け　が　みじかい　です。
はは　は　かみ　の　け　が　みじかい　です。
はは　の　なまえ　は　えみこ　です。
ちち　の　なまえ　は　まさ　です。
わたし　は　せ　が　たかい　です。
わたし　の　なまえ　は　けんじ　です。

Questions

1 おかあさん　の　なまえ　は　なん　です　か。
2 おとうさん　の　なまえ　は　なん　です　か。
3 おかあさん　は　せ　が　たかい　です　か。
4 おとうさん　は　せ　が　たかい　です　か。
5 けんじ　さん　は　せ　が　ひくい　です　か。

- The negative of *takai* and *mijikai* are: たかくない　みじかくない
  Write two sentences in *hiragana* using these two words.

- With a partner:
  1 Read the following two *hiragana* passages aloud.
  2 Answer the questions aloud, in Japanese.
  3 Write the answers in *hiragana*.

A

はは　が　すき　です。
はは　の　なまえ　は　ベリル　です。
せ　が　たかい　です。
かみ　の　け　が　ながい　です。
スポーツ　が　すき　です。
サッカー　を　します。

B

ちち　の　なまえ　は　トム　です。
せ　が　たかい　です。
スポーツ　が　きらい　です。
ほん　を　よみます。
ほん　と　まんが　が　すき　です。
まいにち　テレビ　を　みます。

Questions

1 What is the name of the person referred to in A? In B?
2 Is person A tall or short?
3 What does person B dislike?
4 What does person B like to read?
5 How often does person B watch TV?
6 What game does person A like to play?

Note: *katakana* words

ベリル	*BERIRU*	Beryl
スポーツ	*SUPOOTSU*	sports

サッカー	*SAKKAA*	soccer
トム	*TOMU*	Tom
テレビ	*TEREBI*	TV

- My friend Anisa stayed with a homestay family in Japan. They became her Japanese family. That's Anisa in the photo, with her family. Read the caption. Find out their names, and when Anisa went to Japan.

アニサ　は　ごがつ　に　にほん　に　いきました。これ　は　アニサ　の
にほん　の　かぞく　です。
にほん　の　おかあさん　は　ゆきこ　でした。おとうさん　は　さぶろう
でした。にほん　の　いもうとさん　は　はるこ　でした。
はるこ　さん　は　さんさい　です。

Note: *Nihon no okaasan wa Yumiko deshita.* The Japanese would use *desu* instead of *deshita* because the people's names are the same now as when Anisa visited. However, in English we tend to say "was" and in the passage above we are reporting the information given to us by Anisa.

Unit 3

おとうと が います。あね も います
Otooto ga imasu. Ane mo imasu
I have a younger brother. I have an older sister, too.

NEW WORDS

たいへん	*taihen*	very
いい	*ii*	good
あたま が いい です	*atama ga ii desu*	clever (head is good)
あたま が わるい です	*atama ga warui desu*	not clever (head is bad)
あね	*ane*	own older sister
おとうと	*otooto*	own younger brother

Read this profile of my young brother Nick.

おとうと の なまえ は ニック です。	*Otooto no namae wa NIKKU desu.*
ニック は じゅういっさい です。	*NIKKU wa juuissai desu.*
ちゅうがくせい です。	*Chuugakusei desu.*
わたし は ニック が すき です。	*Watashi wa NIKKU ga suki desu.*
どようび ともだち と サッカー を します。	*Doyoobi tomodachi to SAKKAA o shimasu.*
よる わたし と ビデオ ゲーム を します。	*Yoru watashi to BIDEO GEEMU o shimasu.*
なつ の にちようび は わたし と うみ に いきます。	*Natsu no nichiyoobi wa watashi to umi ni ikimasu.*
ニック は あたま が いい です。	*NIKKU wa atama ga ii desu.*
いい せいと です。	*Ii seito desu.*

Now read this profile of my older sister, Melissa.

あね は メリッサ です。	*Ane wa MERISSA desu.*
じゅうななさい です。	*Juunanasai desu.*
あたま が いい です。	*Atama ga ii desu.*
いい せいと です。	*Ii seito desu.*
せ が ひくい です。	*Se ga hikui desu.*
レコード と カセット テープ が すき です。	*REKOODO to KASETTO TEEPU ga suki desu.*

よる　レコード　と　テープ　を　ききます。	*Yoru REKOODO to TEEPU o kikimasu.*
テレビ　を　みます。	*TEREBI o mimasu.*
ともだち　と　パーティー　に　いきます。	*Tomodachi to PAATII ni ikimasu.*
メリッサ　は　がっこう　が　たいへん　すき　です。	*MERISSA wa gakkoo ga taihen suki desu.*
いつも　しゅくだい　を　します。	*Itsumo shukudai o shimasu.*
わたし　は　しゅくだい　を　しません。	*Watashi wa shukudai o shimasen.*
メリッサ　は　わたし　の　しゅくだい　を　します。	*MERISSA wa watashi no shukudai o shimasu!*
メリッサ　は　たいへん　いい　あね　です　ね。	*MERISSA wa taihen ii ane desu ne!*

Note:

1 *juuissai* is written じゅういっさい
Double the "s" with a half-size *tsu.*

2 Learn how to write *chuugakusei* ちゅうがくせい

Check your understanding

With a partner, or around the class, ask each other questions in English or Japanese to see how well you understood the conversation. Then read the English version below.

My younger brother's name is Nick.
Nick is eleven years old.
He's a Middle School student.
I like Nick.
On Saturdays he plays soccer with his friends.
In the evenings he plays video games with me.
On summer Sundays he goes to the beach with me.
Nick is clever. He's a good student.

My older sister is Melissa.
She's seventeen.
She's clever.
She's a good student.
She's short.
She likes records and tapes.
In the evenings she listens to records and tapes.
She watches TV.
She goes to parties with her friends.
Melissa likes school very much.
She always does her homework.
I don't do homework.
Melissa does my homework. She's a very good older sister, isn't she?

STUDY

- If we wanted to make every sentence super clear we could have put *NIKKU wa* or *MERISSA wa* at the beginning of each sentence but that would get very tedious. It is obvious who we are talking about as long as it has been stated once at the beginning of the paragraph.

- Learn the phrase ***atama ga ii desu***.

- Remember the place you go to has particle ***ni*** after it:
  Umi ***ni*** *ikimasu.*

- ***San*** was not used after the names because we were talking about our own family.

- Learn: *Watashi* ***to*** . . . "with me". For example:
  Haha wa watashi **to** *machi ni ikimashita.*
  My mother went to town with me.
  Watashi wa otoosan **to** *kuruma o sooji shimashita.*
  I cleaned the car with my father.

- Practice sentences that need the ***ni*** particle.
  Use the verbs *ikimasu*, *kimasu* and *kaerimasu* with a place in front of them.

Writing practice

- Read these sentences. Look carefully to see how to write each word.
  わたし　は　なつ　に　にほん　に　いきました。おとうさん　と
  おかあさん　と　にほん　を　みました。やま　を　みました。おおきい
  まち　を　みました。
  Note: ***ookii***. If a word begins with two *o*'s (like *ookii*) write おお
  If two *o*'s occur later in the word (e.g. *kinoo*) following an *o* syllable like *no*, you double the *o* with う

- Read and understand the following sentences.
  いちじ　に　うち　に　かえりました。
  あした　うみ　に　いきます。
  まいにち　うみ　に　いきました。
  きのう　まち　に　いきません　でした。

- Learn how to write the days of the week correctly.
  げつようび　すいようび　きんようび　にちようび
  かようび　もくようび　どようび
  After you have thoroughly learned these words, use them to write sentences of your own.

- Review the double '*s*'; write *issai* いっさい

STUDY

- Time words with ***ni***:

  Natsu no doyoobi ni . . .

  On summer Saturdays . . . (On Saturdays belonging to summer)

  Remember that you use ***ni*** after time words in Japanese if you have the words **on** or **at** in the English sentences.

  Practice substituting other seasons and months to say things like:

Fuyu no nichiyoobi ni . . .	"On winter Sundays . . ."
Hachigatsu no kayoobi ni . . .	"On Tuesdays in August . . ."

  Say what you did on those occasions, using the past tense.

  e.g. *Watashi no kazoku wa fuyu no doyoobi ni FUTTOBOORU o mimashita.*

  "On Sundays in winter my family watched football."

- ***Imasu*** is a new verb. It means: "is/are/exists" and its English equivalent is "There is/there are/I have."

  It is used for things that can move under their own volition — people, animals, insects, birds.

  The Japanese like to state things impersonally, so to say "I have a younger brother" in Japanese, you actually have to say "A younger brother exists". In English that would sound peculiar.

  Imasu works the same way as all the other verbs you have learned:

imasu	there is/there are/(I have)
imasen	there is not/there are not/(I have not)
imashita	there was/(I had)
imasen deshita	there was not/(I didn't have)

  (In English we use the word "have" loosely at times. In the examples above, "have" does not mean ownership as in "I have a camera". In Japanese you will use a different verb for owning things.)

- When talking about a member of your family, *imasu* takes the particle ***ga*** before it. It also takes ***ga*** if you want people to focus on an animal, bird, other person or insect. But use ***wa*** with the negative.

Imooto ***ga*** *imasu.*	I have a younger sister/A younger sister exists.
Ane ***wa*** *imasen.*	I don't have an older sister/An older sister does not exist (in my family).
Inu ***ga*** *imasu.*	I have a dog/A dog exists/There is a dog.

  A complete sentence would be: *Watashi wa imooto ga imasu* "Talking about me I have a younger sister." But as you know it's not necessary to put in *Watashi wa* if people know that you are talking about yourself.

  Ga focuses on the particular item of information that I want to give you about myself. In this case I want you to know that I have a younger sister. There may be many other things I could tell you about myself but at the moment I want you to focus on this particular fact.

  In sentences that don't have the assumption that you are talking about yourself or another person, e.g. *Inu ga imasu* "There is a dog/A dog exists", you are also focusing particularly on the **dog** out of all the things around you that also exist.

- When you want to use ***mo*** to say, for example: "I have an older brother **too**," the ***mo*** replaces the ***ga*** in the sentence.

  Ani ***mo*** *imasu.* "I have an older brother, too."

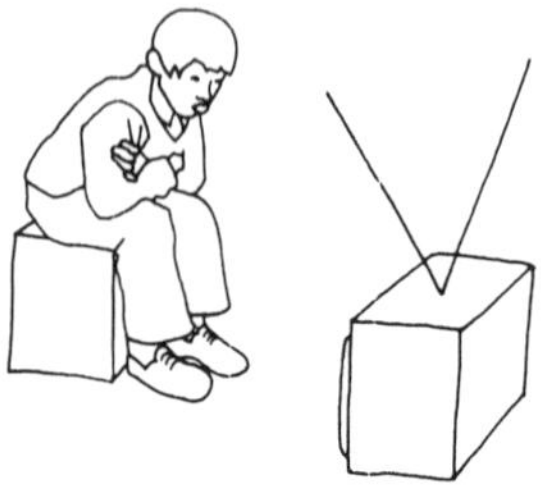

Jon (8)

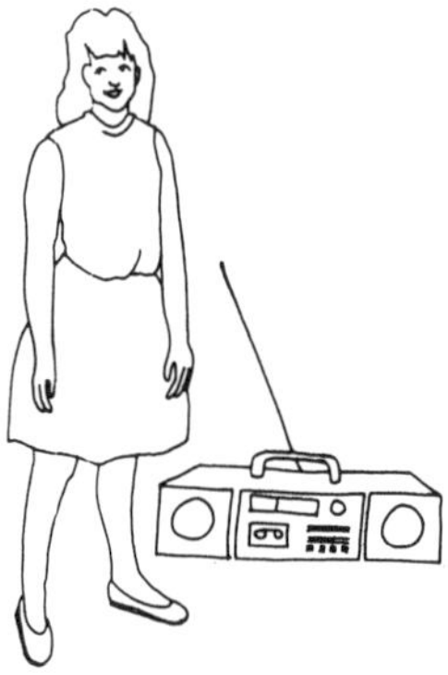

Lisa (14)

Robert (19)

Sarah (2)

Mother (42)

Father (45)

Franky (6)

Jason (10)

ACTIVITIES

- Look at the people illustrated above. Assuming they are your own family, be prepared to describe them in detail. See how much information you need to give before someone recognizes the person you are talking about.

- Draw pictures of fictitious older brothers, older sisters, younger brothers, and younger sisters, or cut out pictures from magazines. Write a story about the person that is true to the picture. Add some more information about interests, assuming that it is **your** family that you are writing about.

  Notes:

  1 Make sure that you really know the words for your own family well before you go on to the next unit.

  2 Don't use ***san*** after your own name or the names of people in your own family.

Writing practice

- Review ***fu*** ふ
  ne ね
  so そ
  go ご

- Review ***okaasan*** おかあさん
  otoosan おとうさん
  Learn ***imooto*** いもうと

- *Katakana* syllables: learn to recognize *TENISU* and *SARA*.
  Learn ***NI*** ニ

- Learn ***SA*** サ

- Review ***TE*** テ
  SU ス
  RA ラ
  TENISU テニス
  SARA サラ

Reading practice

Read the following passage and then answer the questions that follow.

あに　の　なまえ　は　まき　です。
あに　は　まいにち　テニス　を　します。
あに　は　まいにち　まち　に　いきます。
あに　は　まいにち　ほん　を　よみます。

Note: テニス *TENISU* tennis
まち *machi* town

Questions
1 Who does this passage speak about?
2 What does he do?
3 How often does he do this?
4 What is his name?

Read the next *hiragana* passage and then answer the questions that follow.
いもうと　が　います。
いもうと　の　なまえ　は　サラ　です。

いもうと　は　スポーツ　が　すき　です。
まいにち　いもうと　は　まち　に　いきます。
いもうと　は　あたま　が　いい　です。

Questions

1　いもうと　さん　の　なまえ　は　なん　です　か。
2　あたま　が　いい　です　か。
3　どこ　に　いきます　か。
4　なに　が　すき　です　か。

Note: サラ	*SARA*	Sara
スポーツ	*SUPOOTSU*	sports

Unit 4

ごかぞく　は　なんにん　います　か
gokazoku wa nannin imasu ka
How many people are there in your family?

NEW WORDS

ごかぞく	*gokazoku*	someone else's family
きょうだい	*kyoodai*	brothers and sisters
にん	*nin*	counter for people
ひとり	*hitori*	one person
ふたり	*futari*	two people
さんにん	*sannin*	three people
よにん	*yonin*	four people
ごにん	*gonin*	five people
ろくにん	*rokunin*	six people
しちにん	*shichinin*	seven people
はちにん	*hachinin*	eight people
きゅうにん	*kyuunin*	nine people
じゅうにん	*juunin*	ten people
おにいさん	*oniisan*	someone else's older brother
おねえさん	*oneesan*	someone else's older sister
いもうとさん	*imootosan*	someone else's younger sister
おとうとさん	*otootosan*	someone else's younger brother

Note the ***san*** for respect when talking about other people's families. Don't use it for your own family!

Learn these family names **very** carefully so that you don't get them confused.

Maybe the following will help you to keep them straight:

oniisan ***ii*** is tall and straight
oneesan **ee** is soft and feminine

Kim:
ごかぞく　は　なんにん　います　か。 *Gokazoku wa nannin imasu ka.*

Henry:
かぞく　は　ごにん　います。 *Kazoku wa gonin imasu.*

Kim:
おにいさん　が　います　か。 *Oniisan ga imasu ka.*

Henry:
いいえ、あに　は　いません。 *Iie, ani wa imasen.*

Kim:
いもうと　さん　が　います　か。 *Imooto san ga imasu ka.*

Henry:
はい、いもうと　が　います。 *Hai, imooto ga imasu.*
かぞく　は　おかあさん、 *Kazoku wa okaasan,*
おとうさん、　わたし、 *otoosan, watashi,*
いもうと　と　おとうと　です。 *imooto to otooto desu.*

STUDY

- ***Go*** in front of a word has the same function as the honorific ***O*** that you learned in phrases like *Ogenki desu ka.* It is added to show respect for someone else's family. Never use it for your own.

- Learn how to count people, taking particular note of "one person" and "two people".

- Someone asks you: *Imooto san ga imasu ka. Oniisan ga imasu ka* because they are not talking about their own family. They use the "other family" labels.

- Now you can say:
  Ani ga hitori imasu. I have one older brother.
  Ane ga futari imasu. I have two older sisters.
  Note that the number of people is put immediately in front of the verb. The order is: "Older brother one I have."
  Numbers and quantities in Japanese always go in front of the verb.

- When someone asks you how many people there are in your family, they will say: *Gokazoku wa nannin imasu ka*, because they are not talking about their own family. They use the ***wa*** particle because the topic is "your family".
  Likewise, when answering you use the ***wa*** particle: *Kazoku wa gonin imasu.* The topic is "**your** family". Count everybody including yourself.
  Previously, when talking about brothers and sisters you used the ***ga*** particle because you focused on one thing connected with you:
  Anata ***wa*** *oniisan* ***ga*** *imasu ka.*
  "Do you have an older brother?"
  Watashi ***wa*** *ani* ***ga*** *imasu.*
  "I have an older brother."
  Here we ask: "Talking about **you**, the particular thing that I want to know is do you have an older brother?"
  When you are talking about your own family, the ***wa*** particle goes after *kazoku: "Kazoku wa gonin imasu."*

SONG

Juunin no INDIAN

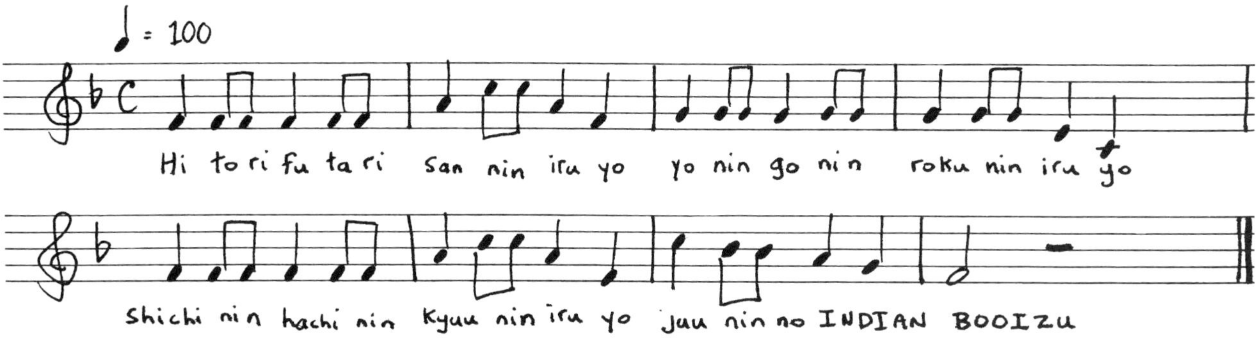
♩ = 100
Hi to ri fu ta ri san nin iru yo yo nin go nin roku nin iru yo
shichi nin hachi nin kyuu nin iru yo juu nin no INDIAN BOOIZU

For your interest only, the *kanji* below show you how *hitori, futari,* etc. are written. You probably recognize the *kanji* for person, *nin.*

The *kanji* before *nin* are the numbers one to ten:

ichi	一
ni	二
san	三
shi/yon	四
go	五
roku	六
nana/shichi	七
hachi	八
kyuu/Ku	九
juu	十

When put together with the *kanji* for person, they become the words you have learned: *hitori, futari, sannin, yonin, gonin, rokunin, shichinin, hachinin, kyuunin, juunin.*

一人 二人 三人 四人 五人

六人 七人 八人 九人 十人

Check your understanding of the conversation at the beginning of this unit.

Kim: How many are there in your family?
Henry: There are five.
Kim: Do you have an older brother?
Henry: No, I don't.
Kim: Do you have a younger sister?
Henry: Yes, I do. My family consists of my mother, father, me, and my younger sister and brother.

ACTIVITIES

- With a partner or around the class, talk about the number of people in your families.

- Practice counting people around the room, up to "ten people". Begin: "One person, two people . . ."

- The following is a list of people. Put them in the correct order from "one person" to "ten people". Check with the New Words list afterwards.
  ごにん　さんにん　じゅうにん　ろくにん
  ひとり　よにん　きゅうにん
  ふたり　はちにん　しちにん

- Which numbers of people are missing in the following list that should be "one person" to "ten people".
  さんにん　ごにん　しちにん　はちにん
  ひとり　よにん　じゅうにん

  Fill in an appropriate "people counter" to complete each of the following sentences. Write out the completed sentences, plus their translation, in your notebook.
  おにいさん が＿＿＿＿＿＿＿＿います か。
  おねえさん が＿＿＿＿＿＿＿＿います か。
  かぞく は＿＿＿＿＿＿＿＿います。
  ＿＿＿＿＿＿＿＿きました。

- Give the English equivalent of the following.
  (Note that the "people counter" always goes in front of the verb.)
  はちにん きました。
  ろくにん いきました。
  まち に ふたり いきました。
  うみ に ごにん いきます。
  うち に ひとり います。

Check your understanding

1 *Ani ga hitori imasu.*
2 *Imooto ga futari imasu.*
3 *Otooto ga sannin imasu.*
4 *Ane ga hitori imasu.*
5 *Ani wa imasen.*
6 *Ane ga futari imasu.*
7 *Imooto wa imasen.*
8 *Otooto ga hitori imasu.*
9 *Imooto ga yonin imasu.*
10 *Ani no namae wa RIKKU desu.*

Match the sentences above with the ones below.

a I have two younger sisters.
b My older brother's name is Rick.
c I have three younger brothers.
f I have no older brothers.
g I have two older sisters.
h I have no younger sisters.

d I have one younger brother.
e I have one older brother.
i I have four younger sisters.
j I have one older sister.

Read the following sentences aloud, and translate them into English. Check against the sentences above to see if you were correct.

1 あに が ひとり います。
2 いもうと が ふたり います。
3 おとうと が さんにん います。
4 あね が ひとり います。
5 あに は いません。
6 あね が ふたり います。
7 いもうと は いません。
8 おとうと が ひとり います。
9 いもうと が よにん います。
10 あに の なまえ は リック です。

Writing practice

- Review **_ku_** く
  Learn **_gu_** ぐ

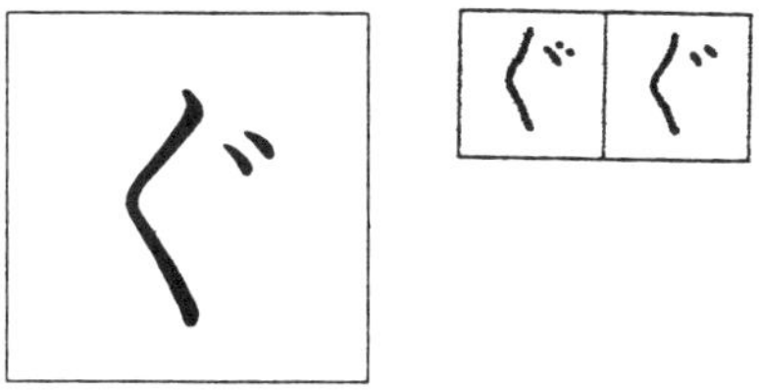

- Review **_ho_** ほ
  Learn **_po_** ぽ

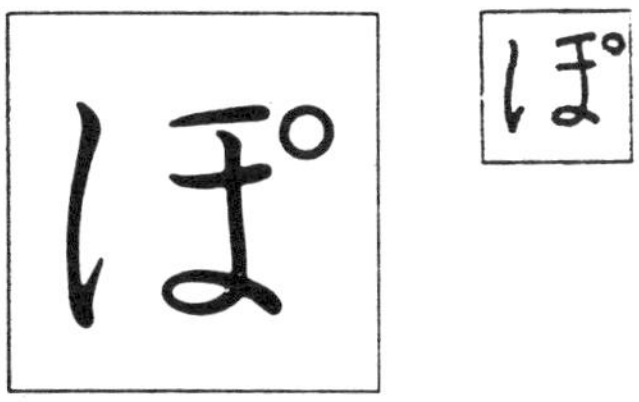

- Review **_ya_** や
  Learn **_gya_** ぎゃ

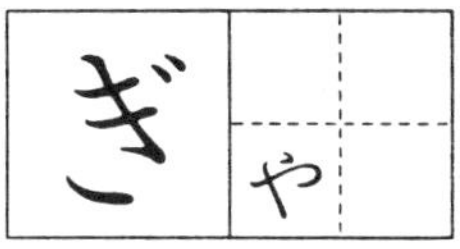

- Review *katakana* words.

Unit 5

おにいさん　が　います　か
oniisan ga imasu ka
Do you have an older brother?

NEW WORDS

ハンサム	*HANSAMU*	handsome/good-looking
ハンサム　じゃない　です/ではありません	*HANSAMU janai desu/ dewa arimasen*	not handsome/ not good looking
きれい	*kirei*	beautiful
きれい　じゃない　です/では　ありません	*kirei janai desu/ dewa arimasen*	not beautiful

Ann:
おにいさん　が　います　か。　*Oniisan ga imasu ka.*

Elizabeth:
はい、あに　が　ふたり　います。　*Hai, ani ga futari imasu.*

Ann:
そう　です　ね。おなまえ　は　なん　です　か。　*Soo desu ne. O namae wa nan desu ka.*

Elizabeth:
マーク　と　トム　です。　*MAAKU to TOMU desu.*

Ann:
なんさい　です　か。　*Nansai desu ka.*

Elizabeth:
マーク　は　じゅうはっさい　です。*MAAKU wa juuhassai desu.*
トム　は　じゅうろくさい　です。　*TOMU wa juurokusai desu.*

Ann:
ハンサム　です　か。　*HANSAMU desu ka.*

Elizabeth:
いいえ、ハンサム　じゃない　です。*Iie, HANSAMU janai desu.*

STUDY

- ***Janai desu***. It is some time since you practiced using *janai* and *dewa arimasen*. Did you remember that they mean the same thing?

- ***HANSAMU*** (which is written in *katakana* because it came from English) and ***kirei*** are both special words in Japanese. They tell us something more about the noun, but they are not true adjectives. (Be very careful with your pronunciation of *kirei*. It is very much like *kirai* in spelling but totally different in meaning!)

  HANSAMU and *kirei* belong to a small group of words called qualitative nouns ("Q Nouns"). We will look at how they behave. You know how to say the following:
  It is not a book.
  Hon dewa arimasen (janai desu).
  It is an umbrella.
  Kasa desu.

  HANSAMU and *kirei* behave in exactly the same way. They follow the *desu* family pattern as shown in the examples above. When you want to say "not handsome" use *HANSAMU dewa arimasen* or *HANSAMU janai desu.* For "not beautiful" use *kirei dewa arimasen* or *kirei janai desu. Kirei* must be learned particularly carefully because it looks like an adjective and you might be tempted to treat it as one.

  Joozu (clever/skillful/good at) is another from the same group. To say "not good at" you therefore say *Joozu janai desu.* Practice using these words in your conversations about families.

- You will learn more about this special group of words as you progress through the course. For the moment be content to memorize these three and the way to use them. Don't worry about remembering their name — qualitative nouns. It only means that you are telling the quality of something, answering the question "What kind of . . .?"

  Adjectives tend to tell you facts about things, not opinions. For example: a **red** car, a **tall** person, a **big** house – all facts. Qualitative nouns will enable you to say what you think about something: "What kind of person is she?" "She's beautiful." "What kind of dog is it?" "It's a clever dog." These two answers may only be your opinion, others may not agree, whereas when using adjectives you would both have to agree, because in most cases the adjectives are telling you facts.

  Using qualitative nouns, you could say things like "I met Mary's older sister yesterday. She's beautiful. (*Kinoo MEERI san no oneesan ni aimashita. Kirei desu ne.*)

- English is not as precise as Japanese. We often say "I saw Mary" when we mean "I met Mary". If you actually met, the Japanese phrase you have to use is ***ni aimasu***. (Remember that *aimasu* usually has the particle *ni* in front of it.)

  If you had only seen Mary in the distance and had not actually come face to face, you would use *mimasu*. If you use *mimasu*, Mary is an object that you had seen in the same way as you see any other object, so you would use the particle ***o***. *MEERI san o mimashita.*

  Look carefully at the following examples:
  Getsuyoobi no niji ni KEN san ni aimashita.
  I saw Ken at two o'clock on Monday.
  Doyoobi no sanji ni MARIA san ni aimasu.

I will see Maria at three o'clock on Saturday.
Kayoobi ni DAN san ni aimasen.
I won't see Dan on Tuesday.
Mokuyoobi no rokuji ni RENE san ni aimasen deshita.
I didn't see Rene at six o'clock on Thursday.
Nichiyoobi no ichiji ni aimashoo.
Let's meet at one o'clock on Sunday.
Practice using this verb in sentences relating to meeting other people's family members.

- Look at the following examples:
  BESU san o mimashita. "I saw Beth" (I didn't talk to her, I just saw her).
  Watashi wa BAABARA san o mimashita. Anata wa BAABARA san o mimashita ka.
  "I saw Barbara. Did you see Barbara?"
  The phrase *o mimasu* is much more limiting than *ni aimasu.*
  If you were going to a rock concert and were going to see your favorite group, you could use *mimasu* only if you were going to see them from a distance.
  Take care – be sure what the intention is when choosing your verb – is it "see" or "meet"?

ACTIVITIES

- Interview each other about your families. Be careful to use the words for other people's families when you ask the questions and your own family words when you reply.
  Report to the group, telling them in Japanese about the person you interviewed.

- Listen to the reports and make notes of the information given. Check with the speaker at the end to see if you took in all the information.

- Michelle is an exchange student on an American Field Scholarship. Here is some information. Figure out the questions you would have to ask Michelle to obtain the information that is given. (Remember you will be talking about someone else's family.)

  Michelle has an older sister. Her name's Rochelle. 17 years old/Studies at a French High School/Likes tennis. Practices tennis every day/Will come to the U.S. in July.

  Michelle has an older brother, Philippe/19 years old/Likes swimming/Sundays goes to the beach and swims/Will also come to the U.S. in July.

  Michelle's mother is Monique/She won't come to the U.S.

  Michelle's father is Claude/He won't come to the U.S. (either)/ Michelle's mother and father will go to Spain (*SUPEIN*) in July.

- Write your questions and the answers Michelle gave you, in Japanese.

- Find the words written below in the *hiragana* list that follows. The words may be written down or across.
  Imperial Goddess
  The present Emperor
  Name of this period of time in Japan
  also
  my own father
  my own mother
  I/me
  father
  mother

あ	ま	て	ら	す	お
き	せ	ら	さ	む	か
ひ	か	ち	ち	へ	あ
と	も	は	は	い	さ
お	か	あ	ね	せ	ん
み	な	ぼ	く	い	あ
わ	た	し	そ	う	し
い	こ	て	え	の	た
お	と	う	さ	ん	く

From the following *hiragana* puzzle, find ten words that belong to family relationships. (The words may be written down or across.)

お	あ	に	ぼ	ち	い
に	か	ぞ	く	ち	も
い	わ	ご	は	は	う
さ	た	お	と	う	と
ん	し	れ	き	あ	ね

- In the next puzzle, find:
  1 Two words that tell you temperature.
  2 Two animals.
  3 One thing you may give as a present.
  4 Two numbers.
  5 Two places you may enjoy visiting.

す	し	あ	つ	い
ず	は	な	か	た
し	れ	わ	た	し
い	ぬ	さ	ん	く
ご	こ	う	え	ん
う	み	さ	ふ	み
の	ね	こ	し	な

- Make cards like the ones below and play Happy Families. Play in groups of three or four. There are five people in each family and there are eight families. Put on the table the cards that tell the composition of each family, so that you know what to ask for.

Kumiko san no kazoku: *otoosan* *okaasan* *imootosan* *otootosan* *Kumiko san* *Nihonjin desu.*	*Kumiko san no otoosan* Age: 46 Name: Jiroo Likes: Tennis	*Kumiko san no okaasan* Age: 42 Name: Kazuko Likes: Cats	*Kumiko san no imootosan* Age: 6 Name: Yukiko Likes: Books	*Kumiko san no otootosan* Age: 8 Name: Masao Likes: Soccer (*SAK-KAA*)
(John) *JON san no kazoku:* *otoosan* *okaasan* *oniisan* *otootosan* *JON san* *AMERIKAjin desu.*	*JON san no otoosan* Age: 46 Name: Jim Likes: Books	*JON san no okaasan* Age: 40 Name: Cathy Likes: Cats	*JON san no oniisan* Age: 19 Name: Carl Likes: Basket-ball	*JON san no otootosan* Age: 11 Name: Richard Likes: Video games
(Megan) *MEEGAN san no kazoku:* *okaasan* *oneesan* *otootosan* *imootosan* *MEEGAN san* *OOSUTORA-RIAjin desu.*	*MEEGAN san no okaasan* Age: 43 Name: Sue Likes: Tennis	*MEEGAN san no oneesan* Age: 18 Name: Mireille Likes: Tennis	*MEEGAN san no otootosan* Age: 12 Name: Sam Likes: Video games	*MEEGAN san no imootosan* Age: 10 Name: Kim Likes: Books
(Chris) *KURISU san no kazoku:* *otoosan* *oneesan* *oniisan* *otootosan* *KURISU san* *IGIRISUjin desu.*	*KURISU san no otoosan* Age: 40 Name: Mark Likes: Soccer (*SAK-KAA*)	*KURISU san no oneesan* Age: 20 Name: Tanya Likes: Tennis	*KURISU san no oniisan* Age: 18 Name: Tim Likes: Soccer	*KURISU san no otootosan* Age: 13 Name: Daniel Likes: Dogs

(Sasha) *SASHA san no kazoku:* *otoosan* *okaasan* *oneesan* *imootosan* *SASHA san* *KANADAjin desu.*	*SASHA san no otoosan* Age: 39 Name: Luke Likes: TV	*SASHA san no okaasan* Age: 39 Name: Hannah Likes: Magazines	*SASHA san no oneesan* Age: 17 Name: Rebecca Likes: Movies	*SASHA san no imootosan* Age: 11 Name: Lucy Likes: Volleyball
(Greer) *GURIA san no kazoku:* *otoosan* *okaasan* *imootosan* *otootosan* *GURIA san* *NYUUJIIRANDOjin desu.*	*GURIA san no otoosan* Age: 47 Name: David Likes: Soccer	*GURIA san no okaasan* Age: 46 Name: Sheila Likes: Parties	*GURIA san no imootosan* Age: 12 Name: Angela Likes: Music	*GURIA san no otootosan* Age: 11 Name: Andrew Likes: Music
(Dion) *DION san no kazoku:* *okaasan* *oniisan* *otootosan* *imootosan* *DION san* *FURANSUjin desu.*	*DION san no okaasan* Age: 44 Name: Sylvie Likes: Music	*DION san no oniisan* Age: 17 Name: Michel Likes: Movies	*DION san no otootosan* Age: 12 Name: Pierre Likes: Music	*DION san no imootosan* Age: 11 Name: Angelique Likes: Parties
(Helena) *HERENA san no kazoku:* *otoosan* *okaasan* *oniisan* *oneesan* *HERENA san* *MEKISHIKOjin desu.*	*HERENA san no otoosan* Age: 47 Name: Luis Likes: Books	*HERENA san no okaasan* Age: 46 Name: Vanessa Likes: Music	*HERENA san no oniisan* Age: 24 Name: Mario Likes: Surfing (*SAAFIN*)	*HERENA san no oneesan* Age: 22 Name: Olivia Likes: Basketball

Your aim is to be the first one to collect a whole family. Ask, for example:
Kumiko san no okaasan ga uchi ni imasu ka.
Is Kumiko's mother at home?

Answer:
Hai, Kumiko san no okaasan ga uchi ni imasu.
Yes, Kumiko's mother is at home.
Or:
Kumiko san no okaasan wa uchi ni imasen.
Kumiko's mother is not at home.

If you are asked the question and you are not holding the card, you become the questioner. If you have the card, you must hand it over, saying *Doozo.* The recipient must say *Arigatoo* or forfeit the card.

If you receive a card it gives you the right to continue asking for other cards until someone says that the person you asked for is not at home.

- (In pairs or small groups.) Using the family cards, take turns giving information about each person on the sheet. Give the person's name and age, and looking at the other members of his or her family, say how many brothers and sisters they have or how many children they have.
  Note: *kyoodai* means "brothers and sisters". For example:

  Kyoodai ga sannin imasu.
  (There are/She has) three brothers and sisters.
  Kodomo ga gonin imasu.
  There are five children.

- Using the family cards find characters who have something in common. For example: tell each other "Both Kazuko and Cathy like cats."

Writing practice

- Review ***he*** へ
  Learn ***pe*** ぺ

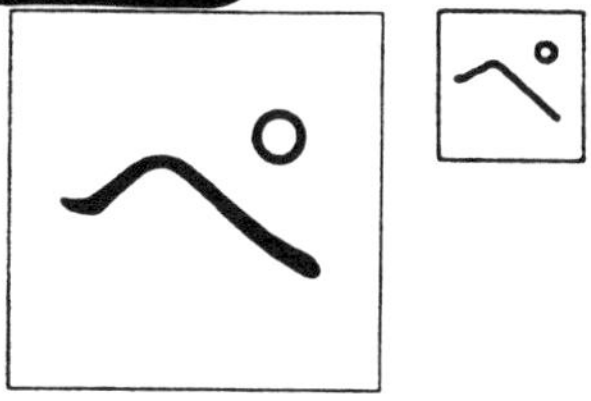

- Review ***fu*** ふ
  Learn ***pu*** ぷ

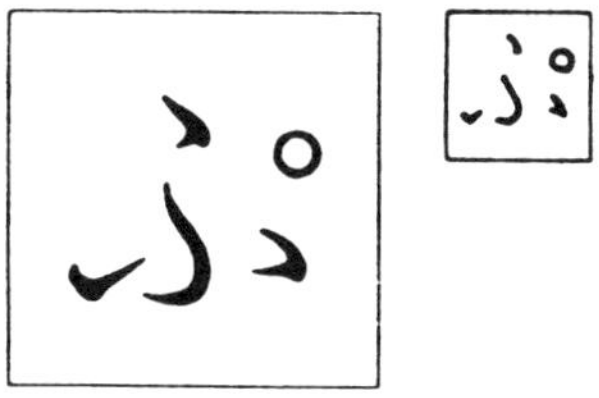

- Review ***bu*** ぶ
- Review ***yu*** ゆ
  Learn ***gyu*** ぎゅ

- Learn to recognize the *katakana* word *AMERIKA*
  アメリカ

Unit 6

STUDY

- If you want to say "either" you can use the ***mo*** particle with a negative verb. Remember that when you use ***mo*** it takes the place of any other particle at this stage of your study. Look at these examples:

Watashi mo ikimasen.	I'm not going either.
KEN san mo kikimasen.	Ken's not going to listen either.
Hon mo yomimasen.	I won't read books either.
Gakkoo ni mo ikimasen ka.	Aren't you going to school either?
Manga mo yomimasen ka.	Don't you read comics either?
REKOODO mo kikimasen deshita.	I didn't listen to the record either.
Watashi mo imooto wa imasen.	I don't have a younger sister either.

So now you can say "I didn't go" *Ikimasen deshita.* You can ask: "Did you go?" with *Ikimashita ka.* And you can understand when a friend replies: *Watashi mo ikimasen deshita.* "I didn't go either".

- ***mo . . . mo*** **Both** and **neither**
Study the following sentences carefully:
Watashi mo HANA mo ikimasu.
Both Hannah and I will go. (I too, Hannah too, will go)
(I also, Hannah also, will go)
BOBU mo ADAMU mo zasshi o yomimasu.
Both Bob and Adam read magazines.
(Or) Both Bob and Adam are going to read the magazines.
(Remember the *masu* form of verbs can be future or habitual action.)

- **Neither**
We want to say "Neither Nicky nor Brian will go." or "Neither Nicky nor Brian go." To say "**neither**", use the negative form of the verb with ***mo . . . mo***. For example:
SARA mo NIKKI mo ikimasen.
Neither Sarah nor Nicky will go.
Ani mo ane mo ikimasen.
Neither my older brother nor my older sister will go.
FIONA san no otootosan mo watashi no imooto mo hanashimasen.
Neither Fiona's little brother nor my little sister will talk
BEN mo PATTO mo benkyoo shimasen.
Neither Ben nor Pat studies.
SUU mo KAIRI mo PIANO o renshuu shimasen.
Neither Sue nor Kylie practices the piano.
KIMU mo KEBIN mo nihongo o benkyoo shimasen.
Neither Kim nor Kevin studies Japanese.
Watashi mo SHARON mo FURANSUgo o hanashimasen.
Neither Sharon nor I speak French as a native language.
(Extension: we could extend the last sentence by saying *Watashi mo KANADAjin no SHARON mo FURANSUgo o hanashimasen.* Neither I nor Sharon, who is a Canadian, speak French as a native language.)

ACTIVITIES

- Make sentences with a partner giving information about family members that includes things like "Both my older brother and my younger brother play tennis" or "Neither my younger sister nor my younger brother likes dogs."

- Use the family cards introduced earlier in this topic to say things like:
  Jiroo san mo JIMU san mo yonjuurokusai desu.
  Both Jiroo and Jim are forty-six years old.
  Kazuko san mo Yukiko san mo TENISU o shimasen.
  Neither Kazuko nor Yukiko plays tennis.
  When you have composed ten sentences read them to another pair and get them to tell you what they mean. Switch roles and see if you can understand their sentences.

Check your understanding

How would you say the following in Japanese?

1 I haven't met your older sister either.
2 Have you met John's older brother?
3 I have two older sisters.
4 I saw both Henry and Fred yesterday.
5 Did you meet my younger sister Ann?
6 Neither Janet's younger sister nor Jim's younger brother came to my party.
7 I have one older sister and two younger brothers.
8 I don't have an older sister.
9 Do you have a younger brother?
10 You haven't met my younger brother Sam.

Answers

1 *Oneesan mo aimasen deshita.*
2 *JON san no oniisan ni aimashita ka.*
3 *Ane ga futari imasu.*
4 *Kinoo HENRI san mo FUREDDO san mo mimashita.*
5 *Imooto no AN ni aimashita ka.*
6 *JANETTO san no imootosan mo JIMU san no otootosan mo watashi no PAATII ni kimasen deshita.*
7 *Watashi wa ane ga hitori imasu, otooto ga futari imasu.*
8 *Ane wa imasen.*
9 *Otootosan ga imasu ka.*
10 *(Anata wa) Otooto no SAMU ni aimasen deshita.*

Those were difficult. If you could do most of them correctly, then: *Taihen yoku dekimashita* — **very** well done. If you made some mistakes don't worry about it but find out what you were doing incorrectly and get it right now. Did you remember not to use *san* for members of your own family?

Writing practice

- Review ***hi*** ひ
  Learn ***pi*** ぴ

- Review ***go*** ご

- Learn ***pa*** ぱ

- Learn ***gyo*** ぎょ

ACTIVITIES

- With a partner, review all the verbs you know, saying that someone else does that too: e.g. *JON san mo manga o yomimasu.* John reads comics too. With the same partner go through all the verbs as before saying that someone does not do that thing **either**.
  e.g. *SANDORA san mo ikimasen.* Sandra is not going to go either.

- Make up questions to ask your partner that require a "Neither (David) nor (Mark) . . ." answer.

- You learned previously how to say "I'll meet you at . . ." or "I play soccer on Mondays" etc. Make up a conversation in which you meet someone after a long time:
  Greet.
  Ask about other people you both know.
  Ask if someone does something **too**.
  Give news about others using comments like "John came too" and "Sam didn't come either" "My brother is . . ." "Last week my sister went to . . ." "Did your younger brother play . . . yesterday?" Say that you will meet again at a particular time, on a particular day, or just say goodbye if you don't want further contact, using *Sorosoro shitsurei shimasu.*

- Look at the Activities and People chart on the following page and construct sentences to include all the information.

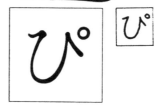

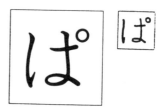

1 Won't play tennis Paula Next Thursday	8 Let's go to the library Fiona and Tania Next Wednesday at 3:30
2 Did not return home Jake Last Thursday	9 Won't watch TV Beth Next week
3 Won't come to school Brett Tomorrow	10 Did not clean the house Patricia Last week
4 Let's go to the park Cherie and friends Tomorrow	11 Won't read comics Jacky Today
5 Won't play video games Stuart Tomorrow	12 Didn't watch video games Jamie Yesterday
6 Did not come to party Susan Yesterday	13 Didn't go to the movies Peter Last Friday
7 Did not watch TV John Last Saturday	14 Didn't go to the library Christine Last Friday

15 Won't go to the park with John June Next Sunday	23 Practice guitar Sally Tuesdays, Thursdays, Fridays
16 Tennis Jan Today at 3 p.m.	24 Go to library Maria Tuesdays
17 Basketball Paul Yesterday at 2 p.m.	25 Watch TV Alexandra Today 4 o'clock
18 Study Jane Every day	26 Volleyball Ken Next Monday 9 o'clock
19 Meet friends Ben Sunday 10 o'clock	27 Cleaning John's mother Every day
20 Return home Steve Next Wednesday 6 o'clock	28 Read Mike Saturday evenings
21 Soccer Tom Tomorrow 1 o'clock	29 Come to the party Elizabeth Friday 7 o'clock
22 Movies Nicky Next Saturday 5 o'clock	30 Volleyball Philip Last Saturday 2:30

Unit 7

しごと
shigoto
work

NEW WORDS

Here are a few job names for interest only.

かんごふ	*kangofu*	nurse
おいしゃ	*oisha*	doctor
はいしゃ	*haisha*	dentist
べんごし	*bengoshi*	lawyer
しゅふ	*shufu*	housewife
みせ　の　ひと	*mise no hito*	shop assistant/store clerk
かいしゃいん	*kaishain*	office worker
うんてんしゅ	*untenshu*	driver
エンジニア	*ENJINIA*	engineer
せんせい	*sensei*	teacher
だいく	*daiku*	carpenter
えきいん	*ekiin*	railway (station) worker
しごと	*shigoto*	work/job

Liam is doing a survey on jobs for his economics class.

Liam:
すみません、ごかぞく　は　なんにん　います　か。
Sumimasen, gokazoku wa nannin imasu ka.

Justin:
ごにん　です。おとうさん　と　おかあさん　と　あに　と　あね　と　わたし　です。
Gonin desu. Otoosan to okaasan to ani to ane to watashi desu.

Liam:
おかあさん　は　しごと　を　します　か。
Okaasan wa shigoto o shimasu ka.

Justin:
はい、そう　です。
Hai, soo desu.

Liam:
おかあさん　の　しごと　は　なん　です　か。
Okaasan no shigoto wa nan desu ka.

Justin:
おかあさん　は　かんごふ　です。
Okaasan wa kangofu desu.

Liam:
おとうさん　の　しごと　は　なん　です　か。
Otoosan no shigoto wa nan desu ka.

Justin:
おとうさん　は　べんごし　です。 *Otoosan wa bengoshi desu.*

Liam:
おにいさん　の　しごと　は　なん　です　か。 *Oniisan no shigoto wa nan desu ka.*

Justin:
あに　は　みせ　の　ひと　です。 *Ani wa mise no hito desu.*

Liam:
おねえさん　の　しごと　は　なん　です　か。 *Oneesan no shigoto wa nan desu ka.*

Justin:
あね　は　かいしゃいん　です。 *Ane wa kaishain desu.*

Liam:
ありがとう　ございます。 *Arigatoo gozaimasu.*
(He asks another student)

Liam:
ごかぞく　は　なんにん　います　か。 *Gokazoku wa nannin imasu ka.*

Terry:
かぞく　は　さんにん　います。 *Kazoku wa sannin imasu.*
おかあさん　と　おとうさん　と　わたし　です。 *Okaasan to otoosan to watashi desu.*

Liam:
おかあさん　の　しごと　は　なん　です　か。 *Okaasan no shigoto wa nan desu ka.*

Terry:
おかあさん　は　しゅふ　です。 *Okaasan wa shufu desu.*
(He continues his survey in this way around the whole group.)

Read as much as possible of the *hiragana*, aloud. Any syllables you don't know check with the word list and then continue. When you have finished, read it to a partner who will follow the text carefully to see if you are correct.

ACTIVITIES

- Using the sentence patterns in this unit, do a survey in your class to find out the size and composition of families. Make a graph to show how many people are from each size of family.

- Make a second graph to show the composition of those families:
  how many boys/girls;
  how many people have brothers/sisters, etc.

- Draw a family tree of your own family, or a fictitious one, and label it in Japanese. Put the age of each person beneath the name. Use the family tree below as a model if you wish.

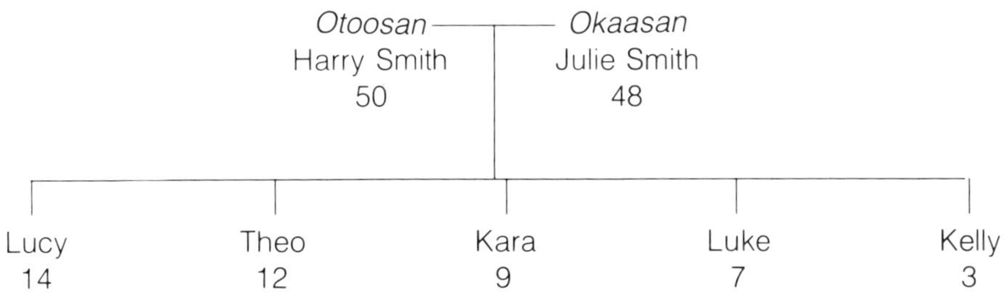

Substitute your own name for one of the above. Label yourself *Watashi* or *Boku* if you are male. Go through your family, carefully explaining the relationship to you. (You will therefore be using your "own family" labels)

- Using several of the family trees, get together, in groups or pairs, to explain the relationships in each different family, remembering that they will be "other family" labels.

- Figure out how many different things you are able to say about yourself, members of your family, or friends. Compare it with the list below:

  Name
  Age
  Nationality
  Native language
  Physical characteristics
  Student/not student
  School attended
  What year student
  Subjects studied at school
  Likes and dislikes
  Leisure time activities
  Sports played
  Friends
  Family members
  Where they've been recently
  What they've done recently
  What they are going to do today/soon
  When their birthdays are

Writing practice

- Review ***pi*** ぴ
- Learn ***pya*** ぴゃ

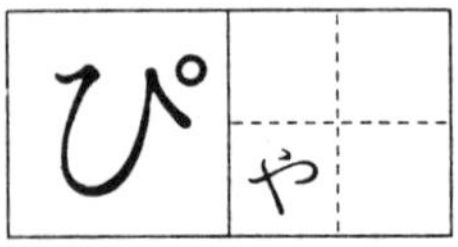

- Learn ***pyu*** ぴゅ

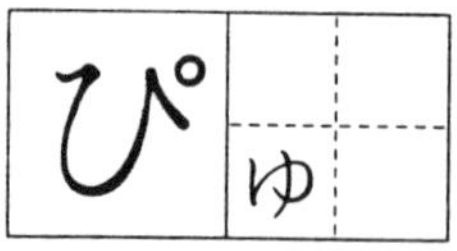

- Learn ***pyo*** ぴょ

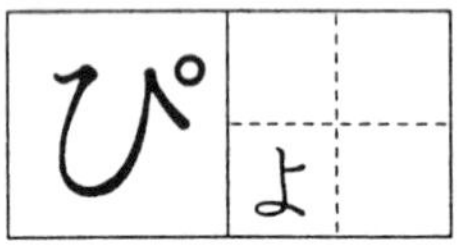

- Learn ***bya*** びゃ

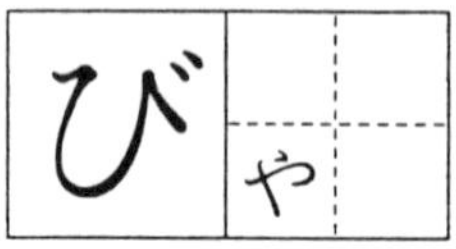

- Learn ***byu*** びゅ

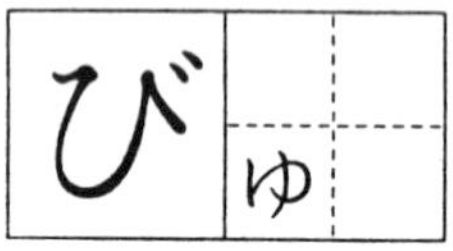

- Learn ***byo*** びょ

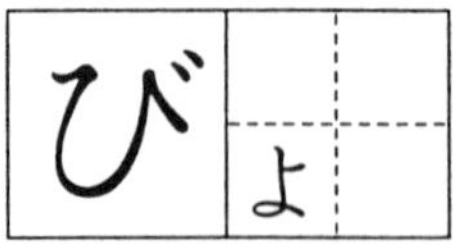

Unit 8

ともだち
tomodachi
Friends

Read the first dialogue in this unit without looking up any vocabulary or grammar and see how much you understand. After you have read it and figured out the meaning, check that your understanding was correct.

Two people meet at a party, set out to find out about each other, and decide to meet again.

A:	
こんばん　は。	*Konban wa.*
B:	
こんばん　は。おなまえ　は　なん　です　か。	*Konban wa. Onamae wa nan desu ka.*
A:	
わたし　の　なまえ　は　クリス　です。	*Watashi no namae wa KURISU desu.*
あなた　の　なまえ　は　なん　です　か。	*Anata no namae wa nan desu ka.*
B:	
バーバラ　です。どこ　の　かた　です　か。	*BAABARA desu. Doko no kata desu ka.*
A:	
イギリスじん　です。あなた　は。	*IGIRISUjin desu. Anata wa.*
B:	
ニュージーランドじん　です。	*NYUUJIIRANDOjin desu.*
スポーツ　を　します　か。	*SUPOOTSU o shimasu ka.*
A:	
はい、スポーツ　が　すき　です。	*Hai, SUPOOTSU ga suki desu.*
あなた　は。	*Anata wa.*
B:	
わたし　は　バスケットボール　や　テニス　を　します。	*Watashi wa BASUKETTOBOORU ya TENISU o shimasu.*
A:	
テニス　が　すき　です　か。	*TENISU ga suki desu ka.*
B:	
はい、あした　テニス　を　しましょう　か。	*Hai, ashita TENISU o shimashoo ka.*

A:	
はい、そう　しましょう。	*Hai, soo shimashoo.*
B:	
すみません　が…あなた　の でんわ　ばんごう　は　なん です　か。	*Sumimasen ga . . . anata no denwa bangoo wa nan desu ka.*
A:	
さん　きゅう　さん　の　に　ろく ぜろ　ご。	*San kyuu san no ni roku zero go.*
あなた　の　でんわ　ばんごう は。	*Anata no denwa bangoo wa.*
B:	
ご　はち　きゅう　の　ろく　ぜろ きゅう ぜろ です。あした　でんわ して　ください。じゃ　また。	*Go hachi kyuu no roku zero kyuu zero desu. Ashita denwa shite kudasai. Ja mata.*
A:	
じゃ　また。	*Ja mata.*

Check your understanding

Here is the translation of the conversation.

A: Hi (Good evening).
B: Hi (Good evening). What's your name?
A: Chris. What's yours?
B: Barbara. Where do you come from?
A: I'm English. What about you?
B: I'm a New Zealander. Do you play sports?
A: Yes, I like sports. How about you?
B: I play tennis and basketball etc.
A: Do you like tennis?
B: Yes, shall we play tennis tomorrow?
A: Yes, let's do that.
B: Excuse me but . . . wnat's your telephone number?
A: 393-2605. What's yours?
B: 589-6090. Please call me tomorrow. See You.
A: See you.

ACTIVITIES

- You know all the constructions used in the above conversation. Practice reading and role playing the conversation. Add information of your own.

- Review nationalities. With a partner, write a profile of one person from the chart in Unit 6. Decide whether you will write it in *hiragana* or *roomaji*. Don't tell the rest of the class which character you are writing about. Don't indicate the name or nationality of the character. Each person will write their own copy of the information. These copies are then given to another pair, who will try to identify the character before any other pairs have solved theirs.

Unit 9

だれ です か
dare desu ka
Who's that?

Tomodachi

In the following conversation Junji and Simon are looking at a photo of one of Junji's friends, who is in Japan.

Simon:
だれ　です　か。 *Dare desu ka.*

Junji:
じろう　くん　です。わたし　の　いい　ともだち　です。 *Jiroo kun desu. Watashi no ii tomodachi desu.*

Simon:
じろう　さん　は　スポーツ　が　すき　です　か。 *Jiroo san wa SUPOOTSU ga suki desu ka.*

Junji:
はい、バスケットボール　を　します。 *Hai, BASUKETTOBOORU o shimasu.*

Simon:
あなた　は　スポーツ　が　すき　です　か。 *Anata wa SUPOOTSU ga suki desu ka.*

Junji:
はい、サッカー　が　すき　です。 *Hai, SAKKAA ga suki desu.*

Reading practice

In the dialogue above:

1 What is the name of the person being discussed in the photo.
2 Is the person male or female? (How do you know?)
3 What does the person like to do?
4 What sport does Junji like?

Use the following passage for practice in reading aloud, reading comprehension, and/or listening comprehension.

Kore wa watashi no ii tomodachi desu.
This is my good friend.

NEW WORDS

かぞく	*kazoku*	your own family (review)
と いっしょ に	*to issho ni*	together with
そして	*soshite*	and then
ちゃん	*chan*	(girl) friend or used by parents for daughters

Tomodachi no Tomoko chan wa watashi no ii tomodachi desu. Ii seito desu. Atama ga ii desu. Kirei desu. Watashi wa kirei janai desu. Mainichi watashi wa Tomoko chan to hachiji ni gakkoo ni ikimasu.

Getsuyoobi no juuniji ni BASUKETTOBOORU o shimasu.

Kayoobi no yoji ni machi no toshokan ni ikimasu. Watashi no uchi ni kaerimasu. Toshokan no hon o yomimasu. Soshite Tomoko chan to issho ni shukudai o shimasu.

Suiyoobi no niji ni machi no mise o mimasu. Yoji ni kaerimasu.

Mokuyoobi no goji ni watashi wa Tomoko chan to tomodachi to eigo no renshuu o shimasu. Soshite TEREBI o mimasu.

Kinyoobi ni Tomoko chan to GITAA no renshuu o shimasu.

Doyoobi no niji ni watashi wa Tomoko chan no uchi ni ikimasu. Tomoko chan no otoosan to okaasan ga suki desu. Itsumo Tomoko chan no kazoku to issho ni kooen ni ikimasu. Tomoko chan mo watashi mo TENISU o shimasu. Tomoko chan no GEEMU o mimasu. Soshite Tomoko chan wa kazoku to watashi no GEEMU o mimasu. Tomoko chan no uchi ni kaerimasu. Goji ni eiga ni ikimasu. Juuji ni kaerimasu.

Nichiyoobi wa Tomoko chan ni aimasen. Watashi wa chichi to haha to issho ni ani no uchi ni ikimasu. Getsuyoobi wa mata Tomoko chan ni aimasu. Ii tomodachi desu ne!

See how much you can read and understand of the *hiragana* version below.

ともだち の ともこ ちゃん は わたしの いい ともだち です。
いい せいと です。あたま が いい です。きれい です。わたし は
きれい じゃない です。まいにち わたし は ともこ ちゃん と
はちじ に がっこう に いきます。
げつようび の じゅうにじ に バスケットボール を します。
かようび の よじ に まち の としょかん に いきます。わたし
の うち に かえります。としょかん の ほん を よみます。そして
ともこ ちゃん と いっしょ に しゅくだい を します。
すいようび の にじ に まち の みせ を みます。よじ に
かえります。
もくようび の ごじ に わたし は ともこ ちゃん と ともだち
と えいご の れんしゅう を します。そして テレビ を みます。
きんようび に ともこ ちゃん と ギター の れんしゅう を
します。どようび の にじ に わたし は ともこ ちゃん の
うち に いきます。
ともこ ちゃん の おとうさん と おかあさん が すき です。
いつも ともこ ちゃん の かぞく と いっしょ に こうえん に
いきます。ともこ ちゃん も わたし も テニス を します。

ともこ　ちゃん　の　ゲーム　を　みます。そして　ともこ　ちゃん　は　かぞく　と　わたし　の　ゲーム　を　みます。ともこ　ちゃん　の　うち　に　かえります。ごじ　に　えいが　に　いきます。じゅうじ　に　かえります。
にちようび　は　ともこ　ちゃん　に　あいません。わたし　は　ちち　と　はは　と　いっしょ　に　あに　の　うち　に　いきます。
げつようび　は　また　ともこ　ちゃん　に　あいます。いい　ともだち　です　ね。

Answer the questions in English:

1 What is the name of my friend? Male or Female?
2 Who is clever?
3 What time do we go to school each day?
4 What do we do at lunchtime on Monday?
5 What are three things we do together on Tuesday?
6 When do we practice English?
7 What musical instruments do we play?
8 Where do I go on Saturday? With whom?
9 Why don't I see Tomoko on Sunday?
10 Who watches my tennis match?

Answers

1 Tomoko (Female).
2 Tomoko.
3 Eight o'clock.
4 Basketball.
5 Go to the town library, go back to my house, read library books, do homework.
6 Thursday.
7 Guitar.
8 Tomoko's family.
9 I go to my older brother's house with my family.
10 Tomoko and her family.

STUDY

- Talking about ***san***, ***chan***, and ***kun***

  San is a bit formal. If Japanese people don't know a person very well, they would use their family name (surname), followed by *san* rather than their first name. For example, Hisako Miyamoto would be called *Miyamoto san*.

  Teachers call students by their family names, not their first names, and often don't even know the first name!

  Most students in Japan who are good friends give each other nicknames or use ***chan*** after the name for girls and ***kun*** for boys, e.g. *Kumiko chan, Hiroshi kun.*

  However, for foreigners, Japanese people don't use *san*, *chan*, or *kun* after first names, once they have become good friends. At first they will call you by your family name, followed by *san.* Once you have gotten to know them a little they may call you by your first name, plus *san.* But once you have become good friends they will probably leave out the *san*, and just use your first name the same way that we do.

So if you listen to Japanese people talking, you can figure out how friendly they are from these clues.

There will always be exceptions, depending on the way the people you meet have been brought up, but in general you can accept this information as true. Remember, though, you never use *san* for yourself or your family members.

- Write an outline of what you do with your friends each day.
- In pairs, read your outlines aloud to each other about three sentences at a time. Ask each other questions in English to test how much has been understood.
- Rewrite your outline in the past tense, changing all the *masu* forms to *mashita, masen* forms to *masen deshita.*
- Read or listen to the following passage about Glenn's trip to Washington.

KAPITORU The Capitol

Senshuu watashi wa gakkoo no tomodachi to WASHINTON ni ikimashita.

Getsuyoobi ni KAPITORU o mimashita, BASUKETTOBOORU o renshuu shimashita.

Kayoobi ni WASHINTON no gakusei to BASUKETTOBOORU o shimashita. Ii Otenki deshita. Ii GEEMU deshita.

Suiyoobi wa kaze to ame deshita. Warui Otenki deshita kara WASHINTON ga suki dewa arimasen deshita.

Mokuyoobi no hachiji ni NYUUYOOKU ni kaerimashita. Mata ani to otoosan ni aimashita.

See how much you can read and understand of the *hiragana* version below.

カピトル

せんしゅう　わたし　は　がっこう　の　ともだち　と　ワシントン　に
いきました。げつようび　に　カピトル　を　みました。
バスケットボール　を　れんしゅう　しました。かようび　に
ワシントン　の　がくせい　と　バスケットボール　を　しました。
いい　おてんき　でした。いい　ゲーム　でした。
すいようび　は　かぜ　と　あめ　でした。わるい　おてんき　でした
から　ワシントン　が　すき　では　ありません　でした。もくようび
の　はちじ　に　ニュー　ヨーク　に　かえりました。また　あに　と
おとうさん　に　あいました。

バスケットボール	*BASUKETTOBOORU*	basketball
ゲーム	*GEEMU*	game
カピトル	*KAPITORU*	The Capitol
ワシントン	*WASHINTON*	Washington
ニューヨーク	*NYUUYOOKU*	New York

Questions to answer in English:

1 Where did Glenn go?
2 When?
3 With whom?
4 What was the first thing they did?
5 What did they do on Tuesday?
6 Did they enjoy it? How do you know?
7 What was the weather like on Monday and Tuesday?
8 Why did Glenn decide he didn't like Washington?
9 What day and time did they return to New York?
10 Who met him?

Read or listen to the following passage about Kathy.
KYASHII wa KARIFORUNIA no SANFURANSHISUKO ni sunde imasu. Watashi no ii tomodachi desu. KYASHII no kazoku wa yonin imasu. Otoosan to okaasan to KYASHII to imootosan ga imasu. Imootosan no namae wa KERI desu.

KYASHII wa juugosai desu. KYASHII wa FURANSUgo o benkyoo shimasu. Gogatsu ni PARI ni ikimashita. FURANSUgo o renshuu shimashita. KYASHII wa PARI ga suki deshita. Ima KYASHII wa FURANSUjin no tomodachi ga imasu.

See how much you can read of the *hiragana* version below.

キャシー　は　カリフォルニア　の　サンフラシスコ　に　すんで　います。
わたし　の　いい　ともだち　です。キャシー　の　かぞく　は　よにん
います。おとうさん　と　おかあさん　と　キャシー　と　いもうとさん
が　います。いもうとさん　の　なまえ　は　ケリ　です。キャシー
は　じゅうごさい　です。キャシー　は　フランスご　を　べんきょう
します。ごがつ　に　パリ　に　いきました。フランスご　を
れんしゅう　しました。キャシー　は　パリ　が　すき　でした。
いま　キャシー　は　フランスじん　の　ともだち　が　います。

キャシー	*KYASHII*	Kathy
カリフォルニア	*KARIFORUNIA*	California
サンフランシスコ	*SANFURANSHISUKO*	San Francisco
ケリ	*KERI*	Kelly
パリ	*PARI*	Paris
フランスご	*FURANSUgo*	French language

Answer the questions that follow in English or Japanese. If you choose to answer the questions in Japanese, choose whether to write in *hiragana* and copy the *katakana* words carefully from the text, or use *roomaji*.

1 What nationality is Kathy?
2 Where does she live?
3 What do you know about her family?
4 When did Kathy go to Paris?
5 What was the result of the visit?

Look at the photo below and using the code key in Topic Six, Review, figure out what the caption says.

Code caption 2
2.18/6./13.40.12./11.24./37

Waiting for friends can be nerve-wracking! Decipher the code caption for this photo.

Code caption 3
10.4.14/46/45.48.51.15/
6./12.25./13.7.24.2.

Writing practice

- Review ***ki*** き
- Learn ***kya*** きゃ

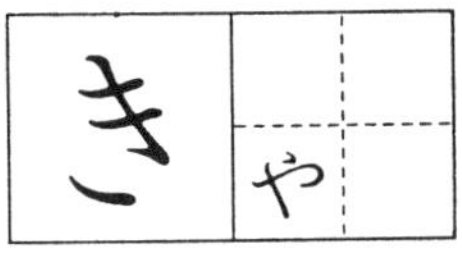

- Learn ***kyo*** きょ

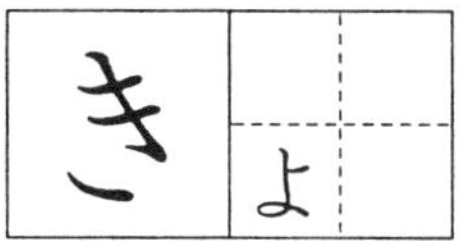

- From ***kyo*** you can make ***kyoo*** きょう

Unit 10

どこ　に　すんで　います　か
doko ni sunde imasu ka
Where do you live?

NEW WORDS

(Review)		
おおきい	*ookii*	big
ちいさい	*chiisai*	small
(New)		
アパート	*APAATO*	apartment
うち	*uchi*	your own house
せまい	*semai*	cramped/narrow
ひろい	*hiroi*	spacious/wide
どこ　に	*Doko ni*	
すんで　います　か。	*sunde imasu ka.*	Where do you live?

Anne is showing photos of her home, family and friends to a Japanese girl she has met at school.

Anne:
これ　は　わたし　の　かぞく　です。 — *Kore wa watashi no kazoku desu.*
おかあさん　です。おとうさん　です。 — *Okaasan desu. Otoosan desu.*
わたし　です。 — *Watashi desu.*

Hiroko:
そう　です　か。あなた　の　うち　です　か。 — *Soo desu ka. Anata no uchi desu ka.*

Anne:
はい、わたし　の　うち　です。 — *Hai, watashi no uchi desu.*

Hiroko:
おおきい　です　ね。 — *Ookii desu ne.*
どこ　に　すんで　います　か。 — *Doko ni sunde imasu ka.*

Anne:
シアトル　に　すんで　います。 — *SHIATORU ni sunde imasu.*

Hiroko:
そう　です　か。わたし　は — *Soo desu ka. Watashi wa*
なごや　に　すんで　います。 — *Nagoya ni sunde imasu.*
わたし　の　うち　は　ちいさい — *Watashi no uchi wa chiisai*

です。アパート　です。せまい	*desu. APAATO desu. Semai*
です。あなた　の　うち　は	*desu. Anata no uchi wa*
ひろい　です　ね。	*hiroi desu ne.*

Japanese homes in general are very much smaller than Western homes. Japanese students visiting other countries are often surprised by the size of rooms they are given to use. Many feel rather insecure with so much space around them and may close the curtains even in the daytime to make themselves feel more comfortable.

STUDY

- **Reminder – using adjectives**. Adjectives can be put right in front of *desu*, e.g. *chiisai desu* It is small, or *ookii desu* It is big. Later you will learn other ways to use them.

  Do you remember how to make the negative? **Take off the *i* and add *kunai***. For example:

  ookii desu is big　　*ookikunai desu* is not big
  chiisai desu is small　　*chiisakunai desu* is not small

ACTIVITIES

- Take turns giving the meaning of the following sentences. Answer are on the following page.

1	*Inu wa chiisai desu.*	7	*Uchi wa chiisakunai desu.*
2	*Kaban wa ookii desu.*	8	*Ima suzushikunai desu.*
3	*Kyoo wa atsui desu.*	9	*Mushiatsui desu ne.*
4	*Sensei wa ii desu.*	10	*Ii otenki desu.*
5	*Ashita samui deshoo.*	11	*Warui inu desu.*
6	*Neko wa ookikunai desu.*	12	*Neko wa warukunai desu.*

- Now how would you say the opposite of all the sentences above?

- Jumbled sentences. Match them with the sentences above and put them in the correct order.
  - a *suzushikunai ima desu*
  - b *desu kyoo atsui wa*
  - c *ookii desu wa kaban*
  - d *desu otenki ii*
  - e *wa chiisakunai uchi desu*
  - f *ne desu mushiatsui*
  - g *inu warui desu*
  - h *wa desu warukunai neko*
  - i *inu wa desu chiisai*
  - j *ii sensei wa desu*
  - k *samui deshoo ashita*
  - l *ookikunai neko desu wa*

- More jumbled sentences. Put the words in the correct order.
  1. *desu chiisai wa inu*
  2. *ookii desu uchi wa*
  3. *uchi chiisakunai desu wa*
  4. *no anata uchi ka desu*
  5. *ka anata no uchi ookii chiisai ka desu desu wa*

- Work in pairs or a small group. Imagine that you are talking about friends you made in Japan on a trip last year.

  Bring out your map of Japan and be prepared to say where your friend lives and show your friends where that place is on the map. Each person takes a different person to talk about from the information below.
  Kimiko lives in Tokyo, she's seventeen and in high school. She's beautiful. She doesn't like sports.

  Masao lives in Hokkaido, he's sixteen and is in high school in Sapporo. He's not handsome but you like him a lot. He plays basketball.

  Saki is fourteen and is in junior high school. He's short. He lives in Nara, likes dogs, doesn't like piano practice.

  Saki is fourteen and is at junior high school. He's short. He lives in Nara, likes dogs, doesn't like piano practice.

  Now continue to make up brief profiles from your own imagination about your friends who live in other cities in Japan.

  Not all of them need to be Japanese! Make sure that you use your maps well to point out where these people live, to help all of your group to become more familiar with Japanese place names.

Answers

1. The dog is small.
2. The bag is big.

3 It's hot today.
4 The teacher is good.
5 Tomorrow will probably be cold.
6 The cat isn't big.
7 The house isn't small.
8 It's not cool now.
9 It's humid, isn't it?
10 It's good weather.
11 It's a bad dog.
12 The cat isn't bad.

(Opposites)
1 *Inu wa ookii desu.*
2 *Kaban wa chiisai desu.*
3 *Kyoo wa samui desu.*
4 *Sensei wa warui desu.*
5 *Ashita atsui deshoo.*
6 *Neko wa chiisakunai desu.*
7 *Uchi wa ookikunai desu.*
8 *Ima atatakakunai desu.*
9 *Mushiatsukunai desu ne.*
10 *Ii otenki dewa arimasen.*
11 *Ii inu desu.*
12 *Neko wa ii desu.*

1 i
2 c
3 b
4 j
5 k
6 l
7 e
8 a
9 f
10 d
11 g
12 h

1 *Inu wa chiisai desu.*
2 *Uchi wa ookii desu.*
3 *Uchi wa chiisakunai desu.*
4 *Anata no uchi desu ka.*
5 *Anata no uchi wa chiisai desu ka, ookii desu ka.*

STUDY

Anne shows Hiroko a photo of her friend Robert.

Anne:
わたし　の　ともだち　です。 *Watashi no tomodachi desu.*

Hiroko:
ともだち　の　なまえ　は　なん　です　か。 *Tomodachi no namae wa nan desu ka.*

Anne:
「Robert」です。 *"Robert" desu.*

Hiroko:
ハンサム　です　ね。 *HANSAMU desu ne.*

They look at a third photo.
Hiroko:
こども　は　だれ　です　か。 *Kodomo wa dare desu ka.*

Anne:
ケイティー　さん　です。ちいさい　です。よんさい　です。 *KEITII san desu. Chisaii desu. Yonsai desu.*

Hiroko:
これ　は　あなた　の　いぬ　です　か。 *Kore wa anata no inu desu ka.*

Ane:
はい、いぬ　の　なまえ　は「*Pooch*」です。 *Hai, inu no namae wa "Pooch" desu.*

ACTIVITIES

- Practice reading the conversation aloud with a friend. Add on more information of your own.
  Practice reading it through, then read it to the rest of the class or to another pair. Then listen to their version.
- Cover the *roomaji* version and see how much of the *hiragana* version you can now read without looking anything up.
- Write the English equivalent of the two dialogues.

STUDY

- Long before this you used *sumimasen ga* to say "Excuse me, but . . ." In the following conversation, ***ga*** is used to say "but" between two sentences. It doesn't have any direct link with the particle ***ga*** that you know as the particle you use to focus on something in particular. The only link is the fact that when you say "but" you are focusing someone's attention on the way you feel about something.

Two boys are looking at vacation photos.
Phil:
おとこ　の　こ　は　だれ　です　か。 *Otoko no ko wa dare desu ka.*

Matt:
マイク　くん　です。 *MAIKU kun desu.*

Phil:
マイク　さん　は　アメリカじん　です　か。 *MAIKU san wa AMERIKAjin desu ka.*

Matt:	
はい、テキサス　に　すんで います。	*Hai, TEKISASU ni sunde imasu.*
Phil:	
あなた　は　テキサス　に いきました　か。	*Anata wa TEKISASU ni ikimashita ka.*
Matt:	
ええ、いきました。	*Ee, ikimashita.*
Phil:	
テキサス　は　おおきい です　ね。	*TEKISASU wa ookii desu ne.*
Matt:	
そう　です　ね。 ハワイ　は おおきくない　です。	*Soo desu ne. HAWAI wa ookikunai desu.*
Phil:	
ちいさい　です　が　すき　です。 きれい　です。　ハワイ は　いい　です　ね。	*Chiisai desu ga suki desu. Kirei desu. HAWAI wa ii desu ne.*
Matt:	
そう　です　ね。	*Soo desu ne.*

ACTIVITIES

(In pairs)

Role play a conversation between two students talking about friends they have in other places. Don't work it out on paper — just let it happen.

For example, Student One says: "My friend Bill lives in Texas." Student Two might ask: "Does he live in Dallas?" Student One therefore has to think quickly and reply either "Yes" or "No". If the answer is "No", say where he does live.

Student Two then has the option of saying something about Dallas or asking something more about Bill, and so on.

If you role play well, you will be able to show genuine interest in this person and will be able to find out a lot of information about him.

EXTRA ACTIVITIES

- Read about the people in the following photo. If necessary look up *hiragana* that you don't know in the chart at the back of the book.
  ともだち　が　さんにん　います。アニサ　と　アナベル　と　アニタ
  です。アニサ　は　ちゅうごくじん　です。アナベル　は
  ニュージーランドじん　です。アニタ　は　ちゅうごくじん　です。
  ごがつ　に　ともだち　は　さんにん　にほん　に　いきました。
  にほん　の　こうえん　に　いきました。

にほん の こうえん が すき でした。
ともだち は みな じゅうごさい です。がっこう の どうきゅうせい です。

アニサ	*ANISA*	Anisa
アニタ	*ANITA*	Anita
アナベル	*ANABERU*	Anabelle
ニュージーランド	*NYUUJIIRANDO*	New Zealand
ちゅうごくじん	*chuugokujin*	Chinese person
どうきゅうせい	*dookyuusei*	classmates

Answer the following questions:

1 アニサ さん も アニタ さん も どこ の かた です か。
2 アナベル さん は なんさい です か。
3 ごがつ に どこ に いきました か。

- Read the following. A Japanese student sent the following photo to her friend, along with a letter. In the letter she explained the photo.
  あね の かぞく です。あね の なまえ は まりこ です。まりこ は さんじゅうさんさい です。こども は おんな の こ が ひとり います。おとこ の こ が ふたり います。おんな の こ は よんさい です。
  おとこ の こ は ひとり じゅっさい です。ひとり はっさい です。にちようび です から かぞく は こうえん に いきました。こうえん は きれい です。

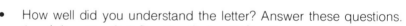

- How well did you understand the letter? Answer these questions.
  1 あね の なまえ は なん です か。
  2 こども は なんにん います か。
  3 なんようび です か。
  4 どこ に います か。
  5 こうえん は きれい です か。

- Think of more questions to ask about the photo.

- Say two or three things about the little girl in the photo.

Answers

1 My older sister's name is Mariko.
2 There are three children (in her family).
3 The day is Sunday.
4 They are in the park.
5 Yes, it is beautiful.

- Look at the next photo and read the caption aloud to a friend. Make up one question each to ask about the photo.

きょう　は　かぞく　の　ともだち　は　テキサス　から　きました。
きょう　の　ハワイ　の　おてんき　は　いい　です。あつい　です。

テキサス	*TEKISASU*	Texas
ハワイ	*HAWAI*	Hawaii
から	*kara*	from

CROSSWORD (TOPIC SEVEN REVIEW)

Complete the puzzle. If the clues are given in English, write the answers in roomaji. If the clues are given in Japanese, write the answers in English.

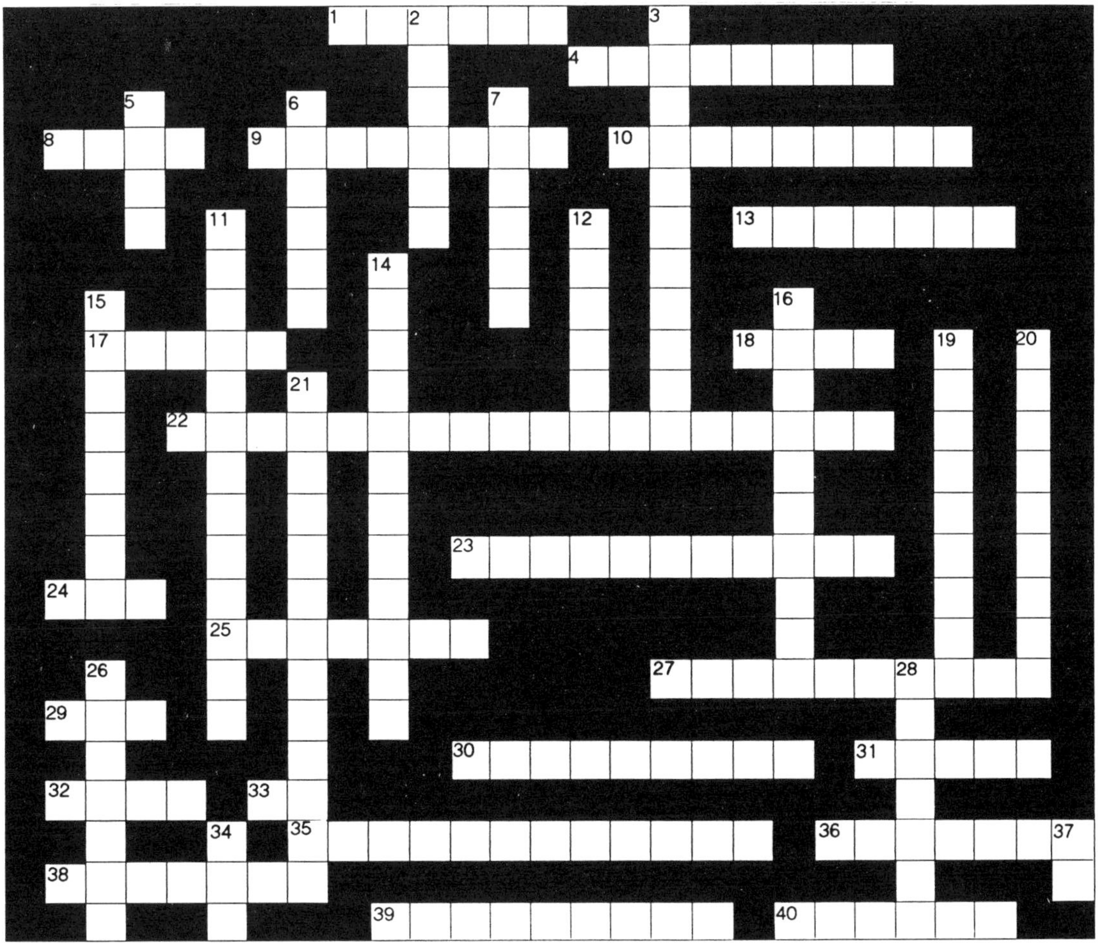

ACROSS

1 own younger sister
4 office worker
8 *atama*
9 lawyer
10 short in height
13 nurse
17 doctor
18 ears
22 *kyoodai*
23 *Okaerinasai*
24 *ten*
25 mother
27 *TEREBI*
29 own older brother
30 someone else's younger brother
31 beautiful
32 *taihen*
33 eyes
35 clean
36 brothers and sisters
38 handsome
39 tall
40 one person

DOWN

2 own younger brother
3 please look
5 *mimi*
6 teacher
7 please wait a minute, . . . *matte ku*
11 this way, please
12 *tomodachi*
14 please listen
15 your family
16 *kyuunin*
19 friend
20 someone else's younger sister
21 clever
26 someone else's older sister
28 job
34 *chichi*
37 good

TOPIC EIGHT homes and daily activities

Introduction

ACHIEVEMENTS

By the end of this topic you will be able to:
- describe your home and other people's homes;
- say what is in each room;
- say what you have and don't have;
- say where you do things.

You will also learn some more of the *hiragana* combined syllables.

Housing
Japanese homes are much smaller on average than homes in Europe and the U.S. Land prices are very high and it is very difficult to own your own home, so the majority of Japanese rent their homes.

Danchi

Most of Japan's one hundred and twenty million people live on the coastal plains. The cities that have grown up there sprawl into one another and it is often hard to see where one city ends and another begins.

To save space, much of Japan's city housing is in apartment blocks. ***Danchi*** are huge complexes of apartment blocks in which as many as one hundred and twenty thousand people can live alongside each other. These *danchi* communities have their own kindergartens, schools, libraries, shopping facilities, medical services and leisure centers. Some of them were built by companies for their workers, to give the workers reasonably priced accommodations close to their work. Others are municipal blocks.

Living in a *danchi* complex, people often have no need to go very far for anything and can spend their working and their leisure time alongside the same people.

There are also very beautiful detached homes, both modern and traditional in design. Just as anywhere else, Japan has a good variety of housing, particularly in the country and outer suburbs where even large and elegant homes can be seen.

Traditionally Japanese country homes were built to accommodate extended families, so houses were large. In the country, families all worked together on the family land. Over the last hundred years, however, there has been a movement toward the cities to the industrial and technological jobs and farming has ceased to be the main occupation. People need to live near their work, and the cities have become huge sprawls of high density housing.

When talking about Japanese homes, therefore, you must realize that there are very many types of housing. They do, however, have some features in common. It is important to know about these features because manners demand certain behavior patterns in the house.

Typical two-story suburban house

APAATO

Inside the home

The entrance to a Japanese home is called the ***genkan***. It is often very small, just enough space for two people to stand inside the front door. Usually the floor immediately inside the front door is of wood or tiles. In that space family and visitors take off their shoes and turn them to face the front door, ready for leaving again. On the step in front of them, slippers will be waiting – unisize slippers for visitors and appropriately sized ones for the family. Before doing anything else, everyone puts on houseslippers.

The step inside the *genkan* is an important barrier between the outside and the inside of the house. Taking off shoes obviously stops a lot of grit and dirt from getting into the house. It also protects the ***tatami*** mats inside the house from damage. Inside the *genkan* there is usually a cupboard for umbrellas, shoes and slippers. The Japanese say ***O agari kudasai*** to invite you into the house which literally means "**Step up please**". The ritual of changing shoes in the *genkan* also has an important symbolic function – the cares and worries of the outside world are left behind as you enter the peaceful sanctuary of the home.

Gate

Genkan

Imagine that you have arrived about five o'clock in the afternoon. Stepping up into the house you will probably be taken to the ***ima*** or living room. In many houses the *ima* doubles as a bedroom at night to make best use of the space. However, nowadays Japanese people like to have one room set up with Western-style furniture and one traditional room if they have the space.

Before you enter the *ima* your hosts indicate that you should take off your slippers before you step on the *tatami* floor. You do so, copying them, and leave your slippers at the door. You walk into the room in your stockinged feet. The golden colored *tatami* mats are actually about three inches thick. Although you can't see their thickness, you can feel their slight springiness as you walk to the table and sit down Japanese style with your legs under you at the table.

The *tatami* mats are beautifully woven and last well with care but would soon disintegrate if shoes were worn on them. Looking around the room, you see that there are six *tatami* mats fitting tightly together to make the total floor covering. You are in a six *tatami* mat room. Other rooms in the house will be measured in *tatami* mats too. When people tell you about their apartment or house, they will indicate the size of the rooms by telling you that they have a 4.5 *tatami* mat room or a six *tatami* mat room, etc. When you rent property it will be advertised by *tatami* mat size. A *tatami* mat is approximately six and a half feet by three and a half feet.

Around the low table in the *ima* there will be either chairs with no legs, cushions, or cushions with backs. In winter the family will sit around this low table, which will usually have an electric heater attached to its underside. This kind of table is called a ***kotatsu***. The table is covered with a kind of blanket *(kotatsu buton)* which comes down to the floor, keeping in warmth around legs and feet. Years ago the warmth was provided by a charcoal burner in a well under the table.

Tatami

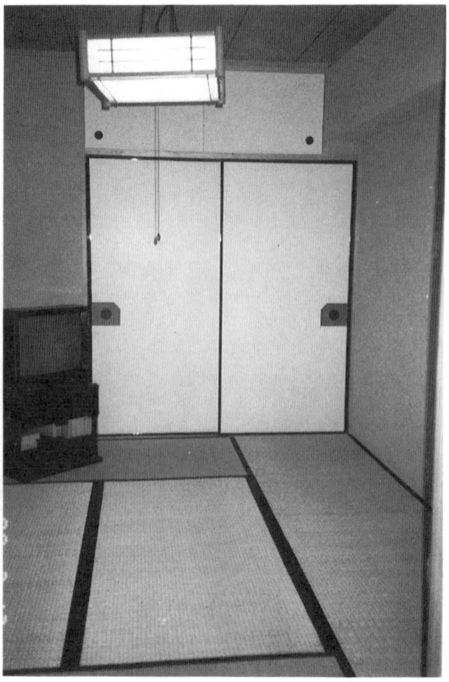

A six-mat room

In this room as you look around you will almost certainly see a TV set and the ***tokonoma*** — an alcove — in which hangs a scroll (***kakejiku***) and where there is usually a flower arrangement or a special piece of pottery. In the *ima* you may also find the family *butsudan*, or small Buddhist altar.

At night the table and chairs will be moved away and from cupboards in the wall called ***todana*** the family will take ***futon*** (mattresses and bedding) and ***makura*** (pillows). Beds will be made up on the floor for possibly the parents, or possibly for you because they have no guest room.

The *futon* are soft and comfortable and are covered with a sheet and have a sort of Japanese comforter on top. The pillows are usually not enjoyed as much by visitors! They are very hard and bulky, usually filled with buckwheat. During the night as you turn your head you can hear the crunchiness of the filling.

The *ima* may also have a clothes rack with coathangers and drawers for clothes storage. In some homes the room has the most amazing clutter of belongings around the walls because storage is a big problem.

The ***daidokoro*** (kitchen) is likely to be small and to be filled to overflowing with modern appliances, food and household utensils. Refrigerators are much smaller than ours, washing matchines too, and come in soft pastel greens, pinks, and mauves as well as white. Because storage is a problem most housewives shop daily.

After giving you something to eat and drink, the family may offer you a bath. Leaving the room you put on your ***SURIPPA*** (slippers) again for the short distance to the bathroom. The toilet, ***otearai***, has its own slippers. So you leave your house slippers outside the toilet (it saves the necessity for "occupied"

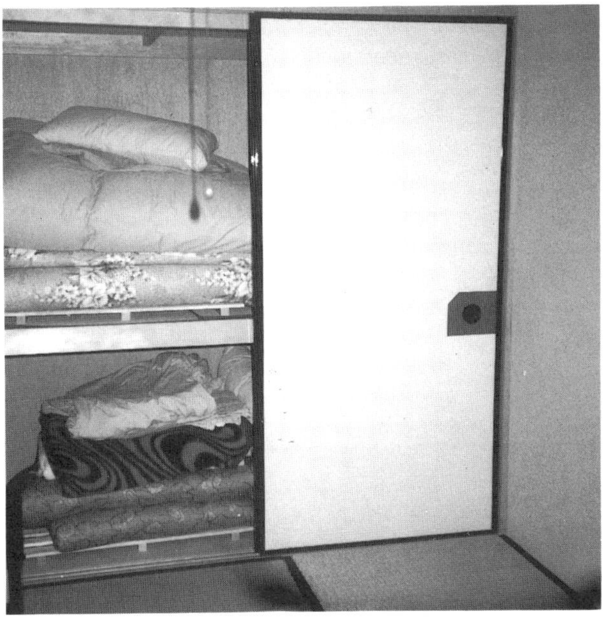

Futon* in the *todana

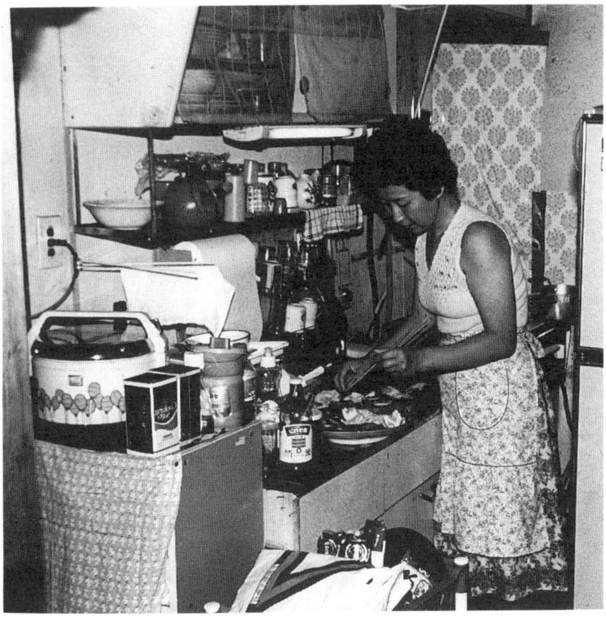

Daidokoro

signs!) and stepping inside you put on the plastic toilet slippers. It is **very** bad manners to wear your house slippers inside the toilet or to wear the toilet slippers outside the toilet. The toilet itself maybe a Western-style one, complete with music, heated seat, and warm water bidet! Or it may be an ordinary Western-style one or a traditional Japanese one. A traditional Japanese toilet is an elongated oval basin set into the floor, with a hood at one end. You squat facing the hood with your back to the door. Sometimes in these toilets there is a bowl on top of the cistern in which you can wash your hands. That water is then used to flush the toilet thus saving water.

We may have baths or showers before going out to dinner and then do our hair while women put on makeup and nice clothes. In traditional families in Japan it is different. The bathroom, ***ofuroba***, is quite small. You will be given a basket to put your clothes in and when you have undressed may have to put it outside the bathroom door to stop your clothes from getting wet. The bathroom will have a tiled floor with a drain in it rather like a shower base, and a small but deep bath with a cover on it.

The biggest sins of all in a Japanese house are to get soap in the bath water, and to let the bath water out after you. The bath, ***ofuro*** is like a hot tub and is for soaking and relaxing **after** you have thoroughly washed. First you notice the taps and possibly a shower with a flexible hose low on the wall. By the side of that there will be a tiny little stool that looks like something from a kindergarten and a small plastic bowl. Sit on the stool facing the taps or the shower hose and fill up the plastic bowl with water. Soap yourself **all over**. Then rinse yourself all over with clean water. Wash again with soap until you are sure that no dirt could possibly be left on you and again rinse and rinse until you are positive that no trace of soap is left on you. Then you may take off the cover and get into the bath to soak. It may feel very hot. It is possible to add cold water but most families would prefer that you don't because it

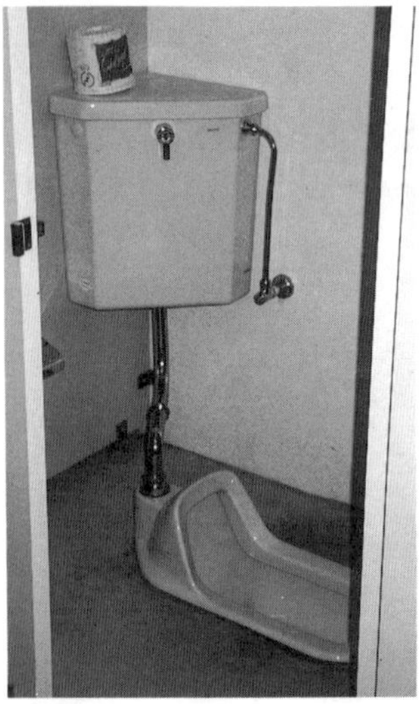

cools it down for everyone else who follows you, sharing the same water. So you tend to come out of the bath warmed and shiny. (Put the cover back on the bath.)

Waiting for you there is likely to be a ***yukata***, a cotton kimono to put on for dinner. Be careful to put it on with the left side overlapping the right, whether you are male or female. The other way is the way corpses are dressed for burial!

Putting on your houseslippers again you walk the few feet to the living room, take off your slippers again at the door and proceed in your socks to the dinner table. The family will usually have their baths after you and then come to the dinner table refreshed and relaxed for their evening meal.

The bedrooms in Japanese houses are called ***shinshitsu***. Many students now have Western style ***BEDDO*** (beds) and Western study furniture, but many still make up a *futon* on the floor each night.

◀ **Traditional style *otearai***

'High tech' — with music, bidet, hot and cold air, musical toilet roll holder

Traditional wooden bathing utensils

A modern *ofuroba*

Unit 1

わたし の うち
watashi no uchi
My house

NEW WORDS

で	*de*	in/at (particle for location of activity)
べんり	*benri*	convenient
だいどころ	*daidokoro*	kitchen
ひろい	*hiroi*	spacious
せまい	*semai*	cramped
れいぞうこ	*reizooko*	refrigerator
いま	*ima*	living room
へや	*heya*	room
テレビ	*TEREBI*	TV
おもしろい	*omoshiroi*	interesting
しんしつ	*shinshitsu*	bedroom
たいへん	*taihen*	very
にんぎょう	*ningyoo*	doll
そう しましょう	*soo shimashoo*	let's do that
あります	*arimasu*	(verb) to be/exist (for things that can't move under their own volition)

Interest vocabulary

ごちゃごちゃ	*gochagocha*	messy/in a mess
おや	*oya*	parents
ポスター	*POSUTAA*	posters
だいすき	*daisuki*	like a lot
ふつう	*futsuu*	usually
ええ と	*ee to*	Let me think (hesitation noise)

Review

こちら へ どうぞ	*kochira e doozo*	please come this way

Maria is showing a Japanese visitor who has come to stay for a few days around her house.

Maria:

わたし の うち です。 *Watashi no uchi desu.*
こちら へ どうぞ。 *Kochira e doozo.*
だいどころ です。 *Daidokoro desu.*

Haruko:

ひろい　です　ね。　れいぞうこ は　おおきい　です　ね。	*Hiroi desu ne. Reizooko wa ookii desu ne.*

Maria:

そう　です　か。	*Soo desu ka.*
これ　は　いま　です。	*Kore wa ima desu.*
かぞく　の　へや　です。	*Kazoku no heya desu.*
だいどころ　で　たべます。	*Daidokoro de tabemasu.*

Haruko:

べんり　です　ね。	*Benri desu ne.*

Maria:

はい、べんり　です。これ　は テレビ　の　へや　です。	*Hai, benri desu. Kore wa TEREBI no heya desu.*

Haruko:

まいにち　テレビ　を　みます か。	*Mainichi TEREBI o mimasu ka.*

Maria:

はい、よる　テレビ　を　みます。	*Hai, yoru TEREBI o mimasu.*
これ　は　わたし　の　へや です。	*Kore wa watashi no heya desu.*
いつも　ごちゃごちゃ　です。	*Itsumo gochagocha desu.*

Haruko:

わたし　の　へや　も ごちゃごちゃ　です。	*Watashi no heya mo gochagocha desu.*

Maria:

そう　です　か。それ　は おもしろい　です。	*Soo desu ka. Sore wa omoshiroi desu.*
これ　は　わたし　の　おや の　しんしつ　です。	*Kore wa watashi no oya no shinshitsu desu.*

Haruko:

あなた　の　へや　は　ひろい です。	*Anata no heya wa hiroi desu.*
わたし　の　うち　は　せまい です。	*Watashi no uchi wa semai desu.*
にほん　の　うち　は　ふつう せまい　です。	*Nihon no uchi wa futsuu semai desu.*
わたし　の　へや　は　たいへん せまい　です。	*Watashi no heya wa taihen semai desu.*

Maria:

この　うち　は　ひろくない です。	*Kono uchi wa hirokunai desu.*
ともだち　の　うち　は　ひろい です。	*Tomodachi no uchi wa hiroi desu.*
あに　の　へや　です。	*Ani no heya desu.*

Haruko:

おにいさん　は　ポスター　が すき　です　ね。	*Oniisan wa POSUTAA ga suki desu ne.*

Maria:	
はい、だいすき　です。	*Hai, daisuki desu.*
これ　は　いもうと　の	*Kore wa imooto no*
へや　です。	*heya desu.*
にんぎょう　が　すき　です。	*Ningyoo ga suki desu.*
Haruko:	
いもうと　が　います。	*Imooto ga imasu.*
くるま　が　すき　です。	*Kuruma ga suki desu.*
Maria:	
これ　は　あなた　の　へや	*Kore wa anata no heya*
です。	*desu.*
Haruko:	
ありがとう　ございます。	*Arigatoo gozaimasu.*
Maria:	
では、テレビ　の　へや　に	*Dewa, TEREBI no heya ni*
きて　ください。	*kite kudasai.*
テレビ　を　みましょう　か。	*TEREBI o mimashoo ka.*
Haruko:	
はい、そう　しましょう。	*Hai, soo shimashoo.*

ACTIVITIES

- Listen while your teacher reads the conversation then practice reading it aloud to a partner. Listen particularly for the long sounds. Practice them carefully.

- Listen carefully to the way the words are grouped. Notice that if you have to take a breath you stop after a particle as if the particle is "glued" to the word before.

Check your understanding

M: This is my house. Please come this way. This is the kitchen.
H: It's spacious isn't it. The refrigerator is big, isn't it?
M: Is it really? (Do you think so?) This is the living room. It's the family room. We eat in the kitchen.
H: It's convenient, isn't it?
M: Yes, it's convenient. This is the TV room.
H: Do you watch TV every day?
M: Yes, in the evenings we watch TV. This is my room. It's always in a mess!
H: My room's always a mess, too.
M: Really? That's interesting. This is my parents' bedroom.
H: Your rooms are really spacious. My house is cramped. Japanese houses are usually cramped. My room is very cramped.

M: This house is not spacious. My friends' houses are. [This] is my older brother's room.
H: Your older brother likes posters, doesn't he!
M: Yes, he likes them a lot. This is my younger sister's room. She likes dolls.
H: I've got a younger sister. She likes cars!
M: This is your room.
H: Thank you.
M Well, come into the family room (TV room). Shall we watch TV?
H: Yes, let's do that.

Bedding is hung out to air in the morning

STUDY

- *Ima de tabemasu.* This is a new particle: ***de***. It is used for the location of your activity. Any place where you do something has to be followed by ***de***. For example:
  Heya **de** *benkyoo shimasu.* I study in my room.
  Ima **de** *TEREBI o mimasu.* I watch TV in the living room.
  Gakkoo **de** *nihongo o benkyoo shimasu.* I study Japanese at school.
  In the next unit you will have more practice using this particle with some new verbs.

- ***Hiroi***, ***semai***, and ***omoshiroi*** are adjectives and change in the negative to ***hirokunai***, ***semakunai***, and ***omoshirokunai***. Remember to put *desu* after the adjective, to make the sentence more polite.

- ***Benri*** is another qualitative noun. Its negative is *benri dewa arimasen.* This is like the words *joozu*, *kirei*, and *HANSAMU* that you learned in the last topic. Keep *benri* separate in your mind from the adjectives.

- ***Futsuu semai*** usually cramped
  Taihen hiroi very spacious
  Semai can also mean "small", in the sense of "cramped" or "narrow".
  Hiroi can mean "wide" and "large" as well as spacious.
  Futsuu means "usually" or "generally". For example:
  Futsuu omoshiroi desu. It is usually interesting.
  Futsuu ookii desu. It is usually big.
  Futsuu chiisai desu. It is usually small.

- ***Gochagocha*** is a colloquial expression meaning "messy", "disorganized", "a mess".

- ***Arimasu*** is the verb for things that cannot move under their own will. For example:
  Nani ga arimasu ka. What is there? (What exists?)
  BEDDO ga arimasu ka. Do you have a bed?/Is there a bed?
  Arimasu is used in the same way as *imasu* but for a different group of things. Again the Japanese prefer to speak impersonally about things they own and say things "exist" rather than saying "I have a . . ."
  Sometimes *arimasu* is described as being used for things that are inanimate (not living) but it is not so. For example:
  Ki ga arimasu. There are trees/There is a tree/We have trees.
  Hana ga arimasu. There are flowers/There is a flower/We have flowers.
  These things are animate (living) but cannot move under their own volition, and always take *arimasu*.

  Look at some more examples:
  Futon ga arimasu ka. Do you have a futon? Is there a futon?
  Heya ga arimasu ka. Do you have a room? Is there a room?
  Hon ga arimasu. I have books./There are books.
  REKOODO ga arimasu. I have records./There are records.
  With this verb you can now say what you have or do not have, though a better way of expressing the idea of ownership will be introduced later when you know more verb forms.
  Remember that, in fact, with *arimasu* you are saying that something exists in an impersonal way, and our way of expressing this in English is often "I have a . . .".
  The negative of *arimasu* is of course ***arimasen***, the past is ***arimashita***, and the past negative is ***arimasen deshita***.
  Like *imasu*, *arimasu* takes the ***ga*** particle. The ***ga*** is focusing on a particular thing:
  Uchi wa daidokoro ga arimasu ka.
  (Talking about) your house, does it have a kitchen?

- ***Ni wa***
  You have learned the particle ***ni*** in sentences like "I will go to town" and in time phrases like "at one o'clock". This unit introduces you to a different use for ***ni***. Look at these sentences:
  Gakkoo ni wa tsukue ga arimasu.
  In school there are desks.
  Toshokan ni wa e ga arimasu.
  In the library there are pictures.
  In these sentences the topic is "In the . . ." "(Talking about) in the library . . ." etc. By putting ***Ni*** in front of ***wa*** we can say "Talking about in the library . . ." or, for example:
  Gakkoo ni wa . . . Talking about in school . . .
  Shinshitsu ni wa . . . Talking about in the bedroom . . .
  When we use ***ni wa*** we will be stating only what exists in that place, not talking about an activity happening there.

Shinshitsu ni wa POSUTAA ga arimasu.
In the bedroom there is a poster.

The use of the verb *arimasu* indicates that the things we are talking about cannot move under their own volition.

Furniture is designed for sitting close to the floor

Check your understanding

Look over the new words and read the conversation. Next, answer the questions that follow.

NEW WORDS

ほんばこ	*honbako*	bookshelves (bookcase)
ようふく	*yoofuku*	(Western) clothes
シャワー	*SHAWAA*	shower
さら	*sara*	plates
ナイフ	*NAIFU*	knives
フォーク	*FOOKU*	forks
ちゃわん	*chawan*	bowls
たくさん の もの	*takusan no mono*	lots of things
に は	*ni wa*	the particles *ni* and *wa* used together to express "talking about in the . . ."

Jim:

いま　に　は　なに　が　あります か。	*Ima ni wa nani ga arimasu ka.*

Liana:

いま　に　は　テーブル　が　あります。	*Ima ni wa TEEBURU ga arimasu.*
とだな　が　あります。	*Todana ga arimasu.*
ほんばこ　が　あります。	*Honbako ga arimasu.*
はな　が　あります。	*Hana ga arimasu.*
いす　が　あります。	*Isu ga arimasu.*
テレビ　が　あります。	*TEREBI ga arimasu.*
まど　が　あります。	*Mado ga arimasu.*
ドア　が　あります。	*DOA ga arimasu.*
え　が　あります。	*E ga arimasu.*

Jim:

しんしつ　に　は　なに　が　あります　か。	*Shinshitsu ni wa nani ga arimasu ka.*

Liana:

しんしつ　に　は　ベッド　が　あります。	*Shinshitsu ni wa BEDDO ga arimasu.*
ほんばこ　が　あります。	*Honbako ga arimasu.*
ほん　が　あります。	*Hon ga arimasu.*
レコード　が　あります。	*REKOODO ga arimasu.*
まんが　が　あります。	*Manga ga arimasu.*
ざっし　が　あります。	*Zasshi ga arimasu.*
ようふく　が　あります。	*Yoofuku ga arimasu.*
ペン　が　あります。	*PEN ga arimasu.*
えんぴつ　が　あります。	*Enpitsu ga arimasu.*

Jim:

おふろば　に　は　なに　が　あります　か。	*Ofuroba ni wa nani ga arimasu ka.*

Liana:

おふろば　に　は　シャワー　が　あります。	*Ofuroba ni wa SHAWAA ga arimasu.*
おふろ　が　あります。	*Ofuro ga arimasu.*

Jim:

だいどころ　に　は　なに　が　あります　か。	*Daidokoro ni wa nani ga arimasu ka.*

Liana:

ナイフ　と　フォーク　が　あります。	*NAIFU to FOOKU ga arimasu.*
さら　が　あります。	*Sara ga arimasu.*
ちゃわん　が　あります。	*Chawan ga arimasu.*
たくさん　の　もの　が　あります。	*Takusan no mono ga arimasu.*

ACTIVITIES

- Draw a plan of your house and label the rooms.
  Write about it. Say what is in each room using the vocabulary above.

- Tell a partner about your house. Explain who belongs in each room.

- A visitor comes to stay and you take him or her around your house. Role play the conversation with a partner, without planning first. Try to put in a few comments as well as just saying "This is the kitchen" etc.

- Write the English translation of the previous conversation.

Writing practice

- Review ***sho*** し

- Learn ***sha*** しゃ

しゃ

- Review ***sho*** しょ

しょ

- From ***shu*** you can make ***shuu*** しゅう

- Review ***chi*** ち

- Review ***cha*** ちゃ

- Learn ***chu*** ちゅ

ちゅ

- From ***chu*** you can make ***chuu*** ちゅう

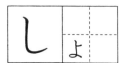

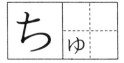

Unit 2

いま に あります か
ima ni arimasu ka
Is it in the living room?

NEW WORDS

ここ	*koko*	here
そこ	*soko*	there
あそこ	*asoko*	over there
また	*mata*	again
いって	*itte*	go
みて	*mite*	look
いって まいります	*itte mairimasu*	I'm leaving now
いって いらっしゃい	*itte irasshai*	Go and come home safely
Review		
どこ	*doko*	where

Learn the last two phrases. ***Itte mairimasu*** is an expression you use when leaving home, and means "I'm leaving now".

The automatic response is ***itte irasshai*** "Go and come home safely".

Mother is in the kitchen when Maria shouts out to her because it is time for school and she can't find her Japanese book.

Maria:
わたし の にほんご の ほん は どこ に あります か。 *Watashi no nihongo no hon wa doko ni arimasu ka.*

Mother:
あなた の へや に あります か。 *Anata no heya ni arimasu ka.*

Maria:
いいえ、わたし の へや に ありません。 *Iie, watashi no heya ni arimasen.*

Mother:
いま に いって、みて ください。 *Ima ni itte, mite kudasai.*

Maria:
ここ に ありません。 *Koko ni arimasen.*

Mother:
また あなた の へや に いって みて ください。 *Mata anata no heya ni itte mite kudasai.*

Maria:
ほん は へや に ありません。 *Hon wa heya ni arimasen.*

Mother:	
おねえさん　の　へや　で みました　か。	*Oneesan no heya de* *mimashita ka.*
Maria:	
いいえ。	*Iie.*
Mother:	
いって、みて　ください…… あります　か。	*Itte, mite kudasai . . .* *arimasu ka.*
Maria:	
はい、あります。ありがとう (ございます)。がっこう　に いきます。いって　まいります。	*Hai, arimasu. Arigatoo* *(gozaimasu). Gakkoo ni* *ikimasu. Itte mairimasu.*
Mother:	
いって　いらっしゃい。	*Itte irasshai.*

Check your understanding of the conversation.

Maria: Where's my Japanese book?

Okaasan (Mother): Is it in your room?

M: No, it's not in my room.

O: Go and look in the living room.

M: It's not here.

O: Go and look in your room again.

M: It's not in my room.

O: Did you look in your older sister's room?

M: No.

O: Go and look. . . . Is it there? (Do you have it?)

M: Yes, it is here. (I have it). Thank you. I'll go to school. Goodbye.

O: Goodbye! (Come home safely!)

STUDY

- Review all the instructions you know, using . . . *kudasai*, e.g. *suwatte kudasai* "please sit". Add the following instructions to your usable expressions:

  Itte kudasai. Please go.
  Mite kudasai. Please look/watch.

- ***Doko ni arimasu ka***.

  Where is it?

  To use this construction you need to put the name of the thing you are talking about, followed by ***wa***, in front of *doko ni arimasu ka*, e.g.

  Kaban wa doko ni arimasu ka. Where is the bag? (Where is there a bag?)

  In your answer you can say, for example;

  Gakkoo ni arimasu. It's in school. or It's at school.

- ***Koko***, ***soko***, ***asoko***

  These words are a family that belong with ***doko***. As with *kore*, *sore*, and *are* (which you already know) they are position words but they are not talking about objects, they are talking about **places**.

The ***ko*** beginning means "close to me". The ***so*** beginning means "closer to you than to me". The ***aso*** beginning means "over there away from both of us". These words let you answer "Here", "There", "Over there".

Someone asks you: *Doko ni arimasu ka.* Where is it?

You can answer:
Koko ni arimasu.
It's here./It's in this place (close to me).
Soko ni arimasu.
It's there./It's in that place there (nearer to you than to me).
Asoko ni arimasu.
It's over there./It's in that place over there (away from both of us).

You can alsc ask about position, e.g.:
Koko ni arimasu ka.
Is it here?

- The ***ni*** means "Is it **in** this place?" and must always be put after *koko, soko, asoko,* or *doko* if you are asking if something is in that place/exists in that place.

- Practice asking each other where things are in the classroom. Answer with: *Koko ni arimasu/Soko ni arimasu/Asoko ni arimasu* as appropriate.

- Practice using *koko, soko,* and *asoko* with animals and people, e.g.
  DAN ga soko ni imasu ka.
  Is Dan in? Is Dan there?
  Okaasan ga koko ni imasu ka.
  Is your mother here?
  Anata no inu ga asoko ni imasu ka.
  Is your dog over there?

- Review *itte/kite kudasai.* In the previous conversation *itte, mite kudasai* means "go and look".

ACTIVITIES

- Practice the conversation with a friend. Be careful with your pronunciation of *itte* – remember you have to give time to both *t*'s.

- Write the English version of the conversation.

- With a friend, make up a similar conversation between a boy or girl and a parent. Let it happen. Don't plan it first.

- Draw a picture of three people in one room of a house. With a partner, ask each other: *Heya ni wa dare ga imasu ka. Okaasan wa heya ni imasu ka.* etc. Answer with: *(DAN) san wa heya ni imasu. Okaasan wa heya ni imasu.* Etc.

Check your understanding

Answer in Japanese, following the hints provided.
1 *Hana wa doko ni arimasu ka.* (living room)
2 *Todana wa doko ni arimasu ka.* (bedroom)
3 *REKOODO wa doko ni-arimasu ka.* (My room — *watashi no heya*)
4 *Sara wa doko ni arimasu ka.* (kitchen)
5 *Daidokoro ni wa nani ga arimasu ka.* (plates, knives, forks)

How would you say the following in Japanese?
1 What is there in the living room?
2 There's a table in the living room.
3 There's a cupboard.
4 There's a bookcase.
5 There are flowers.
6 There are chairs.
7 There is a TV.
8 There are windows.
9 There's a door.
10 There are pictures.
11 What is there in the bedroom?
12 There's a bed.
13 There is a bookcase.
14 There are books.
15 There are records.
16 There are comics.
17 There are magazines.
18 There are clothes.
19 There are pens and pencils.
20 What is there in the bathroom?
21 In the bathroom there's a shower.
22 There's a bath.
23 What is there in the kitchen?
24 There are knives and forks.
25 There are plates.
26 There are bowls.
27 There are lots of things.

Practice the following:
1 There are books.
2 There is a notebook.
3 There is a pen.
4 I have a pencil.
5 There is a tree.
6 I have a car.
7 There is Julie's new bag.
8 There is an interesting film.
9 I have a cramped house.

Answers
1 *Hon ga arimasu.*
2 *NOOTO ga arimasu.*
3 *PEN ga arimasu.*

4 *Enpitsu ga arimasu.*
5 *Ki ga arimasu.*
6 *Kuruma ga arimasu.*
7 *JUURI san no atarashii kaban ga arimasu.*
8 *Omoshiroi eiga ga arimasu.*
9 *Semai uchi ga arimasu.*

Remember ***imasu*** is used for things that can move under their own volition, ***arimasu*** for those that can't.

Draw your own illustrations of things that can move under their own volition and things that can't, e.g.:
horse, bird, cat, dog, person, flowers, trees, house, umbrella, bike, car, book, desk, plates, knives and forks, bowls, fish, beach, school. Make up a sentence for each illustration using either *imasu* or *arimasu*.

Practice the following:
1 I have a cat.
2 I have your notebook.
3 There is a dog.
4 I have a bird.
5 I have an older sister.
6 Do you have a younger brother?
7 What is in the kitchen?
8 Who is in the kitchen?

Answers
1 *Neko ga imasu.*
2 *Anata no NOOTO ga arimasu.*
3 *Inu ga imasu.*
4 *Tori ga imasu.*
5 *Ane ga imasu.*
6 *Otooto san ga imasu ka.*
7 *Daidokoro ni wa nani ga arimasu ka.*
8 *Daidokoro ni wa dare ga imasu ka.*

ACTIVITIES

- In pairs, pointing to things or people you can see, practice using the questions:
  Nani ga arimasu ka.
  Dare ga imasu ka.
  Kyooshitsu ni wa (JON) san ga imasu ka.
  Kyooshitsu ni wa nani ga arimasu ka.
  Kyooshitsu ni wa dare ga imasu ka.
  Kaban ni wa nani ga arimasu ka.
  You will no doubt think of more questions of your own.

- Draw pictures of things that can move under their own volition and things that can't and ask your friends to compose sentences for them. Watch carefully to make sure they don't make mistakes.
  After that, label them with *imasu* and *arimasu* to help you to remember.

- Anne's bedroom: Draw an illustration of a room with books, magazines, table, chair, bed, desk, flowers on the table, pictures on the wall, a dog by the bed.
  Describe what is in the room.

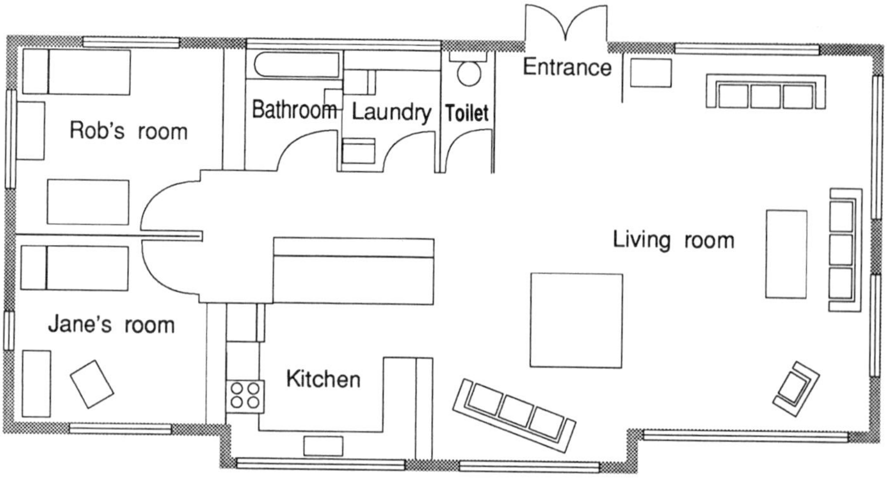

- (In pairs or small groups) Using the illustration above, describe Rob's house.

- Draw an illustration of a living room with easy chairs, a coffee table, a TV, flowers, magazines, a bookcase, window, door, and two people: one sitting at the table, one watching TV.
  Describe what or who is in the room.

- Read the following description and decide which illustration it belongs to.
  へや に は はな が あります。いぬ が います。ほん と ざっし が あります。え が あります。テーブル が あります。つくえ が あります。
  Heya ni wa hana ga arimasu. Inu ga imasu. Hon to zasshi ga arimasu. E ga arimasu. TEEBURU ga arimasu. Tsukue ga arimasu.

- Draw a picture that has the following things in it:
  まんが、ベッド、ほんばこ、とだな、ねこ、ざっし、ほん、レコード、はな、つくえ、にほんご の ほん、いす、まど、ドア。
  Manga, BEDDO, honbako, todana, neko, zasshi, hon, REKOODO, hana, tsukue, nihongo no hon, isu, mado, DOA.
  Label it with the name of the room.

Writing practice

- Review ***ni*** に

- Learn ***nya*** にゃ

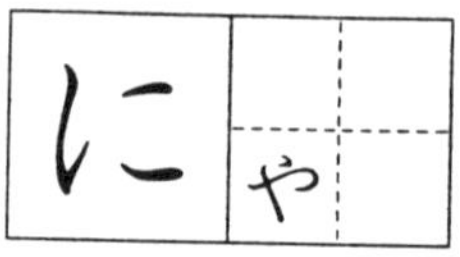

- Learn ***nyu*** にゅ

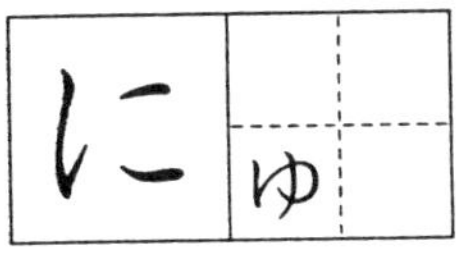

- From ***nyu*** you can make ***nyuu*** にゅう
- Learn ***nyo*** にょ

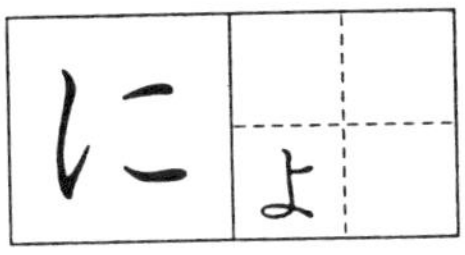

- From ***nyo*** you can make ***nyoo*** にょう

Unit 3

だいどころ で りょうり を します
daidokoro de ryoori o shimasu
I cook in the kitchen

NEW WORDS

で	*de*	particle for location of activity
あらいます	*araimasu*	wash
りょうり を します	*ryoori o shimasu*	cook
シャワー を あびます	*SHAWAA o abimasu*	take a shower

A:
だいどころ で なに を します か。 *Daidokoro de nani o shimasu ka.*

B:
だいどころ で りょうり を します。 *Daidokoro de ryoori o shimasu.*
さら を あらいます。 *Sara o araimasu.*

A:
いま で なに を します か。 *Ima de nani o shimasu ka.*

B:
いま で テレビ を みます。 *Ima de TEREBI o mimasu.*
しゅくだい を します。 *Shukudai o shimasu.*
ほん を よみます。 *Hon o yomimasu.*
レコード を ききます。 *REKOODO o kikimasu.*
ギター を れんしゅう します。 *GITAA o renshuu shimasu.*

A:
おふろば で なに を します か。 *Ofuroba de nani o shimasu ka.*

B:
おふろば で シャワー を あびます。 *Ofuroba de SHAWAA o abimasu.*

Kitchens in Japan tend to be small and cluttered.

Check your understanding of the conversation.
A: What do you do in the kitchen?
B: I cook.
I wash dishes.
A: What do you do in the living room?
B: I watch TV in the living room.

I do my homework.
I read books.
I listen to records.
I practice guitar.

A: What do you do in the bathroom?
B: I have a shower.

STUDY

- There are many places that you know to which you can now apply the particle ***de***, for location of activity:

Toshokan de hon o yomimasu.	I'll read books at the library.
Gakkoo de benkyoo shimasu.	I'll study at school.
Uchi de PIANO o renshuu shimasu.	I practice piano at home.
Kooen de TENISU o shimasu.	I'll play tennis in the park.
Machi de tomodachi ni aimasu.	I'll meet my friend in town.

- The question is: *Doko de . . .*
  Doko de hon o yomimashita ka.
  BEN san no uchi de yomimashita.
  Where did you read the book?
  I read it at Ben's house.
  Doko de REKOODO o kikimashoo ka.
  Where shall we listen to records?
  Watashi no heya de REKOODO o kikimashoo.
  Let's listen to them in my room.
  The reason you did not use ***de*** when using *imasu* and *arimasu* was that you were not actively engaged in doing something. There was no activity — the objects, things, or people just existed, and were not doing anything. When an activity follows you use ***de*** for the place in which the activity occurs.

- Here are some new verbs to extend the possibilities:

おきます	*okimasu*	get up
かいます	*kaimasu*	buy
やすみます	*yasumimasu*	rest
ねます	*nemasu*	lie down/go to bed
のみます	*nomimasu*	drink
つきます	*tsukimasu*	arrive
たべます	*tabemasu*	eat

  Note: all these verbs function in exactly the same way as the ones you already know.

ACTIVITIES

- Practice giving all the forms of the above verbs, e.g. *kaimasu, kaimasen, kaimashita, kaimasen deshita, kaimashoo.*

- Test each other on the different forms, e.g.
  I will eat, I won't eat, He didn't drink, She rested, etc.

- Make up sentences like the following to test each other:
  She lay down in her room.
  He washed the dishes.
  They rested at the park. (Had a rest)
  We bought some sandwiches.
  We bought hamburgers at McDonald's.
  We will eat fish today.
  He won't buy a new car.

- Think of as many ways as possible of using each verb, e.g. wash the car, wash my face, wash my hair, wash the dishes, wash the dog. And think of where you do/did the activity. Use the five verb forms that you know.

Mother ironing in the *ima*

NEW WORDS

サンドイッチ	*SANDOITCHI*	sandwich
ハンバーガー	*HANBAAGAA*	hamburger
ジュース	*JUUSU*	juice
にわ	*niwa*	garden (don't confuse with the separate particles *ni* and *wa*)
じてんしゃ	*jitensha*	bicycle
あそびます	*asobimasu*	play (not used for playing sports)
Review		
いちにち	*ichinichi*	one day
あさごはん	*asagohan*	breakfast
ひるごはん	*hirugohan*	lunch
ばんごはん	*bangohan*	dinner/evening meal
ときどき	*tokidoki*	sometimes
Interest		
マクドナルド	*MAKUDONARUDO*	McDonald's

- How would you say the following:
  1 I ate a sandwich in the kitchen.
  2 I drank juice in the bedroom.
  3 Fred watched TV in the living room.
  4 David listened to records in his room yesterday.
  5 Megan played tennis at school yesterday.
  6 I practiced guitar at home today.
  7 Did you play soccer at school last week?
  8 Did you meet your friend in town yesterday?
  9 Did you buy the record at the department store?
  10 Where did you buy the book?
  11 We played at the park.

Answers

1 *Daidokoro de SANDOITCHI o tabemashita.*
2 *Shinshitsu de JUUSU o nomimashita.*
3 *FUREDDO san wa ima de TEREBI o mimashita.*
4 *Kinoo DEBIDO san wa heya de REKOODO o kikimashita.*
5 *Kinoo MEGAN san wa gakkoo de TENISU o shimashita.*
6 *Kyoo uchi de GITAA o renshuu shimashita.*
7 *Senshuu gakkoo de SAKKAA o shimashita ka.*
8 *Kinoo machi de tomodachi ni aimashita ka.*
9 *DEPAATO de REKOODO o kaimashita ka.*
10 *Doko de hon o kaimashita ka.*
11 *Kooen de asobimashita.*

- You are now in a position to talk about yourself, your family and friends, your house, and where you do activities. Put these together with the times you know and you can give a very good talk about yourself and your life — or about someone else's life. Study Unit 3 carefully and then be prepared to give a 1-2 minute talk about yourself, or a member of your family.

Unit 4

わたし の いちにち
watashi no ichinichi
My day

NEW WORDS

ビスケット (interest only)	*BISUKETTO*	cracker

Note: Review time words that you have learned.

Read the following description of a person's day.

わたし の いちにち	**Watashi no ichinichi.**
ろくじ はん に おきます。	*Rokuji han ni okimasu.*
おふろば で シャワー を あびます。	*Ofuroba de SHAWAA o abimasu.*
だいどころ で あさごはん を たべます。	*Daidokoro de asagohan o tabemasu.*
はちじ に がっこう に いきます。	*Hachiji ni gakkoo ni ikimasu.*
バス で いきます。	*BASU de ikimasu.*
はちじ はん に がっこう に つきます。	*Hachiji han ni gakkoo ni tsukimasu.*
がっこう で べんきょう します。	*Gakkoo de benkyoo shimasu.*
がっこう で じゅうにじ はん に ひるごはん を たべます。	*Gakkoo de juuniji han ni hirugohan o tabemasu.*
さんじはん に かえります。	*Sanji han ni kaerimasu.*
よじ はん に うち に つきます。	*Yoji han ni uchi ni tsukimasu.*
いま で ビスケット を たべます。	*Ima de BISUKETTO o tabemasu.*
ジュース を のみます。	*JUUSU o nomimasu.*
にわ で あそびます。	*Niwa de asobimasu.*
いま で ろくじ に ばんごはん を たべます。	*Ima de rokuji ni bangohan o tabemasu.*
わたし の へや で しちじ に しゅくだい を します。	*Watashi no heya de shichiji ni shukudai o shimasu.*
いま で ときどき テレビ を みます。	*Ima de tokidoki TEREBI o mimasu.*
ときどき ほん を よみます。	*Tokidoki hon o yomimasu.*
ときどき いもうと と あそびます。	*Tokidoki imooto to asobimasu.*
じゅうじ に ねます。	*Juuji ni nemasu.*

ACTIVITIES

- Read the passage. Rewrite it, changing all the verbs to the past tense.

- Write a description of one day in your life, hour by hour. It doesn't have to be the truth. Remember to use ***de*** for location of activities.

- Write a letter to a penpal in Japan.
  1 Introduce yourself and say where you live. Describe yourself.
  2 Describe the composition of your family.
  4 Give descriptions of each member of your family.
  5 Describe your house.
  6 Say where and what you study.
  7 Say what you do in your leisure time.
  8 Say what the weather is like in your country at this time of year. Ask what the weather is like in Japan.

  Here is a format for your letter with the usual polite letter opening and closing.

Your address
(very clearly written)

Name of penpal followed by *san*
(When you know him/her better you can relax into *kun/chan*)

Konnichi wa
O genki desu ka.

. . . .
. . . . (The body of the letter follows) . . . .
O genki de ("Keep well" – used on the end of letters)
Sayonara
Your name (very clearly written)
The date in Japanese (e.g. Year/month/date/day – in numbers or words – 1991, *shigatsu nanoka, kayoobi.* Or: 1991,4,7, *kayoobi*)

- Keep a diary in Japanese for a week. If you do it in *hiragana* it's a very private way of keeping a diary.

Unit 5

NEW WORDS

で	*de*	by means of (particle)
バス	*BASU*	bus
タクシー	*TAKUSHII*	taxi
くるま	*kuruma*	car
じてんしゃ	*jitensha*	bicycle
スケート　ボード	*SUKEETO BOODO*	skate board
スケート	*SUKEETO*	skates
でんしゃ	*densha*	train
ちかてつ	*chikatetsu*	subway/underground train
ひこうき	*hikooki*	airplane
ふね	*fune*	boat, ship

STUDY

- You have learned how to use ***de*** to indicate location of an activity. Another use of ***de*** is for your means of transportation. In this situation ***de*** means "**by means of**", e.g.:

  BASU de ikimasu. I'll go by bus.
  Kuruma de kimashita. I came by car.
  Jitensha de kaerimasen. I won't return by bicycle.

  You can now extend your ability to express what you do or did by adding on the means of transportation:

  BASU de ikimashita. I went by bus.
  Yoji no BASU de machi ni ikimasu. I'll go on (by means of) the four o'clock bus.

  Work together to compose simple sentences with means of transportation.
- "On Monday at five o'clock I went to John's party by bus."
  In this sort of sentence you will put:
  Yourself (as topic) followed by ***wa***
  Time followed by ***ni***
  Place followed by ***ni***
  Means of transportation followed by ***de***
  Verb.

  Try to figure out the next sentence for yourself before looking at the translation.
  Watashi wa getsuyoobi no goji ni JON san no PAATII ni BASU de ikimashita.
  "At five o'clock on Monday, I went to John's party by bus."

- Try the following:
  1 "Next Saturday at six thirty I will go by bus to the cinema with my friend Maria."
  (Who . . . time . . . how . . . where . . . action)
  2 "I will go to John's birthday party on my bike next Sunday."
  (Who . . . when . . . how . . . where . . . action)

  Answers:
  1 *Watashi wa tomodachi no MARIA chan to raishuu no doyoobi no rokuji han ni BASU de eiga ni ikimasu.*
  2 *Watashi wa raishuu no nichiyoobi ni JON san no PAATII ni jitensha de ikimasu.*

  It is possible to vary the order but it may be helpful to get used to this pattern first before trying to alter it. The basic rule however is logic: put it in an order that flows to make sense and remember always to put the verb at the end.

- Practice these sentences.
  1 I'll go to Ben's house on my bike.
  2 I'll come to your school by bus at three o'clock.
  3 I went by train on Monday at six o'clock.
  4 I'll go by boat at five o'clock on Sunday.
  5 John went by subway.
  6 Sam will return home by taxi.
  7 I'll go to Australia by plane.
  8 My mother went to France by boat last week.
  9 Did you go by bus?
  10 Will you go to Glen's house on your skateboard?

  Answers
  1 *BEN san no uchi ni jitensha de ikimasu.*
  2 *Sanji ni anata no gakkoo ni BASU de kimasu.*
  3 *Getsuyoobi no rokuji ni densha de ikimashita.*
  4 *Nichiyoobi no goji ni fune de ikimasu.*
  5 *JON san wa chikatetsu de ikimashita.*
  6 *SAMU san wa uchi ni TAKUSHII de kaerimasu.*
  7 *OOSUTORARIA ni hikooki de ikimasu.*
  8 *Okaasan wa senshuu FURANSU ni fune de ikimashita.*
  9 *BASU de ikimashita ka.*
  10 *GUREN san no uchi ni SUKEETO BOODO de ikimasu ka.*

Reading practice

Read about the five people in the photo on the following page.

1
わたし　の　ともだち　です。
ともだち　の　なまえ　は　アンドル、ピーター、サシャ、ブレット、

リサ　です。みなさん　じゅうろくさい　です。みな　こうこうせい　です。
きょう　さむい　です　が　あかるい　です。きょう　ともだち　は
パーティー　に　いきます。リサ　さん　の　たんじょうび　は　きのう
でした。
らいしゅう　アンドル　さん　は　ブレット　さん　と　ボストン　に
いきます。　サッカー　を　します。
アンドル　さん　は　すいえい　が　じょうず　です。
ブレット　さん　は　ヨット　を　します。
サシャ　さん　は　ダンス　が　すき　です。
ピーター　さん　は　スポーツ　が　きらい　です。まいにち　としょかん
で　ほん　と　ざっし　を　よみます。
リサ　さん　は　いい　せいと　です。いつも　べんきょう　も　スポーツ
も　します。

Note:

あかるい	*akarui*	bright
すいえい	*suiei*	swimming
アンドル	*ANDORU*	Andrew
ピーター	*PIITAA*	Peter
サツャ	*SASHA*	Sasha
ブレット	*BURETTO*	Brett
リサ	*RISA*	Lisa
パーティー	*PAATII*	party
ボストン	*BOSUTON*	Boston
サッカー	*SAKKAA*	soccer
スポーツ	*SUPOOTSU*	sports
ヨット	*YOTTO*	yacht
ダンス	*DANSU*	dancing

2

Think of as many questions as possible to ask a partner about the people in this photo.

3

Hiragana practice: read the following sentences aloud.

おとうさん　は　せ　が　たかい　です。
おとうさん　は　かみ　の　け　が　ながい　です。
おとうさん　は　かみ　の　け　が　あかい　です。
おかあさん　は　せ　が　ひくい　です。
おかあさん　は　かみ　の　け　が　みじかい　です。
おかあさん　は　かみ　の　け　が　あかい　です。

4

Read the following questions aloud, and give answers, in Japanese, using the information above.

1　おかあさん　は　せ　が　たかい　です　か。
2　おとうさん　は　かみ　の　け　が　みじかい　です　か。
3　おかあさん　は　かみ　の　け　が　あかい　です　か。
4　おかあさん　は　かみ　の　け　が　みじかい　です　か。
5　おとうさん　は　せ　が　ひくい　です　か。

5

Translate the following into English.

ごかぞく　は　なんにん　います　か。
かぞく　は　ごにん　います。
おにいさん　が　います　か。
いいえ、あに　は　いません。
いもうとさん　が　います　か。
はい、いもうと　が　います。
かぞく　は　おかあさん、おとうさん、わたし、いもうと、おとうと
です。

Writing practice

- Review ***hi*** ひ
- Learn ***hya*** ひゃ

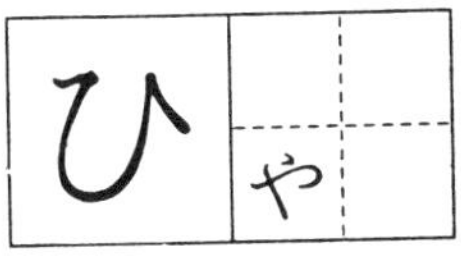

- Learn ***hyu*** ひゅ

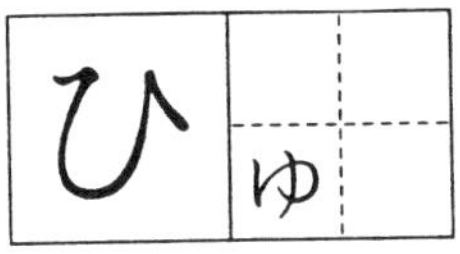

- From ***hyu*** you can make ***hyuu*** ひゅう

- Learn ***hyo*** ひょ

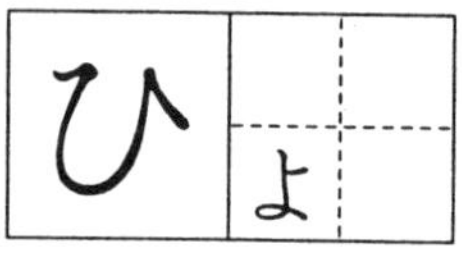

- From ***hyo*** you can make ***hyoo*** ひょう

- Learn to recognize the *katakana* for "England".
IGIRISU イギリス

CROSSWORD (TOPIC EIGHT REVIEW)

ACROSS
6 toilet
7 let's do that
10 mat
11 shrine in house
13 messy
14 entrance hall
16 alcove
18 bathroom
20 pillow

DOWN
1 slippers
2 refrigerator
3 is/are for things that can't move alone
4 scroll
5 table with heater underneath
7 bedroom
8 kitchen
9 mattress . . bed
12 doll
15 like a lot
17 convenient
19 living room

TOPIC NINE health

Introduction

ACHIEVEMENTS

By the end of this unit you will be able to say how you feel and inquire about the health of others.

You will also learn the rest of the *hiragana* combined sounds.

Japan has highly developed health services, with both public and private hospitals and clinics. Doctors are regarded with great respect and are always addressed as ***oisha san*** or ***sensei***. Most doctors practice modern medicine, but there are also numerous practitioners of traditional healing arts including acupuncture, herbal medicine, and various massage treatments.

Health is a popular topic of conversation in Japan. People often discuss ailments, remedies and treatments, exercise and diet. Mothers pass on knowledge of herbal treatments and massage to their daughters and many Japanese women are very good at various forms of massage.

There is a generally high level of awareness of health issues and of the benefits of proper diet and exercise. Most Japanese are quite concerned about being out in the rain without umbrellas and raincoats and worried about the risks to their health by pollution. If they have colds, most will wear masks to keep their face and throat warm and to protect others from infection. Masks are also worn on days when smog is particularly bad.

Exercise

Exercise is a daily part of most people's working or school lives. All over Japan in the morning, people may be seen in parks and open spaces exercising to radio exercise sessions. TV has exercise programs too but people prefer to feel that they are outside in the fresh air, even in big cities where air pollution may in fact be a health hazard!

Many companies have compulsory exercise sessions before work, often on the roof of their company building. Everyone, from the top executives to the junior staff, exercises together.

Office workers regularly give one another shoulder and neck massages to relieve the strain and tension of desk work.

In factories there are set breaks in the working day during which workers stop for a few minutes' exercise beside their machines.

In schools there is usually a session of exercise first thing in the morning as well as physical education and sports periods. Students are also encouraged to take more exercise by joining the after-school sports programs.

Morning exercise outside school

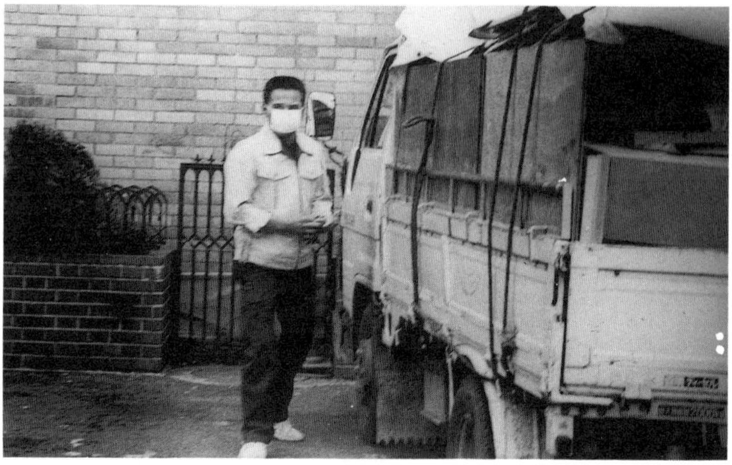

▲ This driver has a cold

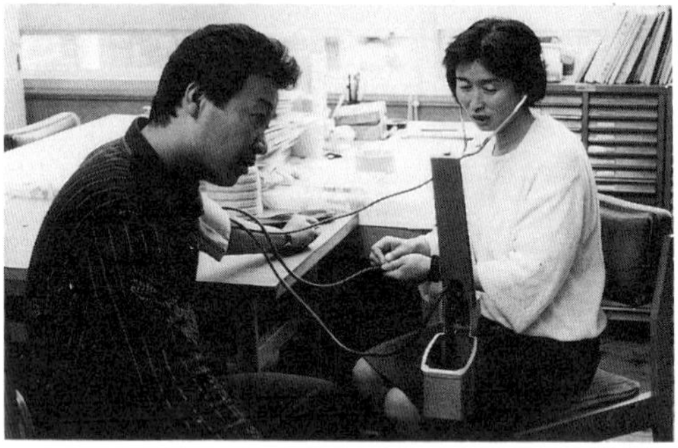

◀ Check-up at the office with a visiting doctor

Diet

The Japanese diet has traditionally been very low in animal fats and high in vegetable and fish protein, with rice as the basic carbohydrate. Unfortunately, contact with the West is changing the excellent dietary habits of the past. Junk foods, cookies, cakes, candies and more meat are now very popular, especially among young people.

The nation's health

The result of a good traditional diet, regular exercise, and an efficient combination of traditional and modern health services, is a generally very healthy nation where the average person lives longer than in most other countries.

However, there are some negative aspects to the health scene in Japan that are worrying Japanese health authorities. One problem, mentioned earlier, is the decline in good eating habits.

Stress is another problem — levels of stress in most people's lives are quite high as they struggle in dense crowds to travel to work, compete at school and work, and work extremely hard to pass their examinations and achieve their ambitions.

Salaried workers (known as ***SARARIIMAN***) are probably the group most at risk from illness in their middle-age years in Japan. These are the young office workers and executives who are working long hours and often drinking alcohol to excess as they try to relax and reduce stress after work. They often smoke heavily as well, and their most common complaint is stomach ulcers.

Smoking is another problem for the nation. Many young people smoke although there are anti-smoking campaigns in every city. To help people stop smoking, there is a great number of patent anti-smoking aids on sale, such as imitation cigarettes, special chewing gums and sweets, but the number of smokers remains high.

Air pollution is still a serious health hazard in some areas, although stringent controls are in place and government and local councils are working hard to combat it.

These negative factors are causing serious concern about the nation's future health.

Superstitions

In all countries there are superstitions concerned with health and sickness. In Japan, people don't take potted plants to people who are in the hospital for fear that their illness will take root and become worse than before. Cut flowers are taken instead. Three, five or seven flowers should be given, as even numbers are associated with bad or unpleasant things.

Never take camellias or chrysanthemums to sick Japanese people as chrysanthemums are the flowers most often used for funerals and it is bad luck to receive camellias if you are sick.

You may remember reading previously that the number four is never used on hospital rooms in Japan because it is an unlucky number.

Unit 1

あたま が いたい です
atama ga itai desu
I have a headache

NEW WORDS

いたい です	*itai desu*	it hurts/is sore/aches
びょうき	*byooki*	sick/ill
げんき	*genki*	well/healthy
あたま	*atama*	head
みみ	*mimi*	ears
め	*me*	eyes
はな	*hana*	nose
くち	*kuchi*	mouth
のど	*nodo*	throat
むね	*mune*	chest
せなか	*senaka*	back
おなか	*onaka*	stomach
あし	*ashi*	legs/feet
て	*te*	hands
うで	*ude*	arms
ゆび	*yubi*	fingers
あしゆび	*ashiyubi*	toes
それ は いけません ね	*sore wa ikemasen ne*	How unfortunate
Interest only		
ぐあい は ちょっと わるい です	*guai wa chotto warui desu*	I don't feel very well
からだ	*karada*	body

STUDY

- Two expressions that are useful:

  Onaka ga sukimashita. I am hungry.
  Nodo ga kawakimashita. I am thirsty.

  They are both in the past tense because they mean, if translated literally:
  My stomach has become empty — so now I am hungry.
  My throat has dried up — so now I am thirsty.
  You may find these expressions useful with this unit.

  The negatives are more difficult and are shown here for interest only. You don't have to learn them but you may like to be able to use them when explaining that you are not hungry or thirsty in this unit.

  Onaka ga suite imasen. I am not hungry.
  Nodo ga kawaite imasen. I am not thirsty.

Don't worry about the grammar involved, just use them as they are.

- The expression ***Sore wa ikemasen ne*** is really useful. It means "What a pity" / "I'm sorry to hear that" / "How unfortunate!" and you can use it with all sorts of situations where you want to say those things, not just in health matters.

- ***Byooki***, "ill", is usually only used when you have been ill enough to stay away from school or work. If you have merely been feeling "under the weather", you can use the phrase *guai wa chotto warui desu*. The word ***chotto*** means "a little bit" in situations where you can't measure the size of "the bit".

- You will recall how to say "How are you?" Earlier it was introduced as a greeting formality when meeting someone after some time. In this unit you can ask it in a genuine inquiry about someone's health.

- ***Dewa*** means "Well then" and is often used where, in English, we would say "Now . . .". A similar word is ***Ja*** じゃ

Read the following conversations:

1 **Akiko:** *Sumimasen ga, atama ga itai desu kara ima anata no REKOODO o kikimasen.*
Hanako: *Sore wa ikemasen ne . . . ashita wa?*
Akiko: *Ashita wa ii deshoo.*

A: Please excuse me but because I have a headache I won't listen to your records at the moment.
H: I'm sorry to hear that. How about tomorrow?
A: Tomorrow will probably be good.

2 Two friends are out hiking.
Reiko: *Chotto matte kudasai. Ashi ga itai desu.*
Kenji: *Watashi mo ashi ga itai desu. Kaerimashoo ka.*
Reiko: *Hai, kaerimashoo!*

R: Please wait a minute! My legs are aching.
K: My legs hurt too. Shall we go home?
R: Yes, let's!

STUDY

- The expression ***itai desu*** can be translated in several ways. We use different expressions depending on the type of pain, for example we say we have a "headache" if our head aches, we say "my head hurts" if we have bumped into something, and we say "My head is sore" for a more localized pain. The Japanese use the same expression to cover all those possibilities. When you translate from Japanese therefore you must be careful to select the expression that is most appropriate.

We can use ***itai desu*** for different pains around the body:

Atama ga itai desu. My head aches/I've got a headache/My head is sore/My head hurts.

Ha ga itai desu. My tooth hurts/I've got toothache/My tooth is sore.

The same variety of expressions occurs with the following:

Nodo ga itai desu. I've got a sore throat.

Senaka ga itai desu. I've got backache.

Ashi ga itai desu. My legs/feet ache.

- The word ***itai*** is an adjective and behaves the same way as other adjectives you know — to make the negative take off the ***i*** and add ***kunai***. So to say "My head does not ache/I don't have a headache" use *Atama ga itakunai desu.*

- ***Ima*** mean's "now" so you can answer the question "Do you have a headache?" with "No, I don't have a headache now."

- The ***ga*** particle is used again when talking about parts of you that hurt because you are focusing on that particular part. ***Ga*** is also used because you feel an emotion about being in pain.

- ***Sumimasen ga*** . . . The ***ga*** in this phrase means "but" as you learned previously. You can also use ***ga*** to say things like "I was sick last week but I'm fine now."
  Senshuu byooki deshita ga ima genki desu.
  Again you are focusing on a particular part of your sentence or the new state, which is now more important than the previous state.

- ***Genki*** is another qualitative noun, not an adjective. You now know several of this group of words:
  kirei, HANSAMU, joozu, genki.
  Kirai and *suki*, *ookii* and *chiisai*, are in fact members of this group too.
  They all behave the same way.

健康・医療

9 いびき防止枕「グーストップ」

1回払 ¥29,800 Ⓐ

申込番号 404292

●材質：ABS樹脂、スポンジ、キルティングカバー●サイズ：巾44×奥30×高11.8cm●重量：約3kg●電源：単1乾電池6本■電子コントロールの「いびき」防止安眠枕です。12秒以内にいびきの音を3回感知するとモーターが作動し枕を左右にゆるやかに傾けます。

10 健康枕ジキドリームN(カバー付)

1回払 ¥8,300 Ⓒ

申込番号 404217

●サイズ：巾50×奥26×高(前部)10cm、(後部) 6cm●重量：700g■睡眠中に首を支え頸椎のズレを防ぎ、磁気の効果でコリと血行を良くします。

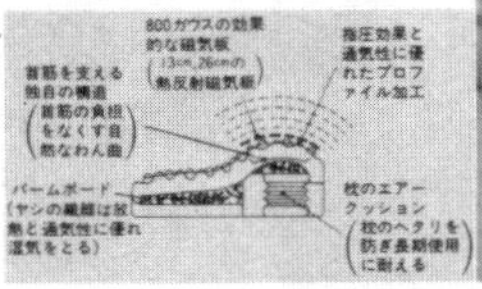

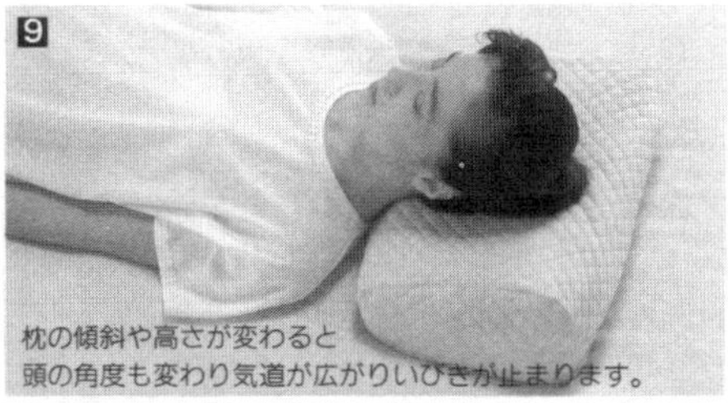

9
枕の傾斜や高さが変わると
頭の角度も変わり気道が広がりいびきが止まります。

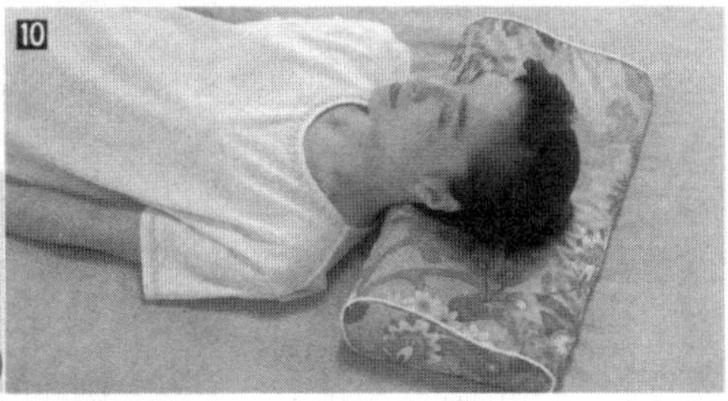

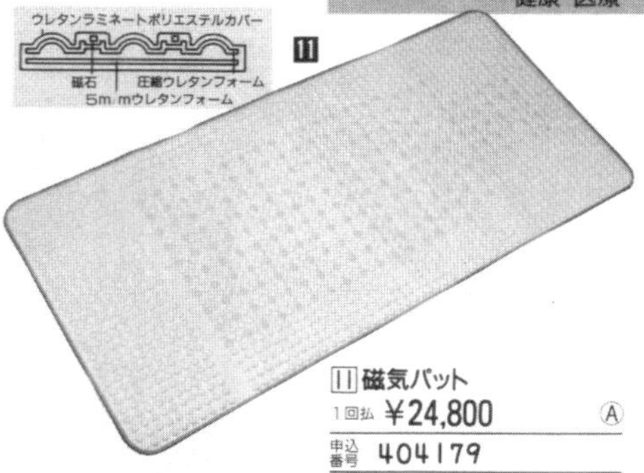

ウレタンラミネートポリエステルカバー

5m/mウレタンフォーム

11 磁気パット

1回払 ¥24,800 Ⓐ

申込番号 404179

●サイズ：巾88×長185×厚2cm●重量：3kg■ご使用の敷布団、ベッドの上に敷くだけで使用できる磁気パットです。212個の永久磁石(1個750ガウス)と圧縮ウレタン層の凹凸で、血行を良くしコリをほぐすとともに体を点でささえ指圧効果が得られます。

12 ニュー中山式快癒器(FK型)

1回払 ¥3,800 Ⓒ

申込番号 404152

●材質：スチロール●サイズ：4球=巾17×奥14×高6.3cm、2球=巾15×奥13.8×高7cm●重量：4球=310g、2球=240g■2球式と4球式の球頭が、指圧師の親指の動きを代用して、首筋・背筋の筋肉をもみほぐします。

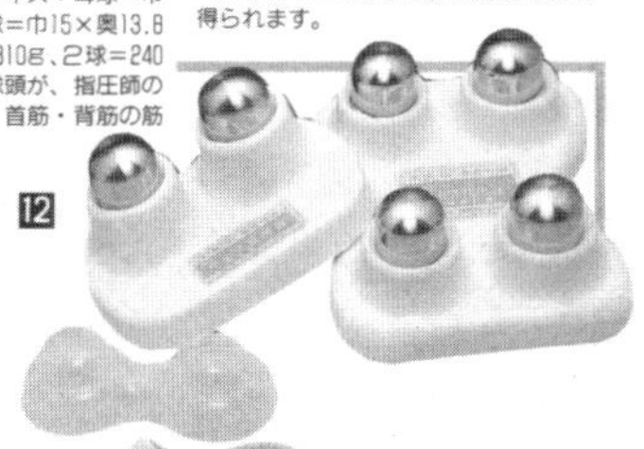

13 磁気腹巻(メッシュタイプ)

1回払 ¥6,600 Ⓐ

●素材：ナイロン、ポリウレタン、ポリエステル●適応ウエストサイズ=M (60~85cm)、L(80~105cm)、LL(90~112cm) ■腰部と腹部に磁石（計36個）を配列、腰のコリをほぐし、腹部の血行を良くします。ボディラインに合った曲線カットによりピッタリフィット、メッシュ構造のため軽くうすくむれません。

⑬申込番号表

サイズ	申込番号	サイズ	申込番号
M	404187	LL	404209
L	404195		

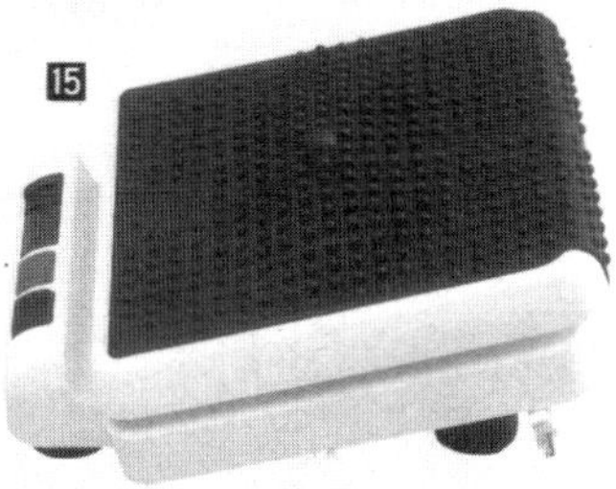

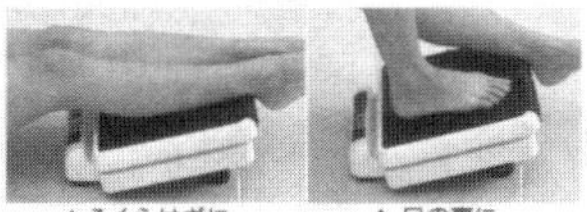

▲ふくらはぎに　▲足の裏に

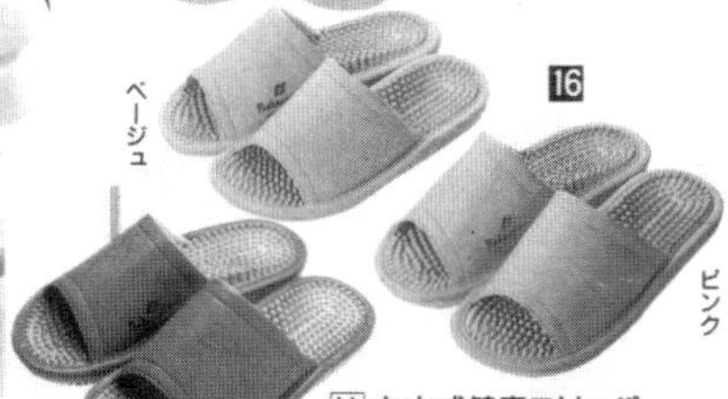

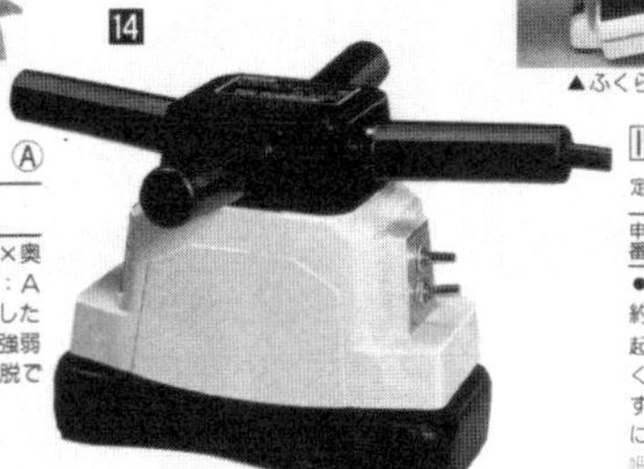

14 温熱マッサージャー

1回払 ¥14,800 Ⓐ

申込番号 404349

●材質：ABS樹脂●サイズ：巾31×奥29.5×高19cm●重量：2.5kg●電源：AC100V、32~42W■パット部に内蔵したヒーターが温熱効果を発揮します。強弱二段階切換式でスペアハンドルは着脱できます。

15「フットバイブ」

定価 ¥39,800 Ⓒ

申込番号 404357

●サイズ：巾30×長37×高17.5mm●重量：約4.5kg●電源=AC100V、21W■上部突起面(指圧ゴム)板が振動し、足の裏・ふくらはぎ等をここちよくマッサージします。スポーツや行楽疲れ、立ち仕事の後にお勧めです。※心臓障害のある方、妊娠している方等は使用できません。組合員価格は生協にお問い合わせ下さい。

16 中山式健康スリッパ(男女兼用)

1回払 ¥2,680 Ⓐ

●材質：天然ゴム、ウレタン樹脂、ビニールレザー●サイズ：M=24.5cm以下、L=25cm以上■約1000個の突起が血行を良くし、疲れをとります。

⑯申込番号表

	ピンク	ベージュ	サックス
M	404098	404071	404080
L	404128	404101	404110

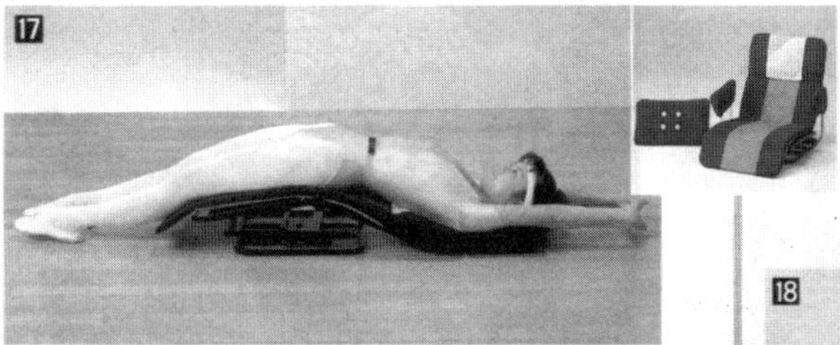

17 のびのび回転座椅子(バイブレータークッション付)

1回払 ¥9,800 組立式 Ⓐ

申込番号 404331

●材質：スチールパイプ（メラミン焼付塗装)、ナイロン他●サイズ：巾62~69×奥60×高60cm●重量：7.5kg■背もたれ部が倒れ、背伸びや腹筋運動ができます。座部は360度回転し、肘掛けは左右にスライドし取りはずしもできます。バイブレータークッション付。

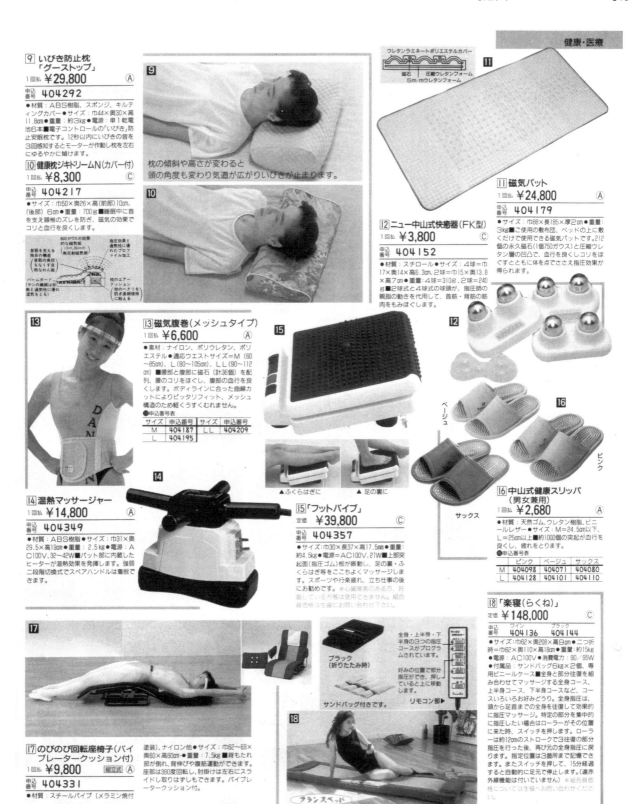

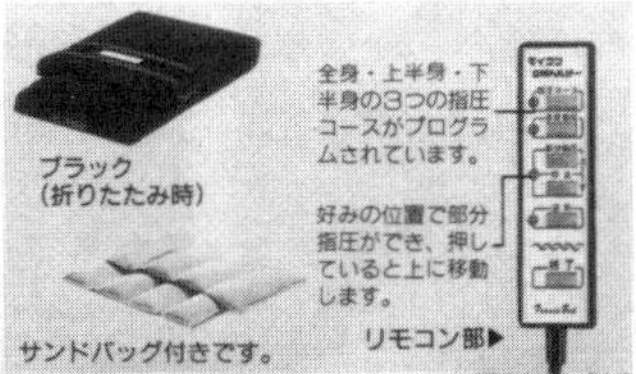

(折りたたみ時)

全身・上半身・下半身の3つの指圧コースがプログラムされています。
好みの位置で部分指圧ができ、押していると上に移動します。
リモコン部▶

フランスベッド

18「楽寝(らくね)」

定価 ¥148,000 Ⓒ

申込番号 ワイン 404136　ブラック 404144

●サイズ：巾62×奥208×高9cm●二つ折時=巾62×奥110×高18cm●重量：約15kg●電源：AC100V●消費電力：90／95W●付属品：サンドバッグ6kg×2個、専用ビニールケース■全身と部分往復を組み合わせてマッサージする全身コース、上半身コース、下半身コースなど、コースいろいろお好みどうり。全身指圧は、頭から足首までの全身を往復して効果的に指圧マッサージ。特定の部分を集中的に指圧したい場合はローラーがその位置に来た時、スイッチを押します。ローラーは約12cmのストロークで3往復の部分指圧を行った後、再び元の全身指圧に戻ります。指定位置は3箇所まで記憶できます。またスイッチを押して、15分経過すると自動的に足元で停止します。(遠赤外線機能は付いていません) ※組合員価格については生協へお問い合わせください。

Health and exercise products abound in Japan

- ***Desu kara*** you have used with weather. You may now extend your use of it with health:
  Atama ga itai desu kara eiga ni ikimasen.
  I won't go to the movies, because I have a headache.

- ***Deshoo*** has not been mentioned for a long time. You will remember that it means "perhaps" or "probably" and may be translated as "I think . . ." as well.
  Now you can say "Perhaps I'll be sick/I think I may be sick/I'll probably be sick."
  AISUKURIIMU o takusan tabemashita kara byooki deshoo.
  Because I ate a lot of ice cream I'll probably be sick.

ACTIVITIES

- Around the class. Practice saying that different parts of you hurt or don't hurt. You can sound like a class of hypochondriacs if you wish!

- Think of reasons why you may be ill tomorrow. Use *deshoo*, e.g.:
  Taihen samui desu kara ashita watashi wa byooki deshoo.
  Because it's very cold I may be ill tomorrow.

Writing practice

- Review ***mi*** み

- Learn ***mya*** みゃ

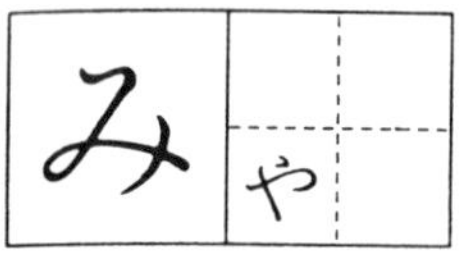

- Learn ***myu*** みゅ

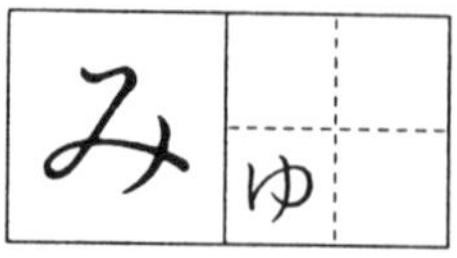

- From ***myu*** you can make ***myuu*** みゅう

- Learn ***myo*** みょ

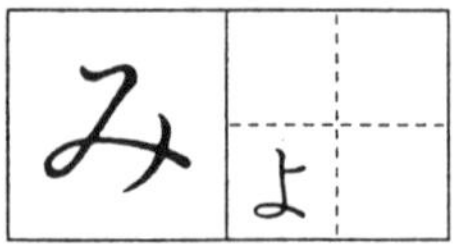

- From ***myo*** you can make ***myoo*** みょう

Unit 2

どう しました か
doo shimashita ka
What's the matter?

NEW WORDS

Interest only

ねつ が あります	*netsu ga arimasu*	(someone) has fever/high temperature
ど	*do*	degrees of temperature

Essential

ジュース	*JUUSU*	juice
みず	*mizu*	water
ぜんぶ	*zenbu*	all
スープ	*SUUPU*	soup
うれしい	*ureshii*	happy
うれしくない	*ureshikunai*	unhappy/not happy
つまらない	*tsumaranai*	boring/worthless
つまらなくない	*tsumaranakunai*	not boring
どう しました か	*doo shimashita ka*	What's the matter?/What happened?
からだ	*karada*	body

Tom's mother is ill so he calls the doctor.

Tom:
おいしゃ さん、きて ください。 *Oisha san, kite kudasai.*
はは は びょうき です。 *Haha wa byooki desu.*

Doctor:
どう しました か。 *Doo shimashita ka?*

Tom:
あたま が いたい です。 *Atama ga itai desu.*
せなか が いたい です。 *Senaka ga itai desu.*
ねつ が あります。 *Netsu ga arimasu.*

Doctor:
じゃ ちょっと まって ください。 *Ja chotto matte kudasai.*
うち に いきます。 *Uchi ni ikimasu.*

Check your understanding of the conversation.
T: Doctor, please come. My mother is sick.
D: What's the matter?

T: She has a headache and a backache. She has a high temperature/a fever.

D: Well, please hold on (wait a minute). I'll come to your house.

Read the following passage and figure out the meaning with a parnter.
Konshuu byooki desu. Netsu ga arimasu. Sanjuukyuu do desu. Karada wa zenbu itai desu. Gakkoo ni ikimasen. Uchi de yasumimasu. Mainichi nemasu. Me ga itai desu kara TEREBI o mimasen. Hon to zasshi o yomimasen. Nodo ga itai desu kara tabemasen. JUUSU to mizu to SUUPU o nomimasu. Raishuu genki deshoo. Ima tsumaranai desu.

こんしゅう　びょうき　です。ねつ　が　あります。さんじゅうきゅう　どです。からだ　は　ぜんぶ　いたい　です。がっこう　に　いきません。うち　で　やすみます。　まいにち　ねます。め　が　いたい　です　からテレビ　を　みません。ほん　と　ざっし　を　よみません。のど　がいたい　です　から　たべません。ジュース　と　みず　と　スープ　をのみます。らいしゅう　げんき　でしょう。いま　つまらない　です。

Work together to explain the following situation:
Imagine that one of your friends is ill. You had arranged to go out with a third person this afternoon. You call the third person and explain the problem. You make arrangements to go next week because your friend will probably be better then.

ACTIVITIES

- Imagine you are on a homestay visit in Japan. You wake one morning feeling unwell.

  With a partner do a role play in which you greet your homestay mother and tell her that you are not well. She questions you to find out what is the matter and maybe takes your temperature. You say that you'll probably feel better tomorrow but won't go to school today. She suggests calling the doctor but you say that it's OK thank you. Tell her that you will lie down and go to sleep.

- In groups or around the class (or in pairs as in a doctor's office) role play a doctor going around the hospital (classroom).
  He/She greets the patient (good bedside manner needed).
  After making the patient feel at ease with some general conversation on the weather or the beautiful flowers, he/she asks what hurts:
  Nani ga itai desu ka.
  The patient can have a lot of aches and pains or just one.
  The doctor commiserates, says he/she will be back later, and moves on to the next patient.

- You have built up a good vocabulary now and can say many useful things in Japanese.

  With a partner or a small group, act out a play in which you use as much as possible of the material that you know.

  Read the following conversation between two students. It may give you a starting point for your play. Or you can use your own ideas.

Yumiko:

おはよう。きょう　さむい　です ね。	*Ohayoo. Kyoo samui desu ne.*

Sachiko:

はい、さむい　です。	*Hai, samui desu.*
おひさしぶり　です　ね。	*Ohisashiburi desu ne.*
おげんき　です　か。	*Ogenki desu ka.*

Yumiko:

いま　げんき　です　が	*Ima genki desu ga*
せんしゅう　びょうき　でした。	*senshuu byooki deshita.*

Sachiko:

それ　は　いけません　ね。	*Sore wa ikemasen ne.*
きっさてん　に　いきましょう か。	*Kissaten ni ikimashoo ka.*
じかん　が　あります　か。	*Jikan ga arimasu ka.*

Yumiko:

はい、いきましょう。	*Hai, ikimashoo.*

In the coffee bar.

Yumiko:

…では、	*. . . Dewa, nani o*
なに　を　しました　か。	*shimashita ka.*

After this they chat about their daily lives, their families and friends, asking and answering questions. The time races by and they suddenly realize they have to separate. They arrange to meet again soon.

Writing practice

- Review ***ri*** り
- Learn ***rya*** りゃ

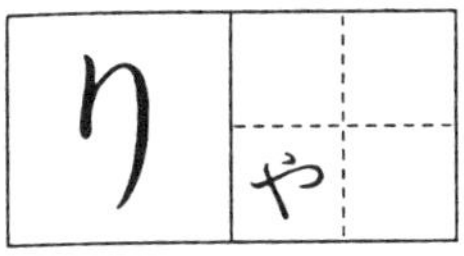

- Learn ***ryu*** りゅ

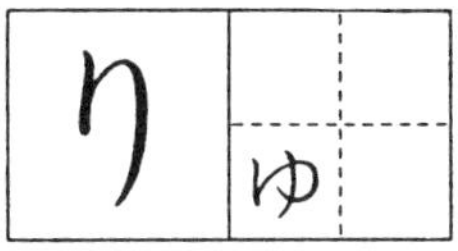

- From ***ryu*** you can make ***ryuu*** りゅう

- Learn ***ryo*** りょ

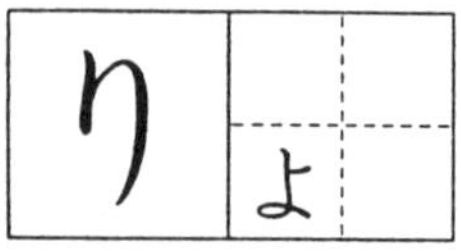

- From ***ryo*** you can make ***ryoo*** りょう

Hiragana faces

What faces can you make using the *hiragana* syllables that you know? The syllables must be clearly readable and as close as possible to the right way up!

CROSSWORD (TOPIC NINE REVIEW)

ACROSS
4 Chest
5 Fingers
10 Soup
12 I don't feel well.
14 Coffee bar
16 Throat
17 Head
19 Toes
21 Nose
22 Legs/Feet
23 How unfortunate!
24 Ears
25 Healthy
27 I'm hungry.

DOWN
1 Not Boring
2 I'm thirsty
3 I have a fever.
6 Sick/Ill
7 Boring
8 All
9 Mouth
11 Back
13 Arms
15 Stomach
18 It hurts.
20 Water
26 Degrees of temperature
28 Eyes
29 Hands

Reading practice (review)

1
Read through the following passage and then answer the questions.

わたし　の　ともだち
わたし　の　にほんじん　の　ともだち　です。おんな　の　こ　は　ごにん　います。
にほん　の　こうえん　に　います。ともだち　の　なまえ　は　ゆきこ、はなこ、さちこ、みちこ、すみこ　です。
みな　じゅうろくさい　です。
みな　にほん　の　なら　に　すんで　います。
なら　の　まち　は　きれい　です。なら　の　こうえん　も　きれい　です。
ともだち　は　こうこうせい　です。みな　は　えいご　を　べんきょう　します。
らいねん　アメリカ　と　カナダ　に　いきます。
こうとうがっこう　で　べんきょう　します。

アメリカ	*AMERIKA*	America
カナダ	*KANADA*	Canada

Questions
1 おんな　の　こ　の　なまえ　は　なん　です　か。
2 どこ　に　すんで　います　か。
3 えいご　を　べんきょう　します　か。
4 なんさい　です　か。
5 なら　は　どこ　に　あります　か。

2

Read the next passage and answer the questions.

こちら　は　イアン　と　サム　です。わたし　の　どうきゅうせい　です。きょう　サッカー　を　します。なつ　です　が　きょう　は　あつい　です。イアン　と　サム　は　せ　が　たかい　です。
イアン　さん　は　じゅうよんさい　です。アメリカじん　です。
サム　さん　は　じゅうごさい　です。カナダじん　です。
きょう　がっこう　で　サッカー　を　れんしゅう　します。あした　こうえん　で　サッカー　を　します。

サム	*SAMU*	Sam
イアン	*IAN*	Ian
サッカー	*SAKKAA*	soccer

Questions

1　サム　は　アメリカじん　です　か。
2　イアン　は　なんさい　です　か。
3　どこ　で　サッカー　を　れんしゅう　します　か。
4　あした　なに　を　します　か。
5　きょう　は　あつい　です　か、さむい　です　か。

3

ブレンドン　は　わたし　の　あに　です。こうとうがっこう　で　べんきょう　します。ブレンドン　の　ともだち　は　リネット　さん　です。ブレンドン　と　リネット　さん　は　カメラ　が　すき　です。ブレンドン　は　いい　せいと　です。いい　あに　です。まいにち　わたし　は　ブレンドン　と　レコード　を　ききます。ゲーム　を　します。ときどき　けんか　を　します。
ブレンドン　と　リネット　は　けんか　を　しません。

ブレンドン	*BURENDON*	Brendon
リネット	*RINETTO*	Lynette
カメラ	*KAMERA*	camera
レコード	*REKOODO*	records
ゲーム	*GEEMU*	game
けんか	*kenka*	quarrel

Questions

1　ブレンドン　は　だれ　です　か。
2　なに　が　すき　です　か。
3　ブレンドン　は　いい　せいと　です　か。
4　ブレンドン　と　リネット　は　いつも　けんか　を　します　か。

4

こちら　は　ちち　と　はは　の　ともだち　です。おとこ　の　ひと　は　デビド　さん　です。おんな　の　ひと　は　ベス　さん　です。デビド　さん　と　ベス　さん　は　カナダじん　です。トロント　に　すんで　います。

デビド　さん　は　ヨット　を　します。
にちようび　と　どようび　いつも　ヨット　を　します。
なつ　と　ふゆ　は　ヨット　を　します。あつい　おてんき　と　さむい
おてんき　は　ヨット　を　します。
ベス　さん　も　ヨット　が　すき　です。かぞく　と　にちようび　に
ヨット　を　します。ベス　さん　の　こども　は　フィオナ　と
カースティ　です。ベス　さん　の　しゅじん　は　アラン　さん　です。
ベス　さん　の　かぞく　が　すき　です。

しゅじん	*shujin*	husband
ベス	*BESU*	Beth
デビド	*DEBIDO*	David
アラン	*ARAN*	Alan
フィオナ	*FIONA*	Fiona
カースティ	*KAASUTI*	Kirsty
トロント	*TORONTO*	Toronto
カナダ	*KANADA*	Canada
ヨット	*YOTTO*	yacht

Questions

1 ベス　さん　と　デビド　さん　は　だれ　の　ともだち　です　か。
2 デビド　さん　は　なに　が　すき　です　か。
3 ベス　さん　は　どこ　に　すんで　います　か。
4 ベス　さん　の　こども　の　なまえ　は　なん　です　か。

5

わたし　の　にほんじん　の　ともだち　の　えみこ　ちゃん　です。えみこ
ちゃん　は　せ　が　ひくい　です。じゅうろくさい　です。いつも
うれしい　です。　がっこう　が　ときどき　きらい　です。ときどき
すき　です。
ニューヨーク　の　こうとうがっこう　に　きました。しゃかい　と
すうがく　と　えいご　と　にほんご　を　べんきょう　します。スポーツ
が　じょうず　です。

うれしい	*ureshii*	happy
ニューヨーク	*NYUUYOOKU*	New York
スポーツ	*SUPOOTSU*	sports

Questions

1 おんな　の　こ　の　なまえ　は　なん　です　か。
2 なんさい　です　か。
3 がっこう　で　なに　を　べんきょう　します　か。
4 なに　が　じょうず　です　か。
5 せ　が　たかい　です　か、せ　が　ひくい　です　か。

Vocabulary Checklist

Topic One

あまど	*amado*	sliding shutters
あなた	*anata*	you
あの	*ano*	that (over there)
アメリカ	*AMERIKA*	America
ありがとう ございます	*arigatoo gozaimasu*	Thank you
ブラウン	*BURAUN*	Brown (name)
ちゅうごく	*Chuugoku*	China
だれ	*dare*	who?
でんわ	*denwa*	telephone
です	*desu*	is/are
では ありません	*dewa arimasen*	is not/are not
ドア	*DOA*	door
ドイツ	*DOITSU*	Germany
どうも	*doomo*	(Thank you) very much
どこ の かた です か	*doko no kata desu ka*	Where are you from?
どうも ありがとう ございます	*doomo arigatoo gozaimasu*	Thank you very much
えんぴつ	*enpitsu*	pencil
フィリッピン	*FIRIPPIN*	Philippines
フランス	*FURANSU*	France
げんき です	*genki desu*	am/is/are well
はい	*hai*	Yes
はな	*hana*	flower
はじめまして どうぞ よろしく	*hajimemashite doozo yoroshiku*	Pleased to meet you for the first time
ひらがな	*hiragana*	hiragana
ひろしま	*Hiroshima*	Hiroshima (city)
ひと	*hito*	person
ほっかいどう	*Hokkaidoo*	Hokkaido (northern island)
ほん	*hon*	book
ホンコン	*HONKON*	Hong Kong
ほんしゅう	*Honshuu*	Honshu (main island)
いいえ	*iie*	No
インド	*INDO*	India
インドネシア	*INDONESHIA*	Indonesia
いぬ	*inu*	dog
イタリア	*ITARIA*	Italy
じゃ また	*ja mata*	See you! Bye!
か	*ka*	(question marker)
かばん	*kaban*	bag, briefcase
カナダ	*KANADA*	Canada

かんじ	*kanji*	kanji
かんこく	*Kankoku*	Korea
かさ	*kasa*	umbrella
カタカナ	*KATAKANA*	katakana
き	*ki*	tree
こんばん　は	*konban wa*	Good evening
こんにち　は	*konnichi wa*	Good afternoon/Hello
コカ　コーラ	*KOKA KOORA*	Coca Cola
くるま	*kuruma*	car
きょうと	*Kyooto*	Kyoto (city)
きゅうしゅう	*Kyuushuu*	Kyushu (southern island)
メキシコ	*MEKISHIKO*	Mexico
めいじ	*Meiji*	(Emperor 1869 – 1912)
みなさん	*minasan*	everybody/everyone
ながさき	*Nagasaki*	Nagasaki (city)
なまえ	*namae*	name
なん	*nan*	what?
なん　です　か	*nan desu ka*	what is it?
なにじん　です　か	*nanijin desu ka*	What nationality are you?
なら	*Nara*	Nara (city)
ねこ	*neko*	cat
にほん	*Nihon*	Japan
にほんご	*nihongo*	Japanese language
にん/じん/ひと/かた	*nin/jin/hito/kata*	person
の	*no*	(particle: "belonging to")
ニュージーランド	*NYUUJIIRANDO*	New Zealand
お	*O*	(Honorific to show respect)
おはよう　ございます	*Ohayoo gozaimasu*	Good morning
おひさしぶり　です　ね	*Ohisashiburi desu ne*	Long time no see!
おげんき　です　か	*Ogenki desu ka*	Are you well?
おかげ　さま　で	*Okage same de. . .*	Thank you for asking. . .
おじぎ	*Ojigi*	bow
おおさか	*Oosaka*	Osaka (city)
オーストラリア	*OOSUTORARIA*	Australia
オランダ	*ORANDA*	Holland
おやすみ　なさい	*Oyasumi nasai*	Sleep well!
パン	*PAN*	bread
レストラン	*RESUTORAN*	restaurant
りんご	*ringo*	apple
ロシア	*ROSHIA*	Russia
さん	*san*	Mr./Mrs./Miss
さっぽろ	*Sapporo*	Sapporo (city)
さよなら	*sayonara*	Goodbye
さようなら	*sayoonara*	Goodbye (formal)
せいと	*seito*	pupil
せんせい	*sensei*	teacher, master
しこく	*Shikoku*	Shikoku (smallest of four main islands)
すみません　が	*sumimasen ga*	Excuse me, but. . . .
スミス	*SUMISU*	Smith (name)
スペイン	*SUPEIN*	Spain
すずき	*Suzuki*	Suzuki (common name)
ただいま	*tadaima*	I'm home!

タイワン	*TAIWAN*	Taiwan
とうきょう	*Tookyoo*	Tokyo (city)
うち	*uchi*	your own home
は	*wa*	(particle showing topic)
わたし	*watashi*	I/me
やま	*yama*	mountain

Topic Two

あけて　ください	*akete kudasai*	Please open
あれ	*are*	that (over there)
ボールペン	*BOORUPEN*	ballpoint pen
ちず	*chizu*	map
ちゅうがっこう	*chuugakkoo*	intermediate/junior high school
どうぞ	*doozo*	Here you are
どれ	*dore*	which? (of more than two things)
え	*e*	picture, painting
ふでばこ	*fudebako*	pencil case
ごみばこ	*gomibako*	garbage can
はこ	*hako*	box
いす	*isu*	chair
じゃない　です	*janai desu*	(informal negative of *desu* "is not")
じん	*jin*	person
じゅく	*juku*	cram school
かいて　ください	*kaite kudasai*	Please write
かみ	*kami*	paper
けしごむ	*keshigomu*	eraser
こくばん	*kokuban*	blackboard
これ	*kore*	this
これ　を　ください	*kore o kudasai*	Please give me this
こうとうがっこう	*kootoogakkoo*	senior high school
きょうしつ	*kyooshitsu*	classroom
まど	*mado*	window
まんが	*manga*	comic
ものさし	*monosashi*	ruler
ノート	*NOOTO*	notebook
ペン	*PEN*	pen
しめて　ください	*shimete kudasai*	Please close
しんぶん	*shinbun*	newspaper
しょうがっこう	*shoogakkoo*	primary school
それ	*sore*	that
つくえ	*tsukue*	desk
ようちえん	*yoochien*	kindergarten
ざっし	*zasshi*	magazine

Topic Three

バイオリン	*BAIORIN*	violin
バレーボール	*BAREEBOORU*	volleyball
バスケットボール	*BASUKETTOBOORU*	basketball
べんきょう　します	*benkyoo shimasu*	study
ちがいます	*chigaimasu*	You're wrong/I beg to differ

ちり	*chiri*	geography
ドイツご	*DOITSUgo*	German language
えいご	*eigo*	English
フランスご	*FURANSUgo*	French
フルート	*FURUUTO*	flute
フットボール	*FUTTOBOORU*	football
がっこう	*gakkoo*	school
ギター	*GITAA*	guitar
はなします	*hanashimasu*	speak/talk
はなしません	*hanashimasen*	don't/won't speak
いけばな	*ikebana*	flower arranging
イタリアご	*ITARIAgo*	Italian
じゅうどう	*juudoo*	(martial art)
かがく	*kagaku*	science
からて	*karate*	(martial art)
けんどう	*kendoo*	kendo (martial art)
ききます	*kikimasu*	listen
ききません	*kikimasen*	don't/won't listen
きらい　です	*kirai desu*	I strongly dislike
こうはい	*koohai*	junior friend of a *senpai*
くん	*kun*	good friend
なにご	*nanigo*	What language(s)?
おんがく	*ongaku*	music
ピアノ	*PIANO*	piano
ラジオ	*RAJIO*	radio
れきし	*rekishi*	history
レコード	*REKOODO*	record (music)
れんしゅう　します	*renshuu shimasu*	practice
サッカー	*SAKKAA*	soccer
せんぱい	*senpai*	special senior friend
しゃかい	*shakai*	social studies
します	*shimasu*	do/will do
しません	*shimasen*	won't/don't do
そう　です	*soo desu*	That's right/That's so
そう　です　か	*soo desu ka*	Is that so?
すき　です	*suki desu*	I like (it)
すき　じゃない　です	*suki janai desu*	I don't like (it)
スポーツ	*SUPOOTSU*	sport
すうがく	*suugaku*	math
たいいく	*taiiku*	Physical Education
カセット　テープ	*KASETTO TEEPU*	casette
テニス	*TENISU*	tennis
や	*ya*	and (in a list)
よみます	*yomimasu*	read
よみません	*yomimasen*	don't/won't read

Topic Four

あした	*ashita*	tomorrow
ばん	*ban*	number
ビデオ　ゲーム	*BIDEO GEEMU*	video games

でんわ　ばんごう	*denwa bangoo*	telephone number
どこ	*doko*	where?
どようび	*doyoobi*	Saturday
どう　いたしまして	*doo itashimashite*	Don't mention it
ええ	*ee*	yes
えいが	*eiga*	film/movie
えき	*eki*	station
げつようび	*getsuyoobi*	Monday
ご	*go*	five
はち	*hachi*	eight
ハイキング	*HAIKINGU*	hiking
はん	*han*	half
へいせい	*heisei*	"accomplishment of peace"
ホノルル	*HONORURU*	Honolulu
ひゃく	*hyaku*	one hundred
いち	*ichi*	one
いえ	*ie*	someone else's house
いきます	*ikimasu*	go
いきましょう	*ikimashoo*	let's go
いつ	*itsu*	when?
いつも	*itsumo*	always
じ	*-ji*	(hour o'clock)
じかん　が　あります	*jikan ga arimasu*	I have time
じかん　が　ありません	*jikan ga arimasen*	I don't have time
じゅう	*juu*	ten
じゅういち	*juuichi*	eleven
じゅうに	*juuni*	twelve
じゅうさん	*juusan*	thirteen
じゅうよん	*juuyon*	fourteen
じゅうご	*juugo*	fifteen
じゅうろく	*juuroku*	sixteen
じゅうなな	*juunana*	seventeen
じゅうはち	*juuhachi*	eighteen
じゅうきゅう/く	*juukyuu/ku*	nineteen
かえります	*kaerimasu*	return home
かようび	*kayoobi*	Tuesday
きます	*kimasu*	come
きのう	*kinoo*	yesterday
きんようび	*kinyoobi*	Friday
こんしゅう	*konshuu*	this week
こうえん	*kooen*	park
くじ	*kuji*	nine o'clock
きょう	*Kyoo*	today
きゅう/く	*kyuu/ku*	nine
まち	*machi*	town
まいにち	*mainichi*	every day
ーません　でした	*— masen deshita*	(past negative ending)
ーました	*— mashita*	(past tense ending)
ーましょう	*— mashoo*	(let's. . .)
みます	*mimasu*	see/look/watch
もくようび	*mokuyoobi*	Thursday
なな	*nana*	seven
なんばん　です　か	*nanban desu ka*	What number is it?
なんようび　です　か	*nanyoobi desu ka*	What day is it?
ニューヨーク	*NYUUYOOKU*	New York

に	*ni*	two
にちようび	*nichiyoobi*	Sunday
にじゅう	*nijuu*	twenty
にじゅういち	*nijuuichi*	twenty-one
オークランド	*OOKURANDO*	Auckland
ピクニック	*PIKUNIKKU*	picnic
プール	*PUURU*	swimming pool
らいしゅう	*raishuu*	next week
れい	*rei*	zero
ろく	*roku*	six
ロサンゼルス	*ROSANZERUSU*	Los Angeles
さん	*san*	three
さんじゅう	*sanjuu*	thirty
せんしゅう	*senshuu*	last week
し	*shi*	four
しち	*shichi*	seven
しょうわ	*shoowa*	(name of Emperor Hirohito's reign)
しゅくだい	*shukudai*	homework
すいようび	*suiyoobi*	Wednesday
たす	*tasu*	added to
としょかん	*toshokan*	library
うち	*uchi*	my house
うみ	*umi*	sea
やきゅう	*yakyuu*	baseball
よじ	*yoji*	four o'clock
よん	*yon*	four
ゼロ	*ZERO*	zero

Topic Five

あかるい	*akarui*	bright
あき	*aki*	autumn
あいます	*aimasu*	meet
あめ	*ame*	rain, rainy
あたたかい	*atatakai*	warm
あたたかくない	*atatakakunai*	not warm
あつい	*atsui*	hot
あつい でしょう か。あめ でしょう か。	*Atsui deshoo ka. Ame deshoo ka*	Do you think it will be hot or rainy?
あつくない	*atsukunai*	not hot
ばいう	*baiu*	rainy season
ボストン	*BOSUTON*	Boston
ふゆ	*fuyu*	winter
はなみ	*hanami*	flower viewing
はる	*haru*	spring
いい	*ii*	good
いい おてんき です	*ii Otenki desu*	It's good weather
か	*ka*	or
かみなり	*kaminari*	thunder
から	*kara*	because
かぜ	*kaze*	wind, windy
きり	*kiri*	fog, foggy
むし あつい	*mushi atsui*	humid

なつ	*natsu*	summer
なぜ　です　か	*naze desu ka*	why (not)?
ね	*ne*	isn't it?
おてんき	*Otenki*	weather
さむい	*samui*	cold
さむくない	*samukunai*	not cold
シカゴ	*SHIKAGO*	Chicago
しも	*shimo*	frost, frosty
すずしい	*suzushii*	cool
すずしくない	*suzushikunai*	not cool
つゆ	*tsuyu*	rainy season
わるい	*warui*	bad
ゆき	*yuki*	snow

Topic Six, Introduction (Interest only)

しち　ご　さん	*shichi go san*	Children's Festival for 3, 5, 7, year olds
ちとせ　あめ	*chitose ame*	a candy for the above festival
かぞえどし	*kazoedoshi*	old system of calculating age
せいじん　の　ひ	*seijin no hi*	adults' day

Topic Six, Unit 1

ちゃん	*chan*	friendly way to speak of girls
こちら	*kochira*	this is (in polite introductions)
ともだち	*tomodachi*	friend
おいくつ　です　か	*Oikutsu desu ka*	How old are you?
なんさい　です　か	*nansai desu ka*	How old are you? (more familiar)
さい	*sai*	counter for age
いっさい	*issai*	one year old
にさい	*nisai*	two years old
さんさい	*sansai*	three years old
よんさい	*yonsai*	four years old
ごさい	*gosai*	five years old
ろくさい	*rokusai*	six years old
ななさい	*nanasai*	seven years old
はっさい	*hassai*	eight years old
きゅうさい	*kyuusai*	nine years old
じゅっさい	*jussai*	ten years old
じゅういっさい	*juuissai*	11 years old
じゅうにさい	*juunisai*	12 years old
じゅうさんさい	*juusansai*	13 years old, etc.
はたち	*hatachi*	20 years old

Topic Six, Unit 2

あたらしい	*atarashii*	new
いちねんせい	*ichinensei*	first-year student
また	*mata*	again.
にねんせい	*ninensei*	second-year student
トロント	*TORONTO*	Toronto
に　すんで　います	*ni sunde imasu*	I live in . . .
オーストラリア	*OOSUTORARIA*	Australia
と	*to*	with/and (in a defined list)

Interest

そろそろ　しつれい　します	*sorosoro shitsurei shimasu*	Excuse me, I must be going

Topic Six, Unit 3

あした	*ashita*	tomorrow
いつ	*itsu*	when
きのう	*kinoo*	yesterday
こんしゅう	*konshuu*	this week
きょう	*kyoo*	today
らいしゅう	*raishuu*	next week
せんしゅう	*senshuu*	last week
たんじょうび	*tanjoobi*	birthday
げつようび	*getsuyoobi*	Monday
かようび	*kayoobi*	Tuesday
すいようび	*suiyoobi*	Wednesday
もくようび	*mokuyoobi*	Thursday
きんようび	*kinyoobi*	Friday
どようび	*doyoobi*	Saturday
にちようび	*nichiyoobi*	Sunday

Topic Six, Unit 3 Festivals (Interest only)

あけまして　おめでとう ございます。	*Akemashite Omedetoo gozaimasu.*	Happy New Year.
はなみ	*hanami*	Flower Viewing (April)
ひなまつり	*hinamatsuri*	Doll Festival (March 3)
こども　の　ひ	*kodomo no hi*	Children's Day (May 5)
こいのぼり	*koinobori*	carp streamers
まつり	*matsuri*	festival
おぼん	*Obon*	Ancestor festival (Aug. 13-15)
おに　は　そと。ふく は　うち。	*Oni wa soto. Fuku wa uchi.*	Devils out! Good luck come in!
さけ	*sake*	rice wine
せつぶん	*setsubun*	Casting Out Devils Day (Feb. 3
しょうがつ	*shoogatsu*	New Year
たなばた	*tanabata*	Star Festival (July 7)
たうえ　まつり	*taue matsuri*	Rice Planting Festival (June 6)
おつきみ	*(O) tsukimi*	Moon Viewing (Sept.)
よい　おとし　を	*yoi O toshi o*	Happy New Year

Topic Six, Unit 4

あき	*aki*	autumn
ふゆ	*fuyu*	winter
はる	*haru*	spring
なつ	*natsu*	summer
お　たんじょうび おめでとう　ございます	*O tanjoobi omedetoo gozaimasu*	Happy Birthday
なんがつ	*nangatsu*	what month?
いちがつ	*ichigatsu*	January
にがつ	*nigatsu*	February
さんがつ	*sangatsu*	March
しがつ	*shigatsu* (not *yon*)	April
ごがつ	*gogatsu*	May
ろくがつ	*rokugatsu*	June
しちがつ	*shichigatsu* (not *nana*)	July
はちがつ	*hachigatsu*	August
くがつ	*kugatsu* (not *kyuu*)	September
じゅうがつ	*juugatsu*	October
じゅういちがつ	*juuichigatsu*	November
じゅうにがつ	*juunigatsu*	December

Topic Six, Unit 5

じょうず です ね	*joozu desu ne*	You're clever, aren't you?
こども の ひ	*kodomo no hi*	Children's Day (5 May)
なんがつ	*nangatsu*	what month
なんにち	*nannichi*	what date
よく できました	*yoku dekimashita*	Well done
ついたち	*tsuitachi*	1st (of a month)
ふつか	*futsuka*	2nd
みっか	*mikka*	3rd
よっか	*yokka*	4th
いつか	*itsuka*	5th
むいか	*muika*	6th
なのか	*nanoka*	7th
ようか	*yooka*	8th
ここのか	*kokonoka*	9th
とおか	*tooka*	10th
じゅういちにち	*juuichinichi*	11th
じゅうににち	*juuninichi*	12th
じゅうさんにち	*juusannichi*	13th
じゅうよっか	*juuyokka*	14th
じゅうごにち	*juugonichi*	15th
じゅうろくにち	*juurokunichi*	16th
じゅうななにち	*juushichinichi*	17th
じゅうはちにち	*juuhachinichi*	18th
じゅうくにち/ じゅうきゅうにち	*juukunichi/ juukyuunichi*	19th
はつか	*hatsuka*	20th
にじゅういちにち	*nijuuichinichi*	21st
にじゅうににち	*nijuuninichi*	22nd
にじゅうさんにち	*nijuusannichi*	23rd
にじゅうよっか	*nijuuyokka*	24th
にじゅうごにち	*nijuugonichi*	25th
にじゅうろくにち	*nijuurokunichi*	26th
にじゅうななにち	*nijuushichinichi*	27th
にじゅうはちにち	*nijuuhachinichi*	28th
にじゅうくにち/ にじゅうきゅうにち	*nijuukunichi/ nijuukyuunichi*	29th
さんじゅうにち	*sanjuunichi*	30th
さんじゅういちにち	*sanjuuichinichi*	31st

Topic Six, Unit 6

も	*mo*	too/also
Interest		
さあ	*saa*	utterance for "well then"

Topic Six, Unit 7

あかい	*akai*	red (adj)
あかくない	*akakunai*	not red
あおい	*aoi*	blue (adj)
あおくない	*aokunai*	not blue
きいろい	*kiiroi*	yellow (adj)
くろい	*kuroi*	black (adj)
みじかい	*mijikai*	short (adj)
みじかくない	*mijikakunai*	not short

ながい	*nagai*	long (adj)
ながくない	*nagakunai*	not long
ちゃいろ	*chairo*	brown color (noun)
みどりいろ	*midoriiro*	green color (noun)
あし	*ashi*	legs/feet
ちゅうがくせい	*chuugakusei*	intermediate/junior high school student
ひくい	*hikui*	short (in height)/low
ひくくない	*hikukunai*	not short
いちにちじゅう	*ichinichijuu*	all day long
いろ	*iro*	color
かみ の け	*kami no ke*	hair
こうこうせい	*kookoosei*	high school student
め	*me*	eyes
めがね を かけます	*megane o kakemasu*	wears glasses
めがね を かけません	*megane o kakemasen*	doesn't wear glasses
おんな の こ	*onna no ko*	girl
おとこ の こ	*otoko no ko*	boy
せ せい	*se/sei*	height
しょうがくせい	*shoogakusei*	primary school student
たかい	*takai*	tall/high/expensive
たかくない	*takakunai*	not tall, etc

Topic Six, Unit 8

あし	*ashi*	legs/feet
あたま	*atama*	head
はな	*hana*	nose
くち	*kuchi*	mouth
め	*me*	eyes
みみ	*mimi*	ears
おなか	*Onaka*	stomach
て	*te*	hand(s)
そうじ します	*sooji shimasu*	to clean
トロント	*TORONTO*	Toronto
Interest		
だいだいいろ	*daidaiiro*	orange (noun)
どうぶつ	*doobutsu*	animal
じゃんけん	*janken*	paper, rock, scissors game
ももいろ	*momoiro*	peach-pink color
むらさきいろ	*murasakiiro*	purple color (noun)
ねずみいろ	*nezumiiro*	grey color (noun)
さくばん	*sakuban*	yesterday evening

Topic Seven, Unit 1

ぼく	*boku*	I/me (males only)
ちち	*chichi*	own father/Dad
ちいさい	*chiisai*	small
ちいさくない	*chiisakunai*	not small
ちょっと まって ください	*chotto matte kudasai*	Please wait a minute
はは	*haha*	own mother/Mom

じゃ　では	*ja/dewa*	well then/then
こちら	*kochira*	this (person) here (for polite introductions)
おかあさん	*Okaasan*	mother (your own and others)
おかえりなさい	*Okaerinasai*	Welcome home
おとうさん	*Otoosan*	father (your own and others)
おおきい	*ookii*	big
おおきくない	*ookikunai*	not big
Review		
みて　ください	*mite kudasai*	please look/watch
きいて　ください	*kiite kudasai*	please listen
と	*to*	with/and (defined list)
ともだち	*tomodachi*	friend

Topic Seven, Unit 2

あに	*ani*	own older brother
いもうと	*imooto*	own younger sister
こちら　へ　どうぞ	*kochira e doozo*	please come this way
Review		
そうじ　します	*sooji shimasu*	to clean
テレビ	*TEREBI*	TV
フィリッピン	*FIRIPPIN*	Philippines

Topic Seven, Unit 3

あね	*ane*	own older sister
あたま　が　いい　です	*atama ga ii desu*	clever
あたま　が　わるい　です	*atama ga warui desu*	not clever
いい	*ii*	good
おとうと	*otooto*	own younger brother
たいへん	*taihen*	very
わるい	*warui*	bad

Topic Seven, Unit 4

にん	*nin*	counter for people
ひとり	*hitori*	one person
ふたり	*futari*	two people
さんにん	*sannin*	three people
よにん	*yonin*	four people
ごにん	*gonin*	five people
ろくにん	*rokunin*	six people
しちにん	*shichinin*	seven people
はちにん	*hachinin*	eight people
きゅうにん	*kyuunin*	nine people
じゅうにん	*juunin*	ten people
ごかぞく	*gokazoku*	someone else's family
いもうとさん	*imootosan*	someone else's younger sister
きょうだい	*kyoodai*	brothers and sisters
おねえさん	*Oneesan*	someone else's older sister
おにいさん	*Oniisan*	someone else's older brother
おとうとさん	*Otootosan*	someone else's younger brother

Topic Seven, Unit 5

ハンサム	*HANSAMU*	handsome
ハンサム　じゃない	*HANSAMU janai*	
です/ では　ありません	*desu/ dewa arimasen*	not handsome
きれい	*kirei*	beautiful
きれい　じゃない	*kirei janai*	
です/ では　ありません	*desu/ dewa arimasen*	not beautiful
Interest		
ハワイ	*HAWAI*	Hawaii

Topic Seven, Unit 7

しごと	*shigoto*	work/job
Interest		
べんごし	*bengoshi*	lawyer
だいく	*daiku*	carpenter
えきいん	*ekiin*	railway worker
エンジニア	*ENJINIA*	engineer
はいしゃ	*haisha*	dentist
かいしゃいん	*kaishain*	office worker
かんごふ	*kangofu*	nurse
みせ　の　ひと	*mise no hito*	shop assistant
おいしゃ	*Oisha*	doctor
せんせい	*sensei*	teacher
しゅふ	*shufu*	housewife
うんてんしゅ	*untenshu*	driver

Topic Seven, Unit 9

ゲーム	*GEEMU*	game
かぞく	*kazoku*	your own family
そして	*soshite*	and then
と　いっしょ　に	*to issho ni*	together with
Review		
ちゃん	*chan*	girl (friend) or used by parents for daughters.
Interest		
パリ	*PARI*	Paris
サンフランシスコ	*SANFURANSHISUKO*	San Francisco
ワシントン	*WASHINTON*	Washington
カリフォルニア	*KARIFORUNIA*	California

Topic Seven, Unit 10

アパート	*APAATO*	apartment
どこ　に　すんで　います　か	*doko ni sunde imasu ka*	Where do you live?
ひろい	*hiroi*	spacious/wide
ひろくない	*hirokunai*	not spacious/wide
せまい	*semai*	cramped/narrow
せまくない	*semakunai*	not cramped/narrow
うち	*uchi*	home/own house
Review		
ちいさい	*chiisai*	small
ちいさくない	*chiisakunai*	not small
から	*kara*	from
おおきい	*ookii*	big
おおきくない	*ookikunai*	not big

Interest

ちゅうごくじん	*chuugokujin*	Chinese person
テキサス	*TEKISASU*	Texas
ダラス	*DARASU*	Dallas

Topic Eight, Introduction

ぶつだん	*butsudan*	family Buddhist shrine
だいどころ	*daidokoro*	kitchen
だんち	*danchi*	apartment/housing estates
ふとん	*futon*	bedding
げんかん	*genkan*	entrance hall
いま	*ima*	living room
かけじく	*kakejiku*	scroll
こたつ	*kotatsu*	covered table with heater
まくら	*makura*	pillow
お　あがり　ください	*O agari kudasai*	Please come in (Step up)
おふろ	*Ofuro*	bath
おふろば	*Ofuroba*	bathroom
おてあらい	*Otearai*	toilet
しんしつ	*shinshitsu*	bedroom
スリッパ	*SURIPPA*	slipper
たたみ	*tatami*	floor mats
とだな	*todana*	closet
とこのま	*tokonoma*	alcove
ゆかた	*yukata*	cotton kimono
ベッド	*BEDDO*	bed

Topic Eight, Unit 1

あります	*arimasu*	exist/be (for things that can't move under own volition)
べんり	*benri*	convenient
べんり　じゃない　です	*benri janai desu*	not convenient
ちゃわん	*chawan*	bowl/dish
フォーク	*FOOKU*	fork
へや	*heya*	room
ほんばこ	*honbako*	bookcase
ナイフ	*NAIFU*	knife
にんぎょう	*ningyoo*	doll
に　は	*ni wa*	talking about in the . . .
おもしろい	*omoshiroi*	interesting
おもしろくない	*omoshirokunai*	not interesting
れいぞうこ	*reizooko*	refrigerator
さら	*sara*	plate
シャワー	*SHAWAA*	shower
そう　しましょう	*soo shimashoo*	Let's do that
ようふく	*yoofuku*	(Western) clothes
で	*de*	at/in (particle for location of activity)

Interest

たくさん　の　もの	*takusan no mono*	lots of things

Review

だいどころ	*daidokoro*	kitchen
ひろい	*hiroi*	spacious/wide

ひろくない	*hirokunai*	not spacious/wide
いま	*ima*	living room
せまい	*semai*	cramped/narrow
せまくない	*semakunai*	not cramped/narrow
しんしつ	*shinshitsu*	bedroom
たいへん	*taihen*	very
Interest		
だいすき	*daisuki*	like a lot
ええ　と	*ee to*	Let me think (hesitation sound)
ふつう	*futsuu*	usually
ごちゃごちゃ	*gochagocha*	messy/in a mess
おや	*oya*	parents
ポスター	*POSUTAA*	poster

Topic Eight, Unit 2

あそこ	*asoko*	over there
いって	*itte*	go
いって　いらっしゃい	*itte irasshai*	go and come back safely
いって　まいります	*itte mairimasu*	I'm leaving now
ここ	*koko*	here
また	*mata*	again
みて	*mite*	look
そこ	*soko*	there
Review		
どこ	*doko*	where

Topic Eight, Unit 3

あらいます	*araimasu*	wash
あそびます	*asobimasu*	play about (not for sports)
で	*de*	particle for location of activity
ハンバーガー	*HANBAAGAA*	hamburger
じてんしゃ	*jitensha*	bicycle
ジュース	*JUUSU*	juice
かいます	*kaimasu*	buy
ねます	*nemasu*	lie down/go to bed
にわ	*niwa*	garden (don't confuse with particles *ni* and *wa*)
のみます	*nomimasu*	drink
おきます	*okimasu*	get up
りょうり　を　します	*ryoori o shimasu*	cook
サンドイッチ	*SANDOITCHI*	sandwich
シャワー　を　あびます	*SHAWAA o abimasu*	take a shower
たべます	*tabemasu*	eat
つきます	*tsukimasu*	arrive
やすみます	*yasumimasu*	rest
マクドナルド	*MAKUDONARUDO*	McDonald's
Review		
あさごはん	*asagahon*	breakfast
ばんごはん	*bangohan*	evening meal
ひるごはん	*hirugohan*	lunch
いちにち	*ichinichi*	one day
ときどき	*tokidoki*	sometimes

Topic Eight, Unit 4

Interest

ビスケット	*BISUKETTO*	cracker

Topic Eight, Unit 5

バス	*BASU*	bus
ちかてつ	*chikatetsu*	underground/subway
で	*de*	by means of (particle)
でんしゃ	*densha*	train
ふね	*fune*	boat/ship
ひこうき	*hikooki*	airplane
くるま	*kuruma*	car
タクシー	*TAKUSHII*	taxi
Interest		
スケート	*SUKEETO*	skates
スケート　ボード	*SUKEETO BOODO*	skateboard

Topic Nine, Introduction

おいしゃ	*Oisha*	doctor
サラリーマン	*SARARIIMAN*	salaried worker

Topic Nine, Unit 1 (For interest only at this stage)
(Some of these words were presented in Topic 6.)

あし	*ashi*	feet/legs
あしゆび	*ashiyubi*	toes
あたま	*atama*	head
びょうき	*byooki*	sick/ill
げんき	*genki*	well
げんき　じゃない　です	*genki janai desu*	not well
はな	*hana*	nose
いたい　です	*itai desu*	it hurts/is sore/aches
いたくない　です	*itakunai desu*	doesn't hurt, etc
くち	*kuchi*	mouth
め	*me*	eyes
みみ	*mimi*	ears
むね	*mune*	chest
のど	*nodo*	throat
おなか	*Onaka*	stomach
せなか	*senaka*	back
それ　は　いけません ね	*sore wa ikemasen ne*	How unfortunate/ I'm sorry to hear that
て	*te*	hands
うで	*ude*	arms
ゆび	*yubi*	fingers
アイスクリーム	*AISUKURIIMU*	ice cream
ぐあい　は　ちょっと わるい　です	*guai wa chotto warui desu*	I don't feel well
からだ	*karada*	body
きっさてん	*kissaten*	coffee bar
のど　が　かわきました	*nodo ga kawakimashita*	I'm thirsty
おなか　が すきました	*Onaka ga sukimashita*	I'm hungry

Topic Nine, Unit 2

どう　しました　か	*doo shimashita ka*	What's the matter?/What happened?
みず	*mizu*	water
スープ	*SUUPU*	soup
つまらない	*tsumaranai*	boring
つまらなくない	*tsumaranakunai*	not boring
うれしい	*ureshii*	happy
うれしくない	*ureshikunai*	not happy
ぜんぶ	*zenbu*	all
Review		
からだ	*karada*	body
ジュース	*JUUSU*	juice
Interest		
ど	*do*	degrees of temperature
ねつ　が　あります	*netsu ga arimasu*	have a fever/temperature

Kanji Checklist

Here is a list of the *kanji* introduced for your interest only. The list will help you recognize and remember them.

日 *ni*
本 *hon* Japan

語 *go* language

人 *hito*
nin person
jin

月 *getsu (yoobi)* Monday

火 *ka (yoobi)* Tuesday

水 *sui (yoobi)* Wednesday

木 *moku (yoobi)* Thursday

金 *kin (yoobi)* Friday

土 *do (yoobi)* Saturday

日 *nichi (yoobi)* Sunday

天気 *tenki* weather

雨 *ame* rain

小学校 *shoogakkoo* junior school

中学校 *chuugakkoo* intermediate school

高等学校 *kootoogakkoo* high school

大学 *daigaku* university

男	*otoko*	man, male			
女	*onna*	woman, female			
子	*ko*	child			
平成	*heisei*	accomplishment of peace			
母	*haha*	mother			
父	*chichi*	father			
一	*ichi*	one	一人	*hitori*	1 person
二	*ni*	two	二人	*futari*	2 people
三	*san*	three	三人	*sannin*	3 people
四	*shi/yon*	four	四人	*yonin*	4 people
五	*go*	five	五人	*gonin*	5 people
六	*roku*	six	六人	*rokunin*	6 people
七	*nana/shichi*	seven	七人	*shichinin*	7 people
八	*hachi*	eight	八人	*hachinin*	8 people
九	*kyuu/ku*	nine	九人	*kyuunin*	9 people
十	*juu*	ten	十人	*juunin*	10 people

Calendar

1st	ついたち	*tsuitachi*
2nd	ふつか	*futsuka*
3rd	みっか	*mikka*
4th	よっか	*yokka*
5th	いつか	*itsuka*
6th	むいか	*muika*
7th	なのか	*nanoka*
8th	ようか	*yooka*
9th	ここのか	*kokonoka*
10th	とおか	*tooka*
11th	じゅういちにち	*juuichinichi*
12th	じゅうににち	*juuninichi*
13th	じゅうさんにち	*juusannichi*
14th	じゅうよっか	*juuyokka*
15th	じゅうごにち	*juugonichi*
16th	じゅうろくにち	*juurokunichi*
17th	じゅうななにち	*juushichinichi*
18th	じゅうはちにち	*juuhachinichi*
19th	じゅうくにち	*juukunichi*
20th	はつか	*hatsuka*
21st	にじゅういちにち	*nijuuichinichi*
22nd	にじゅうににち	*nijuuninichi*
23rd	にじゅうさんにち	*nijuusannichi*
24th	にじゅうよっか	*nijuuyokka*
25th	にじゅうごにち	*nijuugonichi*
26th	にじゅうろくにち	*nijuurokunichi*
27th	にじゅうななにち	*nijuushichinichi*
28th	にじゅうはちにち	*nijuuhachinichi*
29th	にじゅうくにち	*nijuukunichi*
30th	さんじゅうにち	*sanjuunichi*
31st	さんじゅういちにち	*sanjuuichinichi*

People counters

1	ひとり	*hitori*
2	ふたり	*futari*
3	さんにん	*sannin*
4	よにん	*yonin*
5	ごにん	*gonin*
6	ろくにん	*rokunin*
7	しちにん	*shichinin*
8	はちにん	*hachinin*
9	きゅうにん	*kyuunin*
10	じゅうにん	*juunin*
11	じゅういちにん	*juuichinin,* etc.

Age counters

1	いっさい	*issai*
2	にさい	*nisai*
3	さんさい	*sansai*
4	よんさい	*yonsai*
5	ごさい	*gosai*
6	ろくさい	*rokusai*
7	ななさい	*nanasai*
8	はっさい	*hassai*
9	きゅうさい	*kyuusai*
10	じゅっさい	*jussai*
11	じゅういっさい	*juuissai*
12	じゅうにさい	*juunisai*
13	じゅうさんさい	*juusansai*
20	はたち	*hatachi*

ひらがな

あ	a	一	十	あ
い	i	l	い	
う	u	ˋ	う	
え	e	ˋ	え	
お	o	一	お	お
か	ka	フ	カ	か
き	ki	二	キ	き
く	ku	く		
け	ke	l	lー	け
こ	ko	ˉ	こ	
さ	sa	一	ナ	さ
し	shi	し		
す	su	一	す	
せ	se	一	十	せ
そ	so	そ		
た	ta	一	ナ	た
ち	chi	一	ち	
つ	tsu	つ		
て	te	て		
と	to	ˋ	と	
な	na	ナ	ナ丶	な
に	ni	l	lー	に
ぬ	nu	＼	ぬ	
ね	ne	l	ね	
の	no	の		
は	ha	l	lー	は
ひ	hi	ひ		
ふ	fu	ˋう	ふ	ふ
へ	he	へ		
ほ	ho	l	lニ	ほ
ま	ma	一	二	ま
み	mi	ス	み	
む	mu	一	む	む
め	me	＼	め	
も	mo	し	t	も
や	ya	つ	う	や
ゆ	yu	ゆ	ゆ	
よ	yo	-	よ	
ら	ra	ˋ	ら	
り	ri	り		
る	ru	る		
れ	re	l	れ	
ろ	ro	ろ		
わ	wa	l	わ	
を	o	一	ち	を
ん	n	ん		

ひらがな

が ga	ぎ gi	ぐ gu	げ ge	ご go
ざ za	じ ji	ず zu	ぜ ze	ぞ zo
だ da	ぢ ji	づ zu	で de	ど do
ば ba	び bi	ぶ bu	べ be	ぼ bo

ぱ pa	ぴ pi	ぷ pu	ぺ pe	ぽ po

ぎゃ gya	ぎゅ gyu	ぎょ gyo
じゃ ja	じゅ ju	じょ jo
びゃ bya	びゅ byu	びょ byo

きゃ kya	きゅ kyu	きょ kyo
しゃ sha	しゅ shu	しょ sho
ちゃ cha	ちゅ chu	ちょ cho
にゃ nya	にゅ nyu	にょ nyo
ひゃ hya	ひゅ hyu	ひょ hyo
みゃ mya	みゅ myu	みょ myo
りゃ rya	りゅ ryu	りょ ryo

ぴゃ pya	ぴゅ pyu	ぴょ pyo

きゅう kyuu	きょう kyoo
しゅう shuu	しょう shoo
ちゅう chuu	ちょう choo
にゅう nyuu	にょう nyoo
ひゅう hyuu	ひょう hyoo
みゅう myuu	みょう myoo
りゅう ryuu	りょう ryoo

カタカナ

ア	a	⌐	ア		タ	ta	ノ	ク	タ		
イ	i	ノ	イ		チ	chi	´	ニ	チ		
ウ	u	˙	ウ		ツ	tsu	ヽ	˙˙	ツ		
エ	e	ー	エ		テ	te	ー	ニ	テ		
オ	o	ー	オ		ト	to	｜	ト			
カ	ka	⌐	カ		ナ	na	ー	ナ			
キ	ki	ー	ニ	キ	ニ	ni	ー	ニ			
ク	ku	ノ	ク		ヌ	nu	フ	ヌ			
ケ	ke	ノ	⊦	ケ	ネ	ne	´	衤	ネ		
コ	ko	⌐	コ		ノ	no	ノ				
サ	sa	ー	⊦	サ	ハ	ha	ノ	ハ			
シ	shi	˙	˙˙	シ	ヒ	hi	ー	ヒ			
ス	su	フ	ス		フ	fu	フ				
セ	se	⌐	セ		ヘ	he	ヘ				
ソ	so	˙	ソ		ホ	ho	ー	ナ	ホ		

マ	ma	⌐	マ	
ミ	mi	`	ミ	ミ
ム	mu	∠	ム	
メ	me	ノ	メ	
モ	mo	ー	ニ	モ
ヤ	ya	⌐	ヤ	
ユ	yu	⌐	ユ	
ヨ	yo	⌐	ヲ	ヨ
ラ	ra	ー	ラ	
リ	ri	｜	リ	
ル	ru	ノ	ル	
レ	re	レ		
ロ	ro	｜	⌐	ロ
ワ	wa	｜	ワ	
ヲ	o	ー	＝	ヲ
ン	n	`	ン

カタカナ

ガ ga	ギ gi	グ gu	ゲ ge	ゴ go
ザ za	ジ ji	ズ zu	ゼ ze	ゾ zo
ダ da	ヂ ji	ヅ zu	デ de	ド do
バ ba	ビ bi	ブ bu	ベ be	ボ bo

パ pa	ピ pi	プ pu	ペ pe	ポ po

ギャ gya	ギュ gyu	ギョ gyo
ジャ ja	ジュ ju	ジョ jo
ビャ bya	ビュ byu	ビョ byo

キャ kya	キュ kyu	キョ kyo
シャ sha	シュ shu	ショ sho
チャ cha	チュ chu	チョ cho
ニャ nya	ニュ nyu	ニョ nyo
ヒャ hya	ヒュ hyu	ヒョ hyo
ミャ mya	ミュ myu	ミョ myo
リャ rya	リュ ryu	リョ ryo

ピャ pya	ピュ pyu	ピョ pyo